AGRICULTURAL KNOWLEDGE NETWORKS IN RURAL EUROPE, 1700–2000

Boydell Studies in Rural History

Series Editor
Professor Richard W. Hoyle

This series aims to provide a forum for the best and most influential work in agricultural and rural history, and on the cultural history of the countryside. Whilst it is anchored in the rural history of Britain and Ireland, it also includes within its remit Europe and the colonial empires of European nations (both during and after colonisation). All approaches and methodologies are welcome, including the use of oral history.

Proposals or enquiries are welcomed. They may be sent directly to the editor or the publisher at the e-mail addresses given below.

richard@rwhoyle.org.uk

Editorial@boydell.co.uk

Previously published:

Agricultural Knowledge Networks in Rural Europe, 1700–2000

Edited by Yves Segers and Leen Van Molle

THE BOYDELL PRESS

First published 2022
The Boydell Press, Woodbridge

ISBN 978 1 78327 712 4

The Boydell Press is an imprint of Boydell & Brewer Ltd
PO Box 9, Woodbridge, Suffolk IP12 3DF, UK
and of Boydell & Brewer Inc.
668 Mt Hope Avenue, Rochester, NY 14620-2731, USA
website: www.boydellandbrewer.com

A CIP catalogue record for this book is available
from the British Library

The publisher has no responsibility for the continued existence or accuracy of
URLs for external or third-party internet websites referred to in this book, and
does not guarantee that any content on such websites is, or will remain, accurate
or appropriate

This publication is printed on acid-free paper

CONTENTS

Contents

ILLUSTRATIONS

Dries Claeys and Yves Segers, 'The Eye of the Master'. Livestock Improvement and Knowledge Networks in Belgium, 1900–1940

Miguel Cabo and Lourenzo Fernández Prieto, Bridging Rural Culture and Expert Culture: The Agrarian Press in Galicia, *c.*1900–*c.*1950

Laurent Herment, Farmers Facing a Body of Expertise: the Activities and Methods of the Departmental Services for Agriculture in Oise (France), 1945–1955

CONTRIBUTORS

Paul Brassley, University of Exeter, UK

Miguel Cabo, University of Santiago de Compostella, Spain

Dries Claeys, KU Leuven, Belgium and Flanders Heritage

Lourenzo Fernández Prieto, University of Santiago de Compostella, Spain

Laurent Herment, CRH-EHESS, CNRS (UMR 8558), France

Sarah Holland, University of Nottingham, UK

Zsuzsanna Kiss, Eötvös Loránd University, Hungary.

Verena Lehmbrock, Universität Erfurt, Germany

Janken Myrdal, Swedish University of Agricultural Sciences, Uppsala, Sweden

Yves Segers, KU Leuven, Belgium

Pierre-Etienne Stockland, Columbia University, USA and independent scholar

Steven van der Laan, Utrecht University, The Netherlands

Leen Van Molle, KU Leuven, Belgium

ABBREVIATIONS

AAS	Archives de l'Académie des Sciences
ADAS	Agricultural Development and Advisory Service
ANT	Actor-Network Theory
APS	American Philosophical Society
ATB	Agricultural Training Board
AZC	Agricultural Association of Zala County
BOCM	British Oil and Cake Mills
CBV	Centraal Bureau Varkensfokkerij
DA	Doncaster Archives
DAS	Doncaster Agricultural Society
DDSA	Director of the Departmental Services for Agriculture
DSA	Departmental Services for Agriculture
EHF	Experimental Husbandry Farm
ESTC	English Short Title Catalogue
FMS	Farm Management Survey
HGCA	Home Grown Cereals Authority
HSNA	Historical Social Network Analysis
INRA	Institut National des Recherches Agronomiques
IRA	Institut des Recherches Agronomiques
KNA	Knowledge Network Analysis
KSLA	Swedish Academy of Forestry and Agriculture
LCP	Low-Cost Production
MLC	Meat and Livestock Commission
MP	Member of Parliament
NAAS	National Agricultural Advisory Service
NAH	National Archives of Hungary
NFU	National Farmers' Union
NIAB	National Institute of Agricultural Botany

Abbreviations

NSA	National Society for Agriculture
OND	Ordinary National Diploma
RASE	Royal Agricultural Society of England
SLU	Swedish University of Agricultural Sciences
SNA	Social Network Analysis
TNA	The National Archives
UK	United Kingdom
ZCA	Zala County Archive

This book is published with the support of the Interfaculty Centre for Agrarian History (ICAG, KU Leuven) and CORN (Comparative Rural History Network), financed by FWO Flanders, as part of the CORN research programme 'Inequality and Rural Development'.

1

Introduction

Knowledge and its Networks in Rural Europe: From the Early Eighteenth to the Late Twentieth Century

Yves Segers and Leen Van Molle

Farming is imperative to feed the world's population. A massive and still expanding historical literature deals with the development of farming and food provisioning throughout the past centuries: on access to farmland, farming methods and technology, farm labour, agricultural production, productivity and trade, food processing and diets. In this vast literature, processes of agricultural stagnation or growth are often linked to forms of knowledge – about reclamation, drainage, crop rotation, the use of fertilizers and tools, the treatment of cattle plagues, etc. – as self-evident explanations. Knowledge is, in that regard, mentioned as a given, as if it were an 'invisible hand' that steered and changed farming practices and outputs.[1] This book intends to question the creation and, in particular, the exchange of agronomic knowledge in rural Europe from the onset of the so-called modern era, during the course of the eighteenth century until well into the twentieth century, and to explore the spreading of that knowledge through the lens of 'knowledge networks' and related models and analytical concepts.

Where did knowledge come from and how did one learn to run a farm in the European countryside? Was this achieved by imitating one's father

---

[1] This is, for instance, the case in the first and seminal synthesis by B. Slicher van Bath, *De agrarische geschiedenis van West-Europa, 500–1850* (3rd edn, Utrecht-Antwerp, 1976): he specifically counts knowledge and technology among the 'external factors' that influenced the development of agriculture (pp. 12–25, also pp. 328–37 about tools).

or mother, by looking around, over the hedge, by trying things out in the field, by listening and talking to others, and by reading, by means of schooling and by studying, observing, experimenting and trial and error? There is in fact a rich repertoire of verbs in use that refer to the variety of vectors that served, and still serve, for the creation and transmission of knowledge and know-how with regard to farming, ranging from absorbing *tacit* knowledge to inventing and diffusing new agricultural science. Historians studying agricultural knowledge simultaneously find themselves in a Garden of Eden and in a jungle, because knowledge seems to be omnipresent, in all aspects of daily life and everywhere, in town and in the countryside, but its nature, creation, communication, transformation and appropriation are difficult to grasp.

Knowledge on the move, an epistemological issue

According to the well-known definition by the sociologists Peter Berger and Thomas Luckmann, knowledge is 'everything that passes for "knowledge" in a society'. Knowledge is above all a social construction, shaped through communication and negotiation between various actors, through authority, discursive strategies, adjustments and compromises; it is dynamic, polymorphous and capable of travelling through time and space.[2] Consequently, words such as 'transfer', 'vulgarization' and 'reception' are somewhat misleading, because they place too great an emphasis on an assumption that clear-cut knowledge exists in the first place and that there is an effort to pass it on to others who do not possess that knowledge.

Human thinking carries in itself, as the anthropologist Mary Douglas observed, the social configurations of a given time and space.[3] The recent *Wissensgeschichte* asserts that all knowledge is socially, chronologically and geographically situated and, at the same time, on the move.[4] The *geography* of knowledge leads historical research in the first instance to urban centres as the eminent sites of science and arts with their universities and academies, laboratories and museums, libraries and publishing houses.[5] Precisely this focus on cities makes it challenging to question

2   P. Berger and T. Luckmann, *The Social Construction of Reality. A Treatise in the Sociology of Knowledge* (New York, 1966), p. 15; J. Secord, 'Knowledge in Transit', *Isis* 95 (2004), p. 670.
3   M. Douglas, 'Introduction', in M. Douglas (ed.), *Rules and Meanings. The Anthropology of Everyday Knowledge* (2nd edn, New York, 1977), pp. 9–13.
4   Cf. the thought-provoking article by Philipp Sarasin, 'Was ist Wissensgeschichte?', *Internationales Archiv für Sozialgeschichte der deutschen Literatur* 36 (2011), pp. 159–72 (esp. pp. 163–72).
5   D. Livingstone, *Putting Science in its Place. Geographies of Scientific Knowledge* (Chicago, 2003); C. Jacob (ed.), *Lieux de savoir. Espaces et communautés* (Paris, 2007) with its reference to 'Villes phares' (beacon cities); O. Hochadel and

the specific nature and spreading of knowledge within the European countryside and between the rural and the urban world, from Scandinavia to the Mediterranean and from Eastern to Western Europe as reflected in this book. The *chronology* of agricultural knowledge enables us to distinguish between two to four successive phases (which could be called 'revolutions') that have occurred since the eighteenth century, namely the transition from 'traditional' organic farming until late into the nineteenth century to science-based agriculture, including mechanization, chemical and biotechnical farming.[6] But a general periodization does not account for the pace and nature of changes at an individual, local, regional or even (trans)national level. The *social status* of knowledge is unstable, variable and unequal. Knowledge needs to be acknowledged, through sharing, checking and confirmation by others, before it really exists, can move and can attract a larger following. Peter Burke refers to the social difference between 'knowing that' and 'knowing how', or a difference between knowing as an intellectual exercise – rational, systematic and abstract – and popular knowing, associated as it were with beliefs, the concrete and practical.[7] Similarly, Peter Jones, in his thorough study of the agricultural Enlightenment, distinguishes 'savant knowledge' from 'useful knowledge' and questions the complex relationship between both. Academic knowledge that circulated among enlightened landlords and in the salons of intellectual elites could conflict with the empirical 'farm-gate wisdom' of peasants as experts on their fields, but both forms of knowing could also inspire and influence each other.[8] Even 'modern science' is, as the agricultural sociologist Jack Kloppenburg states, socially contingent and the 'historical product of continuous social struggle'.[9]

The history of agricultural knowledge (in the broad sense, including science) has been a frequent topic of study since the 1990s, when

---

    A. Nieto-Galan, *Urban Histories of Science. Making Knowledge in the City, 1820–1940* (New York, 2018).

6   This is not the place to go into the scholarly debates about the nature and timing of agricultural revolutions. Two inspiring references: P. Bairoch, 'Die Landwirtschaft und die industrielle Revolution 1700–1914', in C. Cipolla and K. Borchardt (eds), *Europäische Wirtschaftsgeschichte*, III, *Die industrielle Revolution* (Stuttgart, 1976), pp. 297–332; J. Auderset and P. Moser, 'Die Agrarfrage und die agrarisch-industrielle Wissensgesellschaft. Eine Einführung', in J. Auderset and P. Moser, *Die Agrarfrage in der Industriegesellschaft. Wissenskulturen, Machtverhältnisse und natürliche Ressourcen in der agrarisch-industriellen Wissensgesellschaft (1850–1950)* (Wien, 2018), pp. 31–46.

7   P. Burke, *A Social History of Knowledge. From Gutenberg to Diderot* (2nd edn, Cambridge, 2000), pp. 1–17 (esp. p. 11).

8   P. Jones, *Agricultural Enlightenment. Knowledge, Technology, and Nature, 1750–1840* (Oxford, 2016), pp. 1–13.

9   J. Kloppenburg, 'Social Theory and the De/Reconstruction of Agricultural Science', *Rural Sociology* 56 (1991), p. 524.

German-speaking scholars took the lead. During the last European rural history conference in Paris in September 2019, 52 panels and papers, or nearly 10 per cent of all panels and papers, used the words 'knowledge', 'science', 'research', 'technology', 'innovation' or 'expertise' in their title.[10] The topic continues to gain interest. It benefits, in the first place, from its interplay with the expanding history of sciences and technology (soil science, plant breeding, tropical agriculture, mechanization, veterinary medicine, etc.). It also benefits from the interest in intellectual and cultural history, which focuses on spaces of knowledge production such as savant societies, universities, laboratories and experiment stations. The everyday knowing and know-how of 'ordinary' country dwellers comes to the fore in research on the development of literacy, reading culture, media use and communication in rural communities. Another approach sheds light on the educational and popularization efforts of agricultural colleges, model farms, agricultural exhibitions, housekeeping schools, farmers' unions and the agricultural press. In addition, the gender perspective questions male identification with and female input into the agricultural knowledge society.[11] After the turn of the millennium, German-speaking scholars

---

10   *Rural History 2019. Conference Programme. Abstracts of All Panels and Papers* (Paris, 2019). The interest in knowledge was only a little less marked at the 2019 conference of the American Agricultural History Society Annual Meeting in Washington D.C. in June 2019 (in this case 6.5 per cent of the titles of panels and papers).

11   Telling examples in a chronological order: N. Goddard, 'Agricultural Literature and Societies', in G. E. Mingay (ed.), *Agricultural History of England and Wales*, VI, *1750–1850* (Cambridge, 1989), pp. 361–83; V. Klemm, *Agrarwissenschaften in Deutschland. Geschichte – Tradition, von den Anfängen bis 1945* (St Katharinen, 1992); K. Herrmann and H. Winkler (eds), *Vom 'belehrten' Bauern. Kommunikation und Information in der Landwirtschaft vom Bauernkalender bis zur EDV* (St Katherinen, 1992); M. Lyons, 'What did Peasants Read? Written and Printed Culture in Rural France, 1815–1914', *European History Q.* 27 (1997), pp. 165–97; N. Jas, *Au carrefour de la chimie et de l'agriculture. Les sciences agronomiques en France et en Allemagne, 1850–1914* (Paris, 2000); M. Boulet (ed.), *Les enjeux de la formation des acteurs de l'agriculture, 1760–1945* (Dijon, 2000); H. Inhetveen and M. Schmitt (eds), *Pionierinnen des Landbaus* (Göttingen, 2000); W. Rösener (ed.), *Kommunikation in der ländlichen Gesellschaft vom Mittelalter bis zur Moderne* (Göttingen, 2000); J. Pan-Montojo, *Apostolado, profesion y technologia. Una historia de los ingenieros agronomos en Espana, 1855–2005* (Madrid, 2005); J. Harwood, *Technology's Dilemma. Agricultural Colleges between Science and Practice in Germany, 1860–1934* (Oxford, 2005); L. Van Molle, '"Kulturkampf" in the countryside. Agricultural education, 1800–1940: a multifaceted offensive', in: C. Sarasúa, P. Scholliers and L. Van Molle (eds), *Land, Shops and Kitchens* (Turnhout, 2005), pp. 139–69; N. Vivier (ed.), *Elites et progrès agricole (XVIe-XXe siècle)* (Rennes, 2009); H. Maat, *Science Cultivating Practice. A History of Agricultural Science in the Netherlands and its Colonies, 1863–1986* (Dordrecht, 2009); M. Popplow (ed.), *Landschaften agrarisch-ökonomischen Wissens. Strategien innovativer Ressourcennutzung in Zeitschriften*

started to distinguish between *Wissensgeschichte* (history of knowledge) and *Wissenschaftsgeschichte* (history of science). That distinction, however, is less relevant here because this book focuses on the spread of knowing in the broad sense.

It is not difficult, as many publications do, to prove the development of agricultural science and the availability of knowledge in the countryside. However the working and mobility of science and knowledge through time, regions and social milieus is harder to capture. This leads us to the aim of this book, which is to lay bare in ten case studies how agricultural science, knowledge and know-how was created, and then disseminated, geographically and socially. As the travel of knowledge forms the focal point of this book, the question arises as to which primary sources historians can rely on to unravel and describe the routes of transmission, and which concepts and methods they tend to use. It is relevant to begin this volume with a short account of the conceptual and methodological apparatus from other disciplines that offers an inspiring horizon or lens through which the travel of knowledge can be studied and through which the following chapters can be read.

We are convinced that agricultural and rural history can benefit from insights and ongoing discussions in adjacent disciplines in three ways: theoretically and conceptually, methodologically, and analytically. In more specific terms, the editors invited the authors to explore the usefulness of the concept of 'knowledge networks' – this term is given in the plural form here in order to underline the dynamic and complex relationships between the actors on the scene – to study the exchange of information with regard to farming in the past but, beyond that, they were free to choose their own path.

Imitation, diffusion, mediation and circulation of knowledge

Knowledge seems to have its own, volatile and invisible ways to surface, fix itself, spread, alter and disappear. The attributes that attempt to describe and explain the travel of knowledge have in common that they are founded on abstractions with a suggestive power – such as transfer, diffusion, exchange, percolation and penetration, networks, channels, and many more – that are themselves nevertheless hard to substantiate in qualitative and/or quantitative terms, especially in the case of the past. Much agricultural knowledge was transmitted by literally 'looking over

---

und Sozietäten des 18. Jh.s (Münster, 2010); F. Uekötter, *Die Wahrheit ist auf dem Feld. Eine Wissengeschichte der deutschen Landwirtschaft* (Göttingen, 2010); C. Zimmermann and U. Meiners (eds), 'Mediennützung und Medienaneignung in der ländlichen Gesellschaft', *Zeitschrift für Agrargeschichte und Agrarsoziologie* 58 (2010), 2; P. Jones, *Agricultural Enlightenment* (Oxford, 2016); Auderset and Moser, *Die Agrarfrage* (Vienna, 2018).

the hedge', by noting what worked (and did not work) for other farmers. Emulation is probably the easiest way to explain how (agricultural) knowledge or know-how can pass from A to B. All individuals tend to imitate those whom they look up to, trust and identify with, as explained in *Les lois de l'imitation* or the laws of imitation (1890) of the French intellectual, Gabriel Tarde. His theory advances that the whole social fabric rests on repetition and imitation, and thus on individuals who resemble each other. But this does not equal monotony and immobility: imitation inevitably engenders differentiation and variation, which means that 'inventions' and 'innovation' are rather to be seen as evolutions or new combinations of older findings.[12] Each 'innovation' is subsequently subject to rejection or imitation, at a slow or an increasing pace, and including the variations that it undergoes along the way.[13] This evolutive interpretation of inventions has the important feature that it enables us to (re-)assess the role of all actors as active agents in the societal process of (agricultural) knowledge making.

'Diffusion' (spreading, distribution, dissemination) of knowledge is, furthermore, a vague analytical concept, even when it is accompanied by expressive addenda such as diffusion 'via highways and byways'. The diffusionist model clarifies how science and knowledge spread via social interaction to become a global, universal good. The model displays a clear hierarchical interpretation of spreading: top-down, unidirectional from the expert to the ignorant, from an (active) sender to a (passive) receiver, and from a centre to the periphery.[14] The diffusionist interpretation – a progressive 'trickle-down' and spatial dissemination – rests on the belief in a cultural lag between the (superior) elites and the (inferior) masses, and in spatial terms between the urban and the rural world, and between the West to the rest. This dualistic perception meshes with the theory of the 'two cultures', an appealing image of two contrastive and struggling worlds: a civilized and a rude one.[15]

---

12   F. Djellal and F. Gallouj, 'Les lois de l'imitation et de l'invention: Gabriel Tarde et l'économie évolutionniste de l'innovation', *Revue économique* 68 (2017), pp. 643–71.

13   According to Tarde, the spreading of innovations follows an S-curve: slow in the beginning, followed by a noticeable increase and acceleration, and finally a decline; J. Scott, *What Is Social Network Analysis?* (3rd edn, New York, 2012), pp. 57–8.

14   The diffusionist model of cultural development originated from archaeology and anthropology; it is associated with classical modernization theories. About the 'diffusionist model': R. Cooter and S. Pumfrey, 'Separate Spheres and Public Places: Reflections on the History of Science Popularization and Science in Popular Culture', *History of Science* 32 (1994), pp. 248–50.

15   This theory was elaborated in the early 1920s by the Ukrainian communist Dmytro Lebed to promote the Russification of the region at the expense of the language and culture of the Ukrainian peasantry: see A. Applebaum, *Rode*

Diffusion, in this sense, simply ignores the creative, interactive and interdependent making of science, knowledge and know-how by all layers of society and in all locations, including in the countryside and by the farming classes. This interdependency comes more effectively to the fore when focusing on mediation, a concept that is often used in the context of transmitting scientific knowledge to laypeople. Mediators of different sorts form a bridge between the 'haves and have nots' of science and knowledge by means of its 'popularization' by amateur scientists, advisors, teachers, journalists, sales representatives, etc. They are go-betweens, cross-border workers or 'cultural amphibians',[16] transferring, translating and trading between science and practice in everyday life. Rather than mere carriers of knowledge, they are co-shapers of the news they bring. Mediators connect the urban and the rural sphere, the laboratory and the field, science and practice, as has been studied by Robert Kohler.[17] They circulate, also in the spatial sense. They broaden the flow of knowledge within and beyond a community because they travel back and forth, breaking through local ways of thinking and acting, and linking distant places.

The circulation of knowledge is a recent and even more encompassing concept. It is based on the thesis that knowledge itself has the power to travel: through time and space, through the public and the private sphere, through families, neighbourhoods and institutions, in material and immaterial forms, by means of encounters, communication and negotiation, books and journals, exhibitions, advertisements, etc. Unlike 'diffusion', which sees knowledge rather as a static given to be passed on to the other party, the circulation of knowledge suggests complicated patterns of creating, modifying and moving via tangled paths and permeable borders, up and down, back and forth, in an irregular way, according to common interests and goals and specific local (political, religious, linguistic and other) conditions.[18] As Tarde's interpretation of

---

Hongersnood. Stalins oorlog tegen Oekraïne (Dutch transl., Amsterdam, 2018), p. 85. It should not be confused with the 'two cultures' thesis outlined by the British physicist C. P. Snow in a much-cited lecture of 1959 about the cultural gap between positive sciences and literary circles.

16 This concept comes from M. MacDonald, 'The Secularization of Suicide in England', *Past and Present* 111 (1986), p. 67 and it has been adopted in various contexts.

17 R. E. Kohler, *Landscapes and Labscapes. Exploring the Lab-Field Border in Biology* (Chicago, 2002).

18 An excellent overview of the historiographical introduction and continuing development of the concept of 'circulation of knowledge' by J. Östling *et al.*, 'The History of Knowledge and the Circulation of Knowledge', in: J. Östling *et al.* (eds), *Circulation of Knowledge. Explorations in the History of Knowledge* (Lund, 2018), pp. 9–32. Also Secord, 'Knowledge in Transit'; Sarasin, 'Was ist Wissensgeschichte'; K. Raj, 'Networks of Knowledge, or Spaces of Circulation?

imitation, circulation entails that all actors in the process should be taken seriously, while not necessarily implying that equal weight is applied to the (co-)shaping and transmission of knowledge.

(Historical) Social Network Analysis

The title of this book announces our intention to introduce a new conceptual framework into agricultural history, that of 'knowledge networks'. The concept of a network and the network-related vocabulary are in vogue in a wide variety of sciences and practices: computer networks, business networks, market networks, expert networks, social networks, knowledge networks, self-help networks and so on. Social Network Analysis (SNA) is a sustained and widespread method used in the social sciences. Historians also make use of it, albeit often only in a metaphorical way, by using the network-related vocabulary such as 'links', 'channel' or 'web'. Some embrace (Historical) Social Network Analysis (HSNA), with more or less critical distance, as a methodological tool to tackle larger datasets in order to uncover the structure of social relations in the past.[19] The combination with Digital Humanities has recently gained increased interest and has fuelled new applications, as the up-to-date bibliography for various historical periods and subfields of the Historical Network Research website proves.[20] This forms sufficient reason to outline this conceptual and methodological tool in greater detail.

Network analysis is a methodology that originated in the social sciences and took shape from the 1930s onwards in order to make sense of contemporary social structures on the basis of intended communicative interaction (*ties*) between *actors* that share some common interests, goals or values.[21] SNA considers actors in the first place as persons and, by

---

The Birth of British Cartography in Colonial South Asia in the Late Eighteenth Century', *Global Intellectual History* 2 (2017), pp. 52–4.

[19] Some informative and critical writings about SNA in history: B. H. Erickson, 'Social Networks and History. A Review Essay', *Historical Methods* 43 (1997), pp. 149–57; C. Wetherell, 'Historical Social Network Analysis', *International Review of Social History* 43 (1998), pp. 125–44; E. Fuchs, 'Networks and the History of Education', *Paedagogica Historica* 43 (2007), pp. 185–97; Claire Lemercier, 'Formal Network Methods in History: Why and How?', in G. Fertig (ed.), *Social Networks, Political Institutions, and Rural Societies* (Turnhout, 2015), pp. 281–310.

[20] M. Düring, 'Historical Network Research. Network Analysis in the Historical Disciplines' (2017), see http://historicalnetworkresearch.org/), the *Journal of Historical Network Research* (2017–) and the up-to-date bibliography on this website.

[21] Introductory literature: K. A. Fredericks and M. M. Durland, 'The Historical Evolution and Basic Concepts of Social Network Analysis' (2006, www.

extension, as families, associations, churches, enterprises or even states having face-to-face contacts, meetings, exchanging letters, etc. Creating and participating in a network provides them with social capital: for instance, information, social support, scientific collaboration or political influence. Mapping these structures then becomes a useful method of gaining an understanding of the social position of people and of the social fabric itself. In its pure form, SNA is based on strictly defined concepts, mathematical methods and graphical visualization. It requires homogenous and preferably complete data about a group of individuals: not only descriptive and attributive data (such as age, gender, diploma, occupation, political opinion and religion), but above all *relational* data that reveal the existence and subjective importance (*value*) of more or less *horizontal* and reciprocal ties between persons (kinship, close neighbourhood, distant and close friendships, shared memberships, etc.). SNA considers social relations as meaningful elements of analysis and the 'web' or networks they form as active agents in society.

SNA is therefore not equipped to study anonymous institutional interactions and *vertical* power relations, and certainly not to map the barely tangible pathways of what can be labelled as 'knowing' (acquiring knowledge and understanding through experience, reasoning, evaluation, etc.). SNA is a powerful, but time-consuming method of measuring the pattern of social relationships. It requires qualitative data (the micro-level) and quantifiable data (to create a macro-perspective) about all of the actors in a network, which, in the case of historical research, already poses a formidable barrier. HSNA remains, as Charles Wetherell wrote, an 'inherently problematic enterprise', because historians are not only confronted with lacunae in the available source material and with hidden parts of the past, but also with the biased character of sources.[22] But given the fact that social structures are constructed through time, it is worth taking past structures into account in order to understand the flow of history. (H)SNA can chose two different paths, the first being the *egocentric* approach, namely the (biographical) perspective of one person (or a set of persons in a particular context) and his or her links with others (for instance through correspondence and diaries). More demanding is the *sociocentric* approach that deals with a clearly defined group (a complete network, for instance an enterprise or organization) and allows us to uncover the social relations between its members.[23]

---

interscience.wiley.com); E. Lazega, *Réseaux sociaux et structures relationnelles* (Paris, 2007); Scott, *What is Social Network Analysis?*; J. Scott, *Social Network Analysis* (4th revised edn, London, 2017).

22 Wetherell, 'Historical Social Network Analysis', p. 125.
23 K. Chung, L. Hossein and J. Davies, 'Exploring Sociocentric and Egocentric Approaches for Social Network Analysis' (2005), paper published on Academia.edu.

The method – and here follows a brief account of its specific vocabulary – leads to the identification of all actors (also named *nodes* or *points*) in a network, the direct and indirect ties (*links, lines*) between them, the direction of their interaction (reciprocal and egalitarian or more asymmetric and unequal) and the quality of the ties (formal or informal, multifunctional or singular, strong or weak). The sociologist Mark Gravonetter, who coined the seminal phrase 'the strength of weak ties', considers *strong ties* (family, close friends and workmates for instance) as a form of social security because they are easily mobilizable, but strong ties tend to share more or less the same knowledge. Therefore, the importance of *weak ties* (such as acquaintances and fellow students) may not be underestimated because they can introduce new information and new ideas from more distant parts into a network and thus induce change. Accordingly, as Gravonetter states, weak ties 'provide the bridges over which innovations cross the boundaries of social groups'.[24] Networks can be large or small, strong and cohesive or fragile and unbalanced, and more or less centralized on a few main actors or *centres*. They can be visible, inclusive and willing to accept new members or rather hidden and exclusively open to a 'small world'. Networks have a high or low *density*, according to the number of ties between all the actors, the (spatial or figurative) distance between them, and the frequency and duration of their contacts. They can contain *subgroups* and *intermediaries* bridging between subgroups. Some include actors with specific *roles* in the network, *gatekeepers* to guard the access to the network or *cliques* with intimate links between all its members but intolerant of outsiders, links in their *periphery* or *interlockings* with other networks, and a *star* in their centre to whom most other actors are connected. The results of such analytical and sociometric network research are often graphically presented in the form of sociograms.

Knowledge networks?

The authors in this book were asked to question the trajectories of agricultural knowledge in the past and to investigate whether and, if so, how 'knowledge networks' played a role. It is a fact that examples of network research in agricultural and rural history are thin on the ground. Very few are methodologically grounded in SNA, but nevertheless the idea of networks slips into their reasoning at certain points. The marked exception is the volume edited by Georg Fertig, which puts SNA to the test as a

[24] M. Gravonetter, 'The Strength of Weak Ties', *American Journal of Sociology* 78 (1973), 1360–80; further information about the importance of weak ties in the spreading of information can be found in M. Gravonetter, 'The Strength of Weak Ties: A Network Theory Revisited', *Sociological Theory* 1 (1983), pp. 201–33 (quotation from p. 219).

means of unfolding social relationships in pre-modern and modern rural societies – ranging from kinship and enduring and reciprocal non-kin ties in rural areas, to more formal contacts – and their power to facilitate assets such as the access to land and credit, market participation and political mobilization.[25] Others consciously refer to a 'network' as the best possible description of what is felt as an historical reality that is difficult to capture and prove, a reality that shines through the variety of the available primary sources: namely the agency of important social connections that influenced the thinking and acting of individuals and groups. It is then the expertise of the historian that accounts for the validity of this qualitative interpretation. Peter Jones, for instance, concludes that enlightened 'bookish information', practical wisdom and acquired skills formed a hybrid whole that influenced farmers, and he points at 'social networks and informal competition' that must have played a part in this.[26] Uekötter distinguishes 'dense expert networks' within what he calls the German 'agrarian knowledge system'.[27] Joan Thirsk, when reconsidering the so-called French and British rural divergence, asserts the existence of a 'worldwide network of information on farming' among 'like-minded people' between 1500–1800 and Nadine Vivier advances the functioning of highly active 'European agricultural networks' between 1750 and 1840 who 'intensively exchanged ideas right across Europe'.[28]

The conceptual combination of 'knowledge' and 'networks', however, is perhaps not unproblematic: where and how can historical knowledge research meet network analysis? The history of knowledge has created its own vocabulary and models, as documented above. But there is more: interestingly, and apart from SNA, Knowledge Network Analysis (KNA) has also taken up a position within the landscape of social scientists.[29] It presents itself at first sight as a separate discipline, but it is, when one

25 G. Fertig, 'Rural History and the Analysis of Social Relations', in Fertig (ed.), *Social Networks*, pp. 13–29. All chapters in the volume, excepting one, 'measure' social relations in one way or another, but it should be mentioned that not all explicitly refer to SNA: three of them include the graphical visualization of a network.

26 Jones, *Agricultural Enlightenment*, pp. 220–2.

27 Uekötter, *Die Wahrheit*, pp. 63–80.

28 J. Thirsk, 'The World-Wide Farming Web, 1500–1800' and N. Vivier, 'European Agricultural Networks, 1750–1850: A View from France', both in J. Broad (ed.), *A Common Agricultural Heritage. Revising French and British Rural Divergence* (Exeter, 2009), pp. 13–22 and 23–34; Vivier refers also to a 'real transatlantic network' of corresponding agricultural societies between Europe and North-America around 1800: see 'Conclusions', in Vivier (ed.), *Élites et progrès*, p. 326.

29 The concept KNA was coined by R. W. Helms and C. M. Buysrogge in 2005; see R. W. Helms, J. Cranefield and J. van Reijssen (eds), *Social Knowledge Management in Action. Applications and Challenges* (Cham, 2017), esp. pp. 28–30 and 129.

takes a closer look, rather SNA in disguise, because it uses the same semantic repertoire and the same methodology. KNA studies items such as social interactions in companies to discover bottlenecks in knowledge communication in order to improve knowledge sharing. One specificity of KNA is the distinction it makes between three types of *actors* and *ties* between actors according to their role: the creation, the sharing or the simple using of knowledge. In this way, KNA tends to allocate knowing to specific actors and risks ignoring the complex circulation and transformation of knowledge itself in the course of the process.

Nevertheless, studying the relationship between knowledge and networks, with or without a time-consuming KNA, remains a tempting approach because knowledge is never disembodied, impersonal and disinterested.[30] Examples of historical KNA in the strict sense are rarely found. The very few that are available focus, as one would expect, on interpersonal connections, specifically between scientists and other informed people as the bearers of knowledge and vectors for its spreading.[31] Some other scholars use the concept of 'knowledge networks' in the metaphorical sense.[32] The creation, acknowledgment and circulation of knowledge nevertheless forms part of a constant dialogue, negotiation or bartering process between the bearers of information in its various forms: books, test plots, advertisements, etc. and people, within and beyond groups and networks. This brings objects into the picture as co-actors – or *actants* according to the Actor-Network Theory (ANT) of the French sociologist of science Bruno Latour – within the dynamic process of making knowledge. 'True' knowledge is not a given, but is variable and dynamic as a result of interaction: John Law calls this the 'process of *translation*' in which both humans and non-humans (objects, ideas) have *agency* and cooperate.[33] When one actor (for instance an advisor) succeeds in changing other actors in such a way that they endorse his goals (for instance using more manure), we can describe this actor as a 'primum movens'.[34] This actor influences the other actors, but he changes himself too (the farmers become dependent on the advisory system). What makes

30 Livingstone, *Putting Science in its Place*, pp. 179–86.
31 R. Sigrist and E. D. Widmer, 'Training Links and Transmission of Knowledge in eighteenth-century Botany. A Social Network Analysis', *Redes* 21 (2011), pp. 347–87; F. C. Moon, *Social Networks in the History of Innovation and Invention* (Dordrecht, 2014); K. Raj, 'Networks of Knowledge, or Spaces of Circulation? The Birth of British Cartography in Colonial South Asia in the Late Eighteenth Century', *Global Intellectual History* 2 (2017), pp. 49–66.
32 S. Huigen, J. L. De Jong and E. Kolfin (eds), *The Dutch Trading Companies as Knowledge Networks* (Leiden, 2010).
33 J. Law, *Notes on the Theory of the Actor Network: Ordering, Strategy and Heterogeneity* (Lancaster University, 1992).
34 For instance: M. Callon, 'Some Elements of a Sociology of Translation: Domestication of the Scallops and the Fishermen of St. Brieuc Bay', in J. Law

the ANT model interesting? It does not start from a top-down perspective, but invites us to (re-)consider the role and weight of all *actors* and *actants* within the 'network of allies' that is willing to put new ideas or practices to the test. The result of the negotiation process can be called 'entangled knowledge', a suitable metaphor.[35]

From Scandinavia to Galicia: an introduction to the content

Where does all this lead? This book was set up as an invitation to the authors to critically assess the travel of agricultural knowledge in the past and to unfold the significance of actors and ties as part of that process, the communicative methods they employed and the networks they belonged to. Readers will notice that each of the authors did indeed choose his or her own way of unravelling the paths of agricultural knowledge. Nobody subjected his or her historical sources to a rigorous sociometric analysis. For historians, the models and methods used in the social sciences are clearly not an aim *in se*, nor an outcome, but an inspiring tool as the vocabulary in this volume will prove. The range of approaches in the book varies from the quantification of published sources as a proxy for the circulation of knowledge (the chapter by Myrdal), a careful analysis of a heterogeneous set of sources (including archives of agricultural societies) in order to discover the paths of knowledge exchange (the chapters by Holland and Kiss) and the use of oral history (the chapter by Brassley), to the in-depth study of one exceptional source, written by a farmer (the chapter by Lehmbrock). What prevails is 'thick description' in context, in which attention is paid to the material bearers of knowledge (including a specimen of the grain moth, cf. the chapter by Stockland; to letters, in the chapter by Herment; to the agrarian press, in the chapter by Cabo and Fernández Prieto), to deliberate attempts to spread innovations (in the chapters by Claeys and Segers, and by van der Laan about livestock improvement), to contingencies, and to the spatial, chronological and social circulation of 'news'.

Each contribution in this edited volume serves as a building block that provides an insight into the identity and operation of agricultural knowledge networks in Europe since 1700. More research is of course desirable and necessary; not all periods, countries or regions, sectors and actors are (proportionately) covered. Nevertheless, the insights presented by the articles allow us to formulate some conclusions. What follows is an introduction that can provide an initial framework for the reading of the ten chapters and hopefully also inspire further research.

(ed.), *Power, Action and Belief: A New Sociology of Knowledge* (London, 1986), pp. 196–233.

35 K. Hock and G. Mackenthun (eds), *Entangled Knowledge. Scientific Discourses and Cultural Difference* (Münster, 1912).

More and more complex webs of knowledge

Knowledge production and circulation in agriculture differs fundamentally from that in other economic sectors. The primary sector works with living materials and is highly dependent on factors that are difficult to control, such as climate, weather and soil conditions. Furthermore, agriculture (in the past more than today) relies predominantly on small and medium-sized family businesses, which, in contrast to large industrial groups, for instance, can free up little or no time and money for gathering information, experimenting and innovating. The conventional view of things is that, in the majority of cases, farmers mostly learned their trade from their fathers, in accordance with the traditions of the local community. This pattern was increasingly broken from the eighteenth century onwards: not only did more knowledge circuits develop, but they also displayed increasingly complex mutual relationships. Farmers became the target audience of government bureaucracies, research and educational institutions, agricultural societies, farmers' unions and agricultural cooperatives, political parties, commercial firms and journalists. Yet this does not mean that they were merely receptive actors within the networks concerned. The knowledge production and circulation in and around the agricultural sector took place within a web of economic, social and political interests in which all participants pursued their own interests and, in some cases, multiple objectives.

Janken Myrdal, Etienne Stockland and Verena Lehmbrock each illustrate in their own way how knowledge gained importance in the agricultural sector, and by extension in society as a whole, from the eighteenth century onwards. Both the demand for and the supply of new (and also old) knowledge increased significantly. Myrdal calculates that between 1700 and 1800, an increasing number of books and articles on agricultural topics were published, both in the Anglo-Saxon countries and in Scandinavia. The educated classes set themselves the goal of improving rigid agricultural practices. They focused on observations and experiments, drew conclusions and tried to convey their insights to farmers through publications, with some success. The farmers, for their part, were, according to Myrdal, more open than before to scholarly culture, although this was coupled with a critical attitude, as is also apparent from the contribution of Lehmbrock. The growing supply and improved access to agricultural knowledge went hand in hand with other innovations: new printing techniques made the publication of books, magazines and newspapers cheaper, while the improvement of the transport infrastructure reduced transport costs and allowed scientists to move more smoothly across a longer distance. All this stimulated the circulation of knowledge, at local, regional and gradually also at national, international and even intercontinental level. Those who shared in knowledge could

14

belong to a very informal circuit of initiates, but from the latter part of the eighteenth century onwards, more and more formal knowledge networks were established on the European continent.

Stockland, to start with, shows in his contribution about the French naturalist Henri-Louis Duhamel du Monceau (1700–1782) how a knowledge network was capable of scaling up to a national level. As a savant and agricultural improver, Duhamel du Monceau led the campaign against insect pests. As the linchpin of a web of exchanges, he connected amateur naturalists in the French provinces to experts and government advisers in Paris. His informal network conducted research on the grain moth, fed the debate about this harmful insect and thus created new knowledge through observations, experiments, public demonstrations and the circulation by post of specimens, reports and comments between rural localities and the capital. As a result of these actions, Duhamel du Monceau gave shape to a socio-epistemic alliance between civil servants, scientists and the enlightened rural elite in order to put an end to the problem of insect pests by means of innovative solutions. His ambitions did not exist in isolation. The knowledge network of which he was the driving force formed part of the comprehensive, encyclopaedic and enlightened movement of the time, that epitomized the faith in the reform of routine practices through the union of theory and practice, of savants and practitioners. Stockland concludes that, even in rural areas, socially heterogeneous epistemic networks were established, although we are less well informed about the involvement of local farmers.

Complementary to and, in many cases, arising from the informal networks, formal agricultural networks were established from the latter part of the eighteenth century onwards, of which the agricultural societies were the most prominent. They linked the local with the regional and national level and encompassed multiple goals: educational, political, economic and social. Zsuzsanna Kiss analyses how agricultural societies in nineteenth-century Hungary worked as disseminators of the new 'proper values' attached to agriculture. The National Society for Agriculture (established in 1835) wanted to modernize Hungarian agriculture through the introduction of 'fair' land distribution, a rational form of mixed farming and a 'modern spirit of economy'. To achieve this, it was necessary to disseminate new knowledge and insights. The National Society therefore established regional societies, which were also represented on its central governing board. This created an institutionalized connection between core and peripheral allies. The journals of the national and regional societies in particular acted as a conduit for knowledge between the national and regional levels and between the elite administrations and the members.

To date, and for reasons attributable to the availability of resources, historical research has mainly analysed the functioning and impact of the large, national agricultural societies. Sarah Holland and Zsuzsanna Kiss argue that the agency and dynamics of village or town-based farmers' clubs and of regional societies should not be underestimated. They respectively reveal the working of the agricultural societies in the district of Doncaster (England) and Zala county (Hungary) in the nineteenth century. Like the national associations, both had a strong elitist character and functioned to a large extent as top-down organizations. They were dominated by landlords, large farmers and agronomists who formed the nucleus of the knowledge network around the society: they sat on its board, paid the high membership fee and filled the editorial pages in each associations' magazine. A remarkable detail offered by Kiss is that many members lived in the (capital) city and that not all had practical experience of agriculture. Wherever they were located, membership offered them social prestige as well as access to networks that could serve their economic interests (which were not exclusively in the agricultural sector) and their political ambitions.

It was not until the end of the nineteenth century – when European agriculture was under pressure from overseas competition, farmers' literacy increased and their electoral weight became important – that farmers joined wide-ranging peasant unions that integrated them in large numbers and purposefully in a knowledge offensive. The aim of that knowledge offensive was to modernize the entire European agricultural sector, in other words to bring about a transformative process towards a more efficient, rational way of production and a reorientation towards sectors of production that would be less hindered by overseas competition. The new farmers' unions went to the villages to give lectures and courses, organized agricultural exhibitions of livestock and implements, established model farms and test and demonstration fields, and made arrangements for the cooperative purchase of fertilizers, feeds and tools. The members' magazines fulfilled a central role in the unions' operation: in the first instance, they served as a means of disseminating agricultural knowledge and know-how in an intelligible way and, in the second place, they served as a means of announcing all kinds of activities. Because they also republished articles taken from other newspapers and magazines, they offered a window to the outside world. In this way, these magazines connected individual farmers with their organization, their local community and their region, but also indirectly with what was going on outside. They strengthened the exchange of knowledge between agricultural regions with a similar or different profile and between the countryside and urban knowledge centres.

The media deserve a special mention: the agricultural press, radio and television created their own knowledge offensive and tied farmers directly to themselves. From the mid-nineteenth century until the inter-war period, the agricultural press was a booming business in all European countries. The number of magazines increased noticeably. Some titles continued to appear for a very long time, and a few are still publishing; but many others had an ephemeral existence. Some focused on a specific region, while others focused on a specific sector of production. Some mainly contained advertising, while others aimed at a more highly-educated readership. Miguel Cabo and Lourenzo Fernández Prieto, in their research into the role of the agricultural press in Galicia, distinguish between the agricultural press and the agrarian press. The first they define as press from public or semi-public institutions and professional associations; it mainly contained scientific and technical information for policymakers, agronomists, veterinarians and the like. By the agrarian press they mean the periodicals issued by farmers' unions that promoted the socio-economic and political interests of farmers and rural residents. But the distinction between the two is not always clear: the agrarian press regularly copied articles from the agricultural press, even from foreign periodicals. This shows how knowledge networks were not separate from each other: the agrarian press served the farmers' unions on the one hand and functioned as a translator from the agricultural press to the farmers on the other.

Exclusion or inclusion, indirect or direct

Although access to knowledge in Europe after 1700 was increasingly open and free, 'knowing' was (and is) to a large extent socially shaped and situated. The eighteenth and nineteenth-century agricultural societies, such as the ones in Doncaster and Zala county, had an undeniably elitist character. This meant that their knowledge and expertise were restricted to a fairly closed circuit of equals. Yet it appears that some also tried to involve smaller farmers and even agricultural workers in their activities. After all, *Volksaufklärung* formed part of enlightened thinking. They tried to do this by offering peasants favourably priced membership or by luring them with competitions and prizes, for example for the 'best fat pig kept by a cottager'. Peasants may have been able to build up some agency in the venerable network of a society, although this is hardly visible in the sources and there was certainly no inclusive attitude.

The threshold for smaller farmers was only significantly lowered once farmers' unions and cooperatives converted scientific knowledge into a language accessible and applicable to farmers. This so-called vulgarization narrowed the social divide between the learned elite and the mass of small farmers and farm workers. The farmers' unions explicitly set themselves the goal of improving the living standards of their members. Facilitating access to relevant information and (practical) knowledge was one of their main objectives. In several European countries, they found political and/or financial support for this from regional governments and the central state, which wanted to tackle the agricultural crisis of the years 1880 to 1895 by setting out on a modernization and knowledge offensive. Commercial players, such as manufacturers of fertilizers, animal feeds, tools and sprayers, producers of dairy products, canned goods and so on, also entered that territory. All of these actors, each with their own motives, worked to create 'modern farmers' and used the same wide range of methods and means that the savant agricultural societies had previously tested: the press, lectures, trial fields, demonstrations, (travelling) exhibitions and competitions. But more followed. The government began to invest heavily in agricultural education and extension, research institutions and a corps of consultants to conduct site visits and provide tailored advice to farmers. The farmers' organizations added the joint purchase of inputs (seeds and plants, fertilizers, etc.) and focused, among other things, on credit and insurance. In addition, the communication media boomed. This not only included the autonomous and association press, but, from the inter-war period onwards, radio, film and television as well. Farmers were therefore being approached in a number of different ways, from many sides at the same time and by an increasing number of personnel and resources, in order to drive them to optimize their business operations, according to a well-defined paradigm. In this way, they became the target audience, and, *a fortiori*, central actors within a complex of different networks in which knowledge was generated, vulgarized, passed on, questioned, accepted or rejected.

Nevertheless, this does not mean that all farmers started looking for knowledge and were active participants in knowledge networks from the late nineteenth century onwards, nor does it mean that all media reached them. Laurent Herment unravels the operation and advice provided by the public Agricultural Services of the Oise Department in France (DSA). To that end, he uses the outgoing correspondence of its director during a period of a few months in the year 1950. This state agronomist was well aware that he did not possess all the knowledge, that he could not reach all farmers and that he could not reach them all in the same way. He was personally acquainted with large, prominent farmers and approached them directly. He often reached the much larger group of small farmers indirectly through the channels offered to him by farmers' unions and cooperatives. For information about products and their use, such as pesticides, he mainly called on the knowledge and expertise of commercial firms. He also adapted the language in which he gave advice: in lectures and articles for small farmers, he converted the new scientific insights into practical jargon, a kind of vernacular know-how, dismissing the old practices as outdated and promoting the new as progressive and 'modern'.

Crises as a catalyst

It is striking that moments of crisis increased the call for innovation and the dissemination of knowledge. Crises were, of course, a threat, but at the same time they formed an opportunity to break new ground. They exposed structural problems that called for decisive action, increased readiness for change and innovation, and accelerated decision-making. This is precisely what occurred during the numerous major and minor economic and political crises that have affected European agriculture since the second half of the eighteenth century. Dries Claeys and Yves Segers, for example, discuss how Belgian livestock farming responded to the disastrous consequences of the First World War. The war itself and the immediate post-war period gave an important stimulus to the further introduction and diffusion of 'modern' livestock improvement. Before the war, breeders and farmers focused on the exterior appearance of cattle. Milk yields, quality of meat or fat percentage were hardly recorded or taken into account when selecting animals for breeding. That changed after 1918. Due to the fact that nearly a third of Belgian cattle did not survive the German occupation, the Ministry of Agriculture, the farmers' organizations and the livestock farmers set out to achieve a rapid restoration of the stock. But how?

The reconstruction of the national livestock was hailed by policy-makers and experts as an opportunity to establish a more productive flock by applying improved breeding practices. The necessary knowledge to achieve that goal was already in place before the war in academic and governmental circles, but the gap between theory and practice, experts and farmers, proved to be too wide at the time. After the war, the Belgian government invested in the creation of a new cattle breeding network, including state services (for instance the consultancy of the Livestock Improvement Service), civil society initiatives (breeding syndicates and exploitation syndicates of farmers' unions) and scientific research centres such as the Institute for Zootechnics in Leuven. The breeding syndicates, which received financial support from the government, managed for the first time to involve farmers directly in matters of livestock improvement. State consultants controlled and monitored the progress made. However, not only was the original plan of the Leuven professor Leopold Frateur to improve livestock in the short term delayed, but it also failed to reach the mass of Belgian farmers. By 1930, only 8 per cent of the local branches of the Belgian Farmers' Union had a cattle exploitation syndicate, representing together a meagre 1 per cent of Belgian livestock.

Steven van der Laan analyses how the pig sector in the Netherlands responded to measures taken by the British government in 1926 which banned the import of fresh meat from continental Europe. As a result of this ban, Dutch pig farmers lost a very important sales market. Only processed meat, such as bacon, could still be shipped to the United

Kingdom (UK), but Denmark dominated that product segment. The new situation prompted the Dutch pig sector to launch a knowledge offensive that would allow a switch from meat to the production of high-quality bacon. Several study trips to Denmark yielded the knowledge required to imitate the Danish system. Breeding pigs in Denmark were not only judged on external qualities, as was customary in the Netherlands, but also on production and progeny. The Danish pig farms operated in a controlled environment: some offspring were fattened in a progeny testing station and their meat quality was reported after slaughter. These results were made public and therefore provided pig farmers with the information with which to select the best animals for breeding. Knowledge of Danish practices was quickly adopted by the Dutch to advance their own economic purposes.

Van der Laan argues that the introduction of the progeny testing stations was not the outcome of a straightforward, top-down implementation of (scientific) instructions. Testing stations were but one element in a long search for better breeding practices in which traditional methods had their place and were even considered indispensable by some actors. Innovations were the result of interactions and discussions between the actors involved, including cattle breeders, geneticists, veterinarians, civil servants, farmers' unions and journalists with often diverging opinions. Even so-called experts changed their minds over the course of time. Progeny testing became, as van der Laan concludes, the method by which opinions ultimately converged towards a consensus, as a rational way to improve productivity.

'Cultural amphibians'

Livestock improvement was, therefore, far from being an uncomplicated, linear process, as Claeys and Segers and van der Laan demonstrate. Both in the Netherlands and Belgium, livestock consultants played a significant role in that process from the early twentieth century onwards. They were asked to organize lectures and courses, visits, inspections and travelling exhibitions and to further the collaboration between breeders. Many of them were teachers at agricultural colleges, and many possessed a degree from the agricultural faculties of Gembloux or Leuven in Belgium, or Wageningen in the Netherlands. Given their advanced training, these consultants acted as bridges between science and practice, and introduced a scientific way of thinking and acting into the farming community.

The intermediary role of popularizing publicists and journalists, public advisors, consultants employed by farmers' unions, representatives of commercial firms, as 'cultural amphibians' commuting between the world of scientists and that of farmers, had its roots in the course of the nineteenth century and tended to increase once again after the Second World War. After all, the challenges were great: the national economies had to be rebuilt and food shortages had to be solved. As a result, national governments invested heavily in boosting agricultural productivity by means of fundamental and practice-oriented research and knowledge diffusion. In other words: they invested once again in existing knowledge networks but also created new ones. The Agricultural Extension Service in the United States served as an eminent example for many countries in Europe.

Paul Brassley highlights the role of the UK's National Agricultural Advisory Service (NAAS). In 1950, the service had about 1,500 employees, including many specialists. Its core consisted of the 460 District Advisory Officers, who, as practitioners, were closest to the farmers. Like the directors of the French DSA, they visited farmers, provided tailor-made advice and organized lectures, seminars and shows. They also carried out 'down-to-earth' research themselves, worked closely with local author-ities, published in newspapers and magazines and gave talks on radio and television. They too worked mainly with the larger farms, but it is unclear whether this was a deliberate policy. It is possible that the larger farmers were more receptive to innovations and made more frequent use of the advice of the consultants. Brassley emphasizes that a second circuit of consultants exerted a great influence on agricultural practice: namely the technical and sales representatives of commercial firms. According to a rough estimate by a journalist, British farmers were served in the 1950s–1970s by approximately 40,000 advisors of various sorts (teachers, public servants, consultants of farmers' unions etc.), plus approximately 10,000 representatives of commercial producers. Farmers tended to rely on the products of particular firms and to place their trust in the same sales representative who acted as their personal advisor.

This does not mean, however, that the networks around public advisors, private consultants and commercial representatives were separate worlds. State agronomists were unable to provide all necessary knowledge, given the fast development of specialist science and knowledge during the course of the twentieth century. This is also evident in Laurent Herment's contribution on the DDSA in France. His detailed research offers a unique insight into the problems and challenges faced by farmers in the French region of Oise in the 1950s and into the service's differentiated approach when it came to advising them. Herment concludes that the service was confronted with two types of farmers and therefore also provided 'two levels of knowledge'. It gave the larger and more dynamic farmers access to scientific knowledge to increase their profitability; in order to persuade other farmers, however, it was necessary to 'popularize' the knowledge. This means, Herment writes, that the DDSA simultaneously had to keep its scientific network activated, while advertising good farming practices in a 'how to do' manner. The exchange of information covered a vast region, sometimes reaching abroad, and it was conveyed through various types of actors, including commercial enterprises producing seeds, pesticides and fertilizers. The commercial enterprises also had tentacles at different levels, for each of which they adapted the language they employed, for example, contacts with the scientific world in the production of their merchandise, contacts with the DDSA, farmers' unions, cooperatives and individual farmers for the sale of their merchandise. Commercial companies often took the lead in spreading new knowledge with their marketing strategies. They also had large budgets, no doubt more than other actors such as the DSA, the INRA (Institut National des Recherches Agronomiques) or the farmers' unions.

The crooked paths of agricultural knowledge

The question then remains as to when and how alleged new knowledge led to change. Which communication channels worked the most efficiently: books and journals, lectures, advertisements, public advisors, consultants of farmers' unions, representatives of commercial firms, trial fields, exhibitions? Janken Myrdal shows that the agronomic publications in the Anglo-Saxon countries and Scandinavia in the eighteenth century mainly responded to trends that were already present. After all, changes in agriculture did not always coincide with an increase in publications. In addition, the number of publications remained small and their readership was limited, too limited to be able to explain substantial changes. Rather, an increasing number of publications pointed to changes that had already taken place or were under way. Many authors referred to the practical knowledge they had already acquired.

The buyers and readers of the expensive books and periodicals that Myrdal listed were wealthy and well-educated. Scientific literature was beyond the reach of the majority of the rural population both in price and style of writing; this applied in both the eighteenth and nineteenth centuries, and for many farmers in the twentieth as well. Where farmers could read, they preferred accessible and cheap literature such as agricultural almanacs, the members' magazine of their farmers' union and weekly magazines, which is something that also comes to the fore in the chapters by Cabo and Fernández and by Brassley. Farmers welcomed a mixed content of easy reading material including how to do articles, adapted to the farm work of the season, weather sayings, devotional lyrics, a sequel, jokes, market prices and advertising. Journalists and publishers for their part used all kinds of tactics to get their audiences to read. Cabo and Fernández Prieto underline the importance of the local spoken language in Galicia (Galician instead of Spanish). Cartoons and photos served to make weekly magazines more attractive, capitals and slogans to draw the reader in. Practical advice was conveniently incorporated in the form of fictional dialogues, traditional songs or poetry, which contributed to a smooth memorization. The publishers also advised their readers to read magazines and other printed matter, which was in line with the traditional oral transmission of knowledge and wisdom in Galicia up to the first decades of the twentieth century.

But those pieces of advice were not readily accepted and followed up. Farmers were not the passive recipients of the messages of self-proclaimed experts. Vera Lehmbrock presents a very enlightening case. In 1831, Michael Irlbeck from Liebenstein (near Kötzing in Bavaria) submitted a voluminous manuscript on farming to the Bavarian Agricultural Association for evaluation. Irlbeck had no university education, but ran a medium-sized farm and therefore had a great deal of practical experience. He did not like the Agricultural Enlightenment that had been the 'bon ton' for several decades. He was critical of the new field systems that some 'experts' had touted as superior to the old three-field system. He also knew from his own experience that red clover cultivation in fallow fields was not successful. Irlbeck accused the agricultural publicists of never having farmed themselves, and certainly not 'under the conditions of a peasant economy'. He rejected their advice. What is more, he rejected the idea that they should educate farmers. He only wanted to accept advice from authorized experts, namely experienced farmers and landowners who lived exclusively off agriculture.

However, Irlbeck was not conservative: he accepted that agricultural practice needed to change, but his trust in the advice of agronomists had been undermined several times. Lehmbrock asks why some farmers wanted to blindly follow the advice of so-called enlightened experts and why those protagonists of the *Volksaufklärung* wanted to give advice at all on matters that were not theirs. She concludes that the transmission of knowledge was inadequate because it concerned hierarchical social groups that were separated from one another: the social gap between the hard-working farmers on the one hand and the literate, wealthy and politically powerful elite on the other prevented the exchange of information in both directions. The elite practised 'salon and experimental garden agronomy' and the feedback from the farmers did not reach the enlightened elite or, if it did, was not taken seriously by them. Farmers did have empirical experience, but they did not have the knowledge to explain why certain things worked well and others not at all. The enlightened agronomists honoured knowledge, but looked down on traditional know-how. The Irlbeck case shows that there was a break in communication between the knowledge networks of the enlightened *Volksaufklärung* on the one hand and the local knowledge circuits of farmers on the other. The advice of the learned agronomists did reach some of the farmers, but it did not become part of the current exchange of knowledge among them. The new knowledge was therefore 'socially chambered'. This remained true over most of Europe until the mid-nineteenth century.

Closing the gap did not take place until the latter part of the nineteenth century, when skilled agronomists assumed the role of translators, who devoted themselves to providing hands-on practical advice to farmers and engaging in a dialogue with them. They became, as stated above, the 'cultural amphibians' who, with one foot in the scientific camp and the other in the field, sought to connect these two separate worlds. Ideally, these intermediary actors would provide scientists with feedback regarding the attitude of the farmers, the feasibility of innovations and the specific needs and problems at farm level. This may also have encompassed suggestions and ideas from the farmers themselves. That process did not run smoothly, however. Brassley notes that British farmers continued to express criticism after the Second World War. They regarded a lot of scientific knowledge as insufficiently practical and problem-orientated nor geared to concrete situations, such as the soil type, the size of the business and the local market. The experts in the specialist knowledge circuits above all communicated with each other, but little with farmers. Farmers did not come into direct contact with scientific and technological innovations, but gained a knowledge of them via a mix of other actors (such as teachers, consultants, sales representatives, journalists and fellow farmers), through material evidence and visible results in their own environment (field trials, and demonstrations of tools for instance), or by looking over the hedge.

Cabo and Fernández Prieto found that the knowledge of the experts sent to Galicia, such as agronomists, veterinarians and technicians, was far removed from local practice with which they were not familiar: in addition they spoke in an educated language rather than the local vernacular. In these ways they demonstrated their distance and superiority from the people they had been sent to assist. They were also mistrusted because they were officials of the Spanish state that imposed taxes on farmers and required them to do military service. It was not until the early twentieth century that agronomists began to realize that farmers themselves could take an active role in the innovation process. State agronomists therefore began to encourage the creation of farmers' unions, albeit preferably ones that did not take explicit political positions on questions such as that of the *foro* and full land ownership. The functioning of knowledge networks in the countryside was inevitably deeply influenced by politics and specific economic interests.

Finally, according to many historical sources, a third factor, which is hardly tangible, plays a role in explaining the ineffectual dialogue between experts and farmers, namely the so-called conservative mentality of farmers. This certainly was the case with regard to the improvement of Belgian livestock after the First World War, as farmers were not open to innovation. Farmers did not like school desks, or book farming. In the Belgian context, the small scale of many farms may also have had an influence and the lack of capital to invest in innovations of course played a role. Innovation also went hand in hand with risks and uncertainty. Claeys and Segers conclude that the hesitations of Belgian farmers were not so much a consequence of their conservative mentality, but rather a rational choice based on a pragmatic consideration of costs and profits. Farmers' agency should therefore not be underestimated. They decided what was advantageous to them and what was not, what to adopt and what to discard. Or to put it otherwise, they had the last word. All in all, Irlbeck's conclusion still stands: when it comes to agriculture, agricultural practitioners, not civil servants, must be regarded as the designated experts.

If the chapters in this book make one thing clear, it is that from the eighteenth century onwards, there existed an ever-present tension between science-based or scholarly book-based agriculture and practice-based agriculture, between the expert image of an ideal agriculture and the (less known) self-image of being a good farmer. From the start of the agricultural Enlightenment onwards and increasingly up to the present day, farmers (of both sexes) have been besieged by a growing army of experts and advisors, who fulfil the role of modern prophets, telling them what to do, when and how. They had, and still have, the power to resist and to carve their own path, as did Irlbeck, but it is important to acknowledge that farming became one of the most, if not *the* most patronized profession. The dominant image, which also shines through in this book, is that of an instrumental top-down transmission of knowledge from the laboratory to the field, from government to farmer. But between these two poles, complex and very flourishing networks developed that functioned as a trading zone in which knowledge and experiences circulated, were put to the test, forgotten, altered, rejected or occasionally imposed.

2

Agricultural Literature in Scandinavia and the Anglo-Saxon Countries as an Indicator of a Deep-Rooted Economic Enlightenment, c. 1700–1800

Janken Myrdal

The Economic Enlightenment in the countryside saw a change in the knowledge systems at play and the establishment of a culture of innovation aimed at optimizing agricultural production.[1] To examine this process of change, I will use agricultural literature published in Scandinavia and in the Anglo-Saxon countries during the eighteenth century as an indicator.[2] The hypothesis the chapter wishes to advance is that literature about agriculture was a consequence of changes in agricultural practices, rather than affecting such changes. To put it differently: the authors often

---

[1] For a definition of the Economic Enlightenment see M. Popplow, 'Die Ökonomische Aufklärung als Innovationskultur des 18. Jahrhunderts zur optimierten Nutzung natürlicher Ressourcen', in M. Popplow (ed.), *Landschaften agrarisch-ökonomischen Wissens: Strategien innovativer Ressourcennutzung in Zeitschriften und Sozietäten des 18. Jahrhunderts* (Münster, 2010), pp. 3–4, although he more focuses more on the elite, and I include the general population.

[2] A longer version of this text has been published in Swedish as J. Myrdal, 'Lantbrukslitteraturen under 1700-talet som indikator på djupgående mentalitetsförändringar i samhället', in Per-Magnus Hebbe, *Den svenska lantbrukslitteraturen: bibliografisk förteckning* (2nd edn, Stockholm, 2014), pp. 15–42. For agricultural literature as a source for eighteenth-century agriculture see also Ulrich Lange, *Experimentalfältet: Kungl. Lantbruksakademiens experiment- och försöksverksamhet på Norra Djurgården i Stockholm 1816–1900* (Stockholm, 2000), pp. 34–6; Mats Morell, 'Den agrara ingenjörskonsten', in A. Björnsson and L. Magnusson (eds), *Jordpäron: svensk ekonomihistorisk läsebok* (Stockholm, 2011), pp. 445–71.

addressed issues being discussed more generally in society in formal and informal knowledge networks.

Agricultural literature is one of the oldest and most important non-fictional genres. Columella's work on agriculture from the first century of the Common Era runs to more than 200,000 words.[3] From the sixteenth century there was an expansion of this literature in the West, with a rapid increase from the eighteenth century onwards. Though these works were not widely disseminated, and the direct influence seems to have been rather limited, the proliferation of texts offering a more practical, hands-on approach was a burgeoning part of an even faster growing general intellectual debate within society.

If this agricultural literature reflected the discourses in society at large, they can also be used to study new attitudes, such as the greater appreciation of novelty and innovations. This was a deep, underlying current that was transforming the countryside, an increasingly critical discussion, also among farmers, about how to manage farming, which was combined with growing communication between different social strata where the literate upper class was not only delivering information, but perhaps even more obtaining information from below.

I am not proposing that tradition and stagnation were totally prevalent before then, and I do not argue that this literature provides us with accurate information about what was on the agenda at village meetings or general discussions in the churchyard. However, when the literature does begin to become more widespread, it is in fact one of the few indicators we have about broader societal discussion on these issues. Agricultural literature allows us to reach further back into history than most other sources, as we try to understand the contemporary discussions on farming from any given time.

In order to provide a premise for the hypothesis, I will present statistics on the annual publication of agricultural literature in the Anglo-Saxon countries (England, Scotland, Wales, Ireland, North America) and in Scandinavia (Schleswig-Holstein, Denmark, Norway, Sweden-Finland, Iceland) during the eighteenth century (for Scandinavia to the 1820s). These two regions of Europe have good databases of agricultural literature.

In addition to books, other texts published (in Scandinavia) will also be analysed. Shifting the focus from books to articles is important, as the role of the latter was fast growing from the second half of the eighteenth century. The content of articles is often much more specific than books covering a variety of topics, and thus articles reveal the issues raised during different periods.

---

[3] J. Myrdal, 'Agricultural Treatises in Eurasia before ca. 1500: The Iceberg Method, a Survey, and a Grand Hypothesis', *The Medieval Globe*, 6 (2020), pp. 1–47.

The circulation of agricultural literature and the networks

One important question concerns the circulation of these books and their reach. To obtain information about the number of copies published is no simple feat, but some indicators can be used. Establishing how much they were read is much more difficult.

In an article on Scotland, published in 2006, Heather Holmes analysed four subscription lists contained in books from the late eighteenth and early nineteenth centuries (three of them written by David Young). The number of subscribers varies between 121 and 576, and subscribed copies between 138 and 956 (since many subscribers ordered several copies). She also refers to a few examples of English agricultural books from the same period published in runs of 500 to a thousand copies.[4] Nicholas Goddard gives the example of Arthur Young, the most successful of all agricultural writers of the time in England, whose *Farmer's Kalendar* peaked with a run of around two thousand copies for a new edition printed at the beginning of the nineteenth century.[5]

In Sweden, an investigation into subscription lists includes two books on agriculture. One of these is a work about crop rotation from 1812 and had 489 subscribers ordering 907 copies. About a hundred of the subscribers were farmers. The other book was about agricultural chemistry published in 1831–1832, which had 207 subscribers, none of them farmers. Instead the key group were students (apparently it was used as a university text book). The book on crop rotation was almost the only book included in the selection that farmers subscribed to: a few copies of a county description were also sold to wealthy farmers.[6]

Hushållningsjournalen was an important journal, published by the Royal Patriotic Society (Kungl. Patriotiska Sällskapet) in Sweden, which carried articles on agriculture. In 1779, 600 copies were printed, but most of them remained unsold, so the number of copies printed was gradually reduced to 450 by 1784, which still left many unsold. There was even an attempt to distribute unsold copies at a county market, though this proved fruitless.[7]

Each individual copy may have been read by several persons. For instance, in a letter from 1802, a subscriber to *Hushållningsjournalen* complained that the journal passed through the whole parish and was

---

4   H. Holmes, 'The Circulation of Scottish Agricultural Books during the Eighteenth Century', *Agricultural History Rev.* 54 (2006), p. 56.
5   N. Goddard, 'Agricultural Literature and Societies', in G. E. Mingay (ed.), *The Agrarian History of England and Wales,* VI, *1750–1850* (Cambridge, 1989), pp. 362–5.
6   B. Dal, *Med kolorerade figurer: handkolorering i Sverige under 1700- och 1800-talen* (Lund, 2001), pp. 221, 347.
7   S. Högberg, *Kungl. Patriotiska sällskapets historia: med särskild hänsyn till den gustavianska tidens agrara reformsträvanden* (Stockholm, 1961), pp. 134–5.

well-thumbed when it was eventually returned to him.[8] The actual books themselves may carry signatures revealing ownership, or bookplates. However, such information only hints at whether these books were actually shared amongst multiple people. For the purpose of this study, it is sufficient to say that eighteenth-century agricultural literature, though not insignificant, did not reach out to the peasantry. Almanacs, however, were widely available and often contained some information about agriculture, though of a rather rudimentary sort. I have not included almanacs in this study, as it would demand another kind of study; focusing on what kind of information they contain.[9]

An interesting case is France during the French Revolution. Over a period of two decades, the state invested in educating the general population, and several thousand copies of agricultural treatises were distributed across the country. With the Restoration, this project was gradually wound down.[10] But on the whole, agricultural literature did not have a greater impact in France than in other countries. For the Paris region in the eighteenth century, Jean-Michel Chevet has shown that agrarian change started before the expansion of agricultural literature.[11] In the same volume, François Sigaut claimed that published agricultural science was of little practical importance before the late nineteenth century.[12]

Another indicator is the number of members in agricultural societies. The Royal Patriotic Society in Sweden had about a thousand members, though most of them were not active in its affairs.[13] In the first decades of the nineteenth century, a nationwide organization was established under the control of the Royal Academy of Agriculture, with about 20 provincial agricultural societies. In the years 1801–1820, these had typically about 300 members each, so thousands were affiliated to it, though again most of

---

[8] Högberg, *Kungl. Patriotiska*, p. 135.

[9] In the chapter 'Printing and the People' in N. Zemon Davis, *Society and Culture in Early Modern France* (Stanford, 1965), Davis discusses almanacs and other early literature about agriculture in relation to popular culture. See also M. Vaquero Piñeiro, 'Readings for the Farmers: Agrarian Almanacs in Italy from the Eighteenth to the Twentieth Century', *Agricultural History Rev.* 63 (2015), pp. 243–64.

[10] J. Boulaine, 'Vingt an de vulgarisation au XVIe siècle', in M.-C. Amouretti and F. Sigaut (eds), *Traditions agronomiques européennes: élaboration et transmission depuis l'Antiquité* (Paris, 1998), pp. 43–52.

[11] J.-M. Chevet, 'La transmission des savoirs dans le processus de croissance économique aux XVIIIe-XIXe siècles: L'exemple de la région parisienne', in Amouretti and Sigaut (eds), *Traditions agronomiques européennes*, pp. 182–7.

[12] François Sigaut, 'Entre pratiques raisonnées et science efficace: l'âge des doctrines en agronomie', in Amouretti and Sigaut (eds), *Traditions agronomiques européennes*, pp. 197–221.

[13] Högberg, *Kungl. Patriotiska*, pp. 64–5.

these were inactive. The nobility and the clergy dominated, while wealthy farmers only occasionally made up more than a tenth of the membership. (In one society in the north, half of the members were farmers.)[14]

Such societies were founded all over Europe in the eighteenth and nineteenth centuries.[15] In Germany, the question of membership has been examined in relation to the Economic Enlightenment. Information regarding three societies in the late eighteenth century, in Potsdam, Kurpfalz and Hannover, show that membership was not just a formality: many members were farmers or agents. The number of members varied between 150 and 350.[16] The agricultural societies themselves were mainly elite-based knowledge networks that connected to other formal and informal networks in the countryside, such as village communities and parish organizations, with much of the literature published by members of these societies.

A useful source in studying the influence of this literature are documents produced by the farmers themselves: diaries and account books. I will only briefly touch upon this source as much more research is needed. These documents became quite common in much of north-western Europe from the eighteenth century onwards. I organized a project aimed at collecting them in Sweden, orchestrating the creation of a national catalogue.[17] During the eighteenth century, they contain hardly any mention of agricultural literature, but in the early nineteenth century such comments are found.[18] A survey of peasant diaries, including similar material produced by parish priests and local noblemen, would shed light on the influence of agricultural literature, as well as the local knowledge networks.

---

14 J. Stattin, *Hushållningssällskapen och agrarsamhällets förändring* (Uppsala, 1980), pp. 87–97. In the 1830s and 1840s the proportion of farmers increased to around a fifth to a half of the members in most of these provincial societies.

15 Goddard, 'Agricultural Literature', pp. 370–4 mentions a number of such societies in eighteenth-century England, but does not present any membership numbers. In the mid- nineteenth century the Royal Agricultural Society, founded 1838, had several thousand members.

16 F. Tosch, 'Der Aufklärertypus Friedrich Eberhard von Rochow (1734–1805) und die Märkische Ökonomische Gesellschaft zu Potsdam', in Popplow (ed.), *Landschaften agrarisch-ökonomischen Wissens*, p. 159; K. F. Hünemörder, 'Die Celler Landwirtschaftsgesellschaft und das Hannoverische Magazin: Schnittstellen der ökonomischen Aufklärung in Kurhannover (1750–1789)', in Popplow (ed.), *Landschaften agrarisch-ökonomischen Wissens*, p. 241; Popolow, 'Die Ökonomische', p. 191.

17 J. Myrdal (ed.), *Alla de dagar som är livet. Bondedagböcker om arbete, resor och umgänge under 1800-talet* (Stockholm, 1991); B. Larsson, *Svenska bondedagböcker: ett nationalregister* (Stockholm, 1992).

18 This observation is based on my own extensive reading of this material, and I have also discussed it with Mats Morell.

Agricultural literature and a knowledge-based society

Jan Luiten van Zanden – among others – has argued that the economic expansion in Europe was linked to the emergence of a knowledge-based society. Every society is of course knowledge-based, but what ensued here was a rapid increase in the existing knowledge and of the methods used to apply this knowledge to practical activities (the circulation of knowledge).

Investments in knowledge shaped an increase in human capital among larger portions of the population. Van Zanden has used the number of books as an indicator of the formation of human capital.[19] He has highlighted important general trends, as for instance north-western Europe's advancement and the waning of the Mediterranean countries, which is something that he attributes to a change in the literacy levels with, for example, Sweden making great progress in this regard during the eighteenth century.[20]

Increased book production was not limited to economic topics, and the relative proportion of books on scientific subjects – in England and Scandinavia – actually stagnated during the eighteenth century. Other fields, such as fiction and politics, increased, while books on theology exhibited a clear downward trend.[21] The increase in book production in Europe was, however, on such an enormous scale that absolute change for certain subjects was just as important as relative change.

Van Zanden refers to Joel Mokyr's definition of a knowledge economy as one that produces useful knowledge of relevance to economic growth.[22] Mokyr has, in a series of publications, discussed how technical change occurs, and he has used a survey of books and of the different subjects covered by them in a detailed study of change in Britain, which is assumed to have spearheaded development during the eighteenth century. Mokyr uses agricultural literature, in combination with other indicators, such as agricultural societies, to highlight an accumulation of 'agricultural knowledge'. He considers it doubtful as to whether these agricultural books actually helped raise agricultural productivity and questions whether peasants actually read them. He then goes on to say that such a judgement probably misses the true significance of the change. These books represented a thirst for knowledge and indicate that

---

[19] J. L. van Zanden, *The Long Road to the Industrial Revolution: The European Economy in a Global Perspective, 1000–1800* (Leiden, 2009), pp. 294–5.

[20] *Ibid.*, pp. 185, 195.

[21] J. Mokyr, *The Enlightened Economy: Britan and the Industrial Revolution, 1700–1850* (New Haven, 2009), pp. 46–7; J. Myrdal and J. Söderberg, 'Bokproduktion och sekularisering 1500–1800: Agrarlitteraturen under 1700-talet som exempel', in M. Wallenberg Bondesson *et al.* (eds), *Människans kunskap och kunskapen om människan: en gränslös historia* (Lund, 2012), pp. 47–66.

[22] Van Zanden *The Long Road*, p. 9.

the idea of increased knowledge was a good thing.[23] This is in line with the hypothesis I have put forward.

A number of scholars have made use of statistics on agricultural literature. However, the first one to be mentioned did not: G. E. Fussell (1889–1991). He published an extremely detailed review of English agrarian literature (including some published in Scotland), over several volumes. Fussell had been a librarian at the Ministry of Agriculture and Fisheries, and he made it his ambition to read all the old literature on agriculture. In 1947, two years prior to his retirement, he began publishing a series of books about agricultural literature. In 1950, the volume covering the period 1731–1793, the period that is of greatest interest to this study, appeared.[24] Publication of further volumes did not resume until the 1980s.

His books are descriptive bibliographies, in which book after book and author after author are accorded a few lines each. His selection is somewhat subjective, and even includes the work of the Swedish biologist Carl Linnaeus. For the years 1731–1793, he lists roughly four hundred books. When viewed year by year, there is a certain correlation with the curve in the graph below (Figure 2.1). Fussell identifies certain key individuals: Jethro Tull during the 1730s, and Arthur Young and William Marshall from the end of the eighteenth century.

In 1984, Richard Sullivan published an article on the development of books on agricultural production techniques in England from the sixteenth to the nineteenth century, based on the well-known bibliography by Walter Frank Perkins, which was published in the 1930s.[25] Sullivan compares this to the number of patents that were granted and finds a high correlation. In fact, he suggests that books may be an even better measure of general technological change than patents themselves. His diagram depicts information on books per decade and features two curves, one for first editions and the other for subsequent editions. The number of extra editions tends to decrease over time, especially during the latter half of the eighteenth century when the number of titles increases.[26] He also notes that the number of periodicals increased, which means that it is unlikely that book titles reflect the full scope of topics covered.

---

23 Mokyr, *Enlightened Economy*, pp. 187–9.
24 G. E. Fussell, The Old English Farming Books, II, *More Old English Farming Books: From Tull to the Board of Agriculture, 1731 to 1793* (London, 1950).
25 W. F. Perkins, *British and Irish writers on Agriculture* (3rd edn, Lymington, 1939); R. Sullivan, 'Measurement of English Farming Technological Change, 1523–1900', *Explorations in Economic History* 21 (1984), pp. 270–89; and see D. Grigg, *The Transformation of Agriculture in the West* (Cambridge, MA, 1992), p. 116, but he has no reference to Sullivan.
26 Sullivan, 'Measurement', p. 275.

Extensive bibliographies that include all articles published in journals have been published for Denmark and Sweden (see below). The results for Denmark were analysed by Gerd Malling in 1982 and were subsequently used in an article by Thorkild Kjaergaard in 1986.[27] Kjaergaard compares this information with national agricultural bibliographies from Germany, Italy, England (Perkins) and France, and states that these are incomplete, mainly because they do not include articles published in journals. He has a diagram of all Danish agricultural publications and argues that this demonstrates how the introduction of the printing press was crucial for the modernization of Europe.

Books about agriculture

In this study I have concentrated on the production of texts, books and articles in the Anglo-Saxon countries and Scandinavia, partly because of the high standard of the databases that are available and partly because of the drastic increase of books and articles in these regions. Several problems arise when measuring the number of books and articles, not least the use of databases. I discussed this at length in an article from 2014 in Swedish and, though important, I have omitted much of this discussion here.[28]

Firstly, I discuss individual publications – mainly books, but also pamphlets. I compare Anglo-Saxon countries with Sweden. Then I move on to address all texts on agriculture, including articles published in journals. This part of the study includes Sweden (and Finland until 1809) and Denmark.

The database used for Anglo-Saxon literature is the English Short Title Catalogue (ESTC).[29] It contains titles of publications found in the catalogue of the British Library, as well as two thousand other institutions. Hundreds of thousands of titles are registered, and I have selected all those published in England, Scotland, Wales, Ireland and North America between 1473 and 1800. Searches have been done for 'agriculture', 'gardening' and 'forestry', but in the diagram below (Figure 2.1) only agriculture has been included.

There is an overlap between these categories. Due to a potentially unclear categorization of the catalogue, I checked each publication individually under the category 'agriculture' and these results were

---

[27]   G. Malling, *1700-tallets danske landbrugslitteratur* (Copenhagen, 1982); Thorkild Kjaergaard, 'Origins of Economic Growth in European Societies since the XVIth Century: The Case of Agriculture', *Journal of European Economic History* 15 (1986), pp. 591–8.

[28]   Myrdal, 'Lantbrukslitteraturen', pp. 24–31.

[29]   English Short Title Catalogue (http://estc.bl.uk).

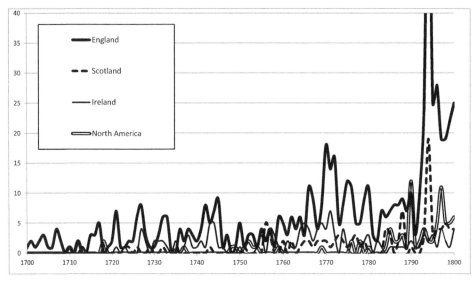

FIGURE 2.1. Printed publications about 'agriculture', per annum in the ESTC.

compared with those from the database search.[30] I was somewhat stricter in identifying agriculture (from the titles), and my numbers were slightly lower than in the database, although the two curves do follow each other closely. The important conclusion is that the identification of publications classified under 'agriculture' is in line with the identification of the Swedish material, and thus I can compare the two databases, covering English and Swedish literature.

For the Anglo-Saxon database, only publications written in English have been chosen, and the criteria were that these had to have been printed in 'England', 'Scotland', 'Ireland' or the 'United States' (also including the period prior to 1776). Publications printed in France and other countries have been excluded. Wales is excluded as there were only five hits in the catalogue during the 1790s and none before that. There are only two hits for 'Canada' from around 1790 and these have been included in the North America category. It should be stated that these publications from the outer periphery at the end of the period are in line with the results presented below.

The earliest part of the dataset consists of books published in England during the sixteenth and seventeenth centuries (the earliest book on agriculture is from 1523), and these have already been presented in another related study. It shows that from the early sixteenth century in England, on average two to three books about agriculture were published

---

30   Myrdal, 'Lantbrukslitteraturen', pp. 24–5.

each year until the beginning of the eighteenth century.[31] In other English-speaking countries, the production of agricultural literature did not really begin until the eighteenth century (Figure 2.1).

Expansion began in the 1720s, with other countries within the UK catching up later. From the middle of the eighteenth century, there was quite an extensive production of books on agriculture in Scotland and Ireland. This production stagnated in Ireland towards the end of the century, while it continued to increase in Scotland. North America witnessed a very rapid increase at the end of the century, essentially after 1776. Books had been of importance before the revolution but were then mainly about religion and politics.[32]

The curves for England and Scotland peak in around 1794, with the former reaching 72 hits (off the scale on the graph). The explanation for this is that the Board of Agriculture was founded in the UK in 1793 and it initiated a number of local surveys, which had already commenced before the organization was officially formed.[33] These generally appeared in 1794. However, even if these are excluded, there is still a strong increase in England and Scotland during the 1790s.

The declining rate of publication during the 1770s can partly be explained in the same way as its decline in Sweden (see below): a decrease in book production was compensated for by an increase in articles published in journals. Before 1764, journals were published in only a few years (1727, 1740, 1739) but, from then on, issues were more or less consistently published throughout the rest of the century, with at least one or two journals being published every year. Few of them were of any significance.[34] Almost all of them were the result of private initiatives. After the turn of the nineteenth century, the number of journals increased, while book production also expanded.

The sharp rise in around 1800 was also matched by considerable sales of both books and magazines at that time.[35] There are several possible explanations for this more deliberate focus on agrarian topics. The French Revolution had highlighted the need for change in the countryside in an effort to pacify revolutionary tendencies. Food supply also became an important issue during wartime, and we thus see an

---

31 Myrdal, 'Agricultural Treatises', pp. 9–10 with diagram.
32 L. Sidney Thompson, *Boktryckarkonstens uppkomst i Förenta Staterna* (Stockholm, 1956).
33 Goddard, 'Agricultural Literature', pp. 379–80.
34 Perkins, *British and Irish Writers*, pp. 210–14; F. A. Buttress, *Agricultural Periodicals of the British Isles, 1681–1900, and their Location* (Cambridge, 1950); N. Goddard, 'The development and Influence of Agricultural Periodicals and Newspapers 1770–1880', *Agricultural History Rev.* 31 (1983), pp. 116–31; Goddard, 'Agricultural Literature', pp. 366–70.
35 *Ibid.*, pp. 362, 369–70.

interesting parallel with the mass production of literature on agriculture in France at this time (see above).

'Agriculture' is the only category to be included in the diagram, but a comparison with the other two categories, 'gardening' and 'forestry', is certainly interesting. In England, the number of publications on gardening was higher than those on agriculture during the first two decades of the century. Of the total number of published works, books on agriculture constituted circa 0.2 per cent from 1700 to 1720, compared to 0.25 per cent on gardening. During much of the rest of the century, agriculture's share remained at this level before increasing during the last decades to 0.5 per cent. Gardening's share gradually fell and, at the end of the century, it was down to circa 0.1 per cent. (Gardening also declined in absolute terms.) There are only a few hits for forestry, and those there are come almost exclusively at the beginning of the century. Forestry has so few hits that any calculations of the relative share are meaningless.

The publications on gardening were, according to the titles, and at least initially, largely for the enjoyment of the upper class (and many of them were specifically targeted at women). This differentiates them from books on agriculture that, according to the titles, had a distinctly practical focus, even if many of these are also explicitly directed at 'gentlemen', i.e. of the middle and upper class.

I will now turn my attention to Sweden. The National Library of Sweden (Kungliga Biblioteket, literally The Royal Library), has a database for all Swedish literature: Libris (also known as LIBRIS). This has been gradually developed over the last decades and has registered every single book ever published in Sweden. Categorization is complete up until 1829, but there are still some gaps in categorization for the period after that (though all books are registered). I have used the category 'agriculture' ('Qd' is the sign used for this in the Swedish National Library system).

Figure 2.2 shows the number of individual printed publications per annum in Sweden. A comparison with England illustrates that Sweden, with almost no agrarian publications at all during the seventeenth century (three publications appeared towards the end of the century), quickly reached the same number of publications as that of the larger nation in absolute terms during the 1740s. This was partly caused by the rapid general rise in book production that Sweden witnessed during this century (see above), but also by a relatively fast increase in agricultural books as shown in Figure 2.2. It is thus astonishing that Sweden actually had a larger annual output of agricultural books than England in the middle of the eighteenth century. The relative proportion was also much higher, though falling during the second half of the century. During the second and third quarters of the century it was around 2–3 per cent of total book production, and in some of those years even more, gradually falling to around 1 per cent by the beginning of the nineteenth century.

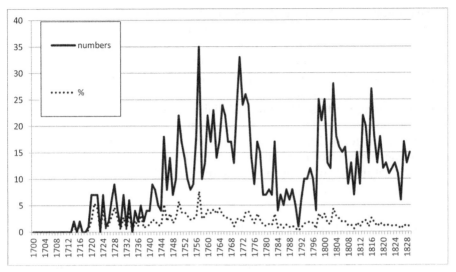

Figure 2.2 Agricultural books produced in Swedish, per annum (absolute and relative in relation to all books). Source: Libris (National Library of Sweden).

The rapid advancement gave Sweden influence in other countries. In the Danish agricultural bibliography (see below) the number of translations from other languages is quite low (under two hundred works in total). However, in the 1740s translations from Swedish were fairly common.[36] Sweden was seen as a pioneering country with respect to agricultural publishing in Germany and Switzerland. The world famous biologist Carl Linnaeus played a role in this.[37] Bern Oekonomische Gesselschaft (the economic society) published a collection of translations from Swedish in the 1760s, inspired by a similar, earlier collection of Swedish texts in translation published in Göttingen.[38] Also, in northern Germany translations from Swedish were not uncommon and were second only to English.[39] An English contemporary author even spoke of a Swedish intellectual miracle.[40] Other than that, much less attention was paid to Swedish contributions in England than in German-speaking countries. The Swedish interest in other countries' agriculture, judging by

36 Malling, *1700-tallets danske*, p. 16.
37 Popplow, 'Die Ökonomische', pp. 36, 41.
38 M. Stuber, '"Dass gemeinnüzige wahtheit gemein gemacht werden": Zur Publikationstätigkeit der Oekonomischen Gesellschaft Bern, 1759–1798', in Popplow (ed.), *Landschaften agrarisch-ökonomischen Wissens*, p. 136.
39 Hünemörder, 'Die Celler', p. 250.
40 A. Önnerfors, 'Die Nutzbarmachung der Natur als Tema der schwedischen augeklärten Presse', in Popplow (ed.), *Landschaften agrarisch-ökonomischen Wissens*, p. 325.

the number of translated texts, was mainly focused on Germany – interest in England was greater during the nineteenth century.

From the 1760s onwards there was a decrease in book production. This was partly, as in England, caused by the fact that debate was now increasingly being conducted in the periodical press, though this is not the entire explanation. What can be seen is a real decrease of interest in these issues among readers. The international interest in Swedish publications also waned. In Sweden there was a massive upsurge in the number of publications following the Freedom of Press Act in 1766. However, the resulting plethora of pamphlets concerned not agriculture, but politics. In fact, natural science was in relative retreat in Sweden by the end of the eighteenth century.[41]

Books and articles on agriculture

The next step is to include all the articles, using two specialist bibliographies of Danish and Swedish agricultural literature. These are among the most comprehensive bibliographies of this type of literature in Europe.

The Swedish bibliography was put together by Per Magnus Hebbe and appeared in two volumes, the first in 1939 (detailing publications up to 1800) and the second in 1945 (up to 1850 – published posthumously as Hebbe had died in 1942).[42] From 1932, he had been the librarian at the Agricultural College of Sweden (Lantbrukshögskolan), which became the core of the Swedish University of Agricultural Sciences (SLU), founded in 1977. The bibliography was created on his initiative and he worked on it for many years. It was then published by the Royal Swedish Academy of Agriculture (now the Swedish Academy of Forestry and Agriculture, KSLA).

Ole Karup Pedersen compiled the Danish bibliography. This project was inspired by the Swedish project. Such mutual stimulus is a common phenomenon in the Nordic countries. It was published by the Kongl. Landhusholdningsselskab in 1958.[43] This volume covered the period up to 1814; a planned second volume never appeared.

The advantage of working with all text, including articles, instead of just individual publications and books, can be shown by comparing the numbers in Hebbe's bibliography – covering both articles and books – with the number in the Libris database covering separate publications

---

[41] K. Johannisson, 'Naturvetenskap på reträtt. En diskussion om naturvetenskapens status under svenskt 1700-tal', *Lychnos 1979–1980* (1981), pp. 109–54.

[42] P. M. Hebbe, *Den svenska lantbrukslitteraturen: bibliografisk förteckning I-II* (Stockholm, 1939–45). A second edition, a facsimile with new introductions, was published in 2014, see n. 2.

[43] O. Karup Pedersen, *Dansk landbrugsbibliografi I: Indtil 1814* (Copenhagen, 1958).

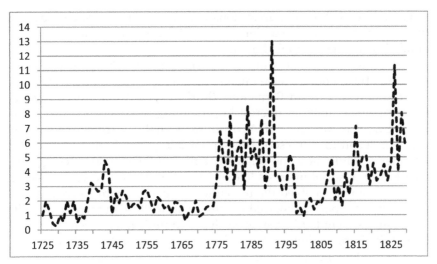

FIGURE 2.3 The number of texts mentioned in Hebbe's bibliography compared with the number of publications in the national database (Libris) where Libris equals 1.0. This mainly shows the number of articles plus books compared to only books.

only: see Figure 2.3. On average, there are two to three times more texts in Hebbe's work and, for some decades (the 1770s and 1780s), as much as ten times more.

The changed circumstances for publication must also be considered. The publication of journals in Sweden was linked to learned societies. There is no equivalent to the English private initiatives. The Royal Swedish Academy of Sciences (Kungl. Vetenskapsakademien) was founded in 1739 and immediately began publishing its 'transactions' (*Vetenskapsakademiens handlingar*). This journal was, at least initially, largely aimed at promoting the economy, not least agriculture. Interest then gradually shifted to a more purely scientific focus.[44] It was felt that the need for a more practical focus existed, and this resulted in the foundation of the Royal Patriotic Society (Kungl. Patriotiska Sällskapet) in 1766. It began publishing at once, and from 1776 issued the monthly *Hushållningsjournalen*. From around 1790, the number of articles published annually declined.

We can now return to the total number of texts. A comparison between the curve for Swedish publications in Figure 2.4 shows that the dip in the 1770s and 1780s does not represent the collapse that Figure 2.2 indicates, but nevertheless there was stagnation. The increase in the early nineteenth century is also more evident. This was a part of a longer trend. During the whole of the nineteenth century, book production on agriculture

---

44 Morell, 'Den agrara', pp. 450–1.

stagnated just below 20 publications per year (or perhaps, considering the gaps in categorization under Qd/agriculture, slightly more), while the number of articles continued to increase.

Part of the expansion during the early nineteenth century can be explained by a renewed state interest. During the 1820s, the government and the new king, Jean Bernadotte (Karl Johan XIV), a French revolutionary general, took an interest in promoting Sweden's economy. The Royal Swedish Academy of Agriculture (Kungl. Lantbruksakademien) was founded in 1811 and soon began publishing periodicals.[45] Bernadotte, a former revolutionary and originally a man of the people, acted against a backdrop of social interests like all historical figures. Nevertheless, he was the one who enabled the revolutionary period, with its concern for agriculture, to spark a renewed interest in agriculture in Sweden as well.

Finland is included in the Swedish graph until 1809, when it became part of the Russian Empire. Here I have identified works dealing specifically with Finland (and not only books and journals published in Finland), as a part of all texts about provinces of Sweden ('landskap'). This increases from about 15–20 per cent of all texts to about 30 per cent during the decades at the turn of the nineteenth century (part of a general expansion of the periphery in European agricultural publishing). In the graph, the 'loss' of Finland can be identified as a dip after 1809, but then a fast recovery follows according to a general expansion during the 1810s.

Turning now to Denmark, it has already been noted that Sweden introduced the Freedom of the Press Act in 1766. Denmark introduced a similar law in 1771 but, as in Sweden, it did not have any effect on the average number of articles published on agriculture. (Both in Denmark and Sweden the freedom of press was restricted again after a few years.) What is specific to Denmark is the tremendous increase of agricultural texts from the 1780s and over the following two decades. This peak occurred at a time when the country was experiencing a kind of peaceful revolution, with the social structure of the countryside undergoing total change: the 'Stavnsbåndets ophævelse', the abolition of a serfdom-like institution, in 1788. The state's subsequent concern was to support agriculture and a free peasant class. This had a significant impact on agrarian literature – an increase that commenced prior to 1788 and paved the way for social and economic transformation.[46] In one sense, this can be seen as part of the general increase in agricultural publishing at the time of the French Revolution, but under very specific Danish historical circumstances.

Schleswig-Holstein, the southernmost part of Denmark that was also part of the German Empire, witnessed an increased rate of publication in

45   Lange, *Experimentalfältet*, pp. 291–4.
46   Thorkild Kjaergaard, 'The Rise of Press and Public Opinion in Eighteenth-Century Denmark-Norway', *Scandinavian Journal of History* 14 (1989), p. 229.

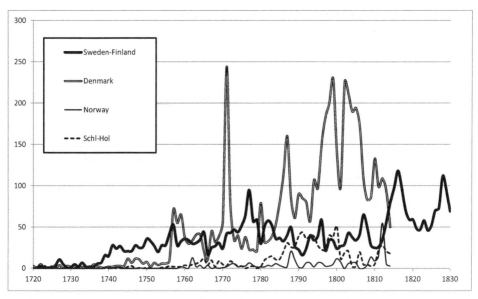

FIGURE 2.4 Annual production of agricultural literature in the Nordic countries (including articles), 1720–1814/1829 (Schl-Hol = Schleswig-Holstein).

the decades before 1800. Norway's curve rises gradually, and this is part of the general expansion of the periphery in Europe. Even in Iceland (not included in Figure 2.4) there was a small upsurge in agricultural publication in the 1780s and 1790s, which reached an average of two texts per year. This eventually faded away in the first decade of the nineteenth century but is, nevertheless, an example of the general increase in publications on agriculture in the outermost periphery of Europe.

The increase in the total number of texts on agriculture was generally in line with agrarian expansion, in the sense that cultivation was expanding, and new methods were being introduced, although there was no close alignment. The expansion of agrarian literature in these further reaches of Europe was also a result of these regions being increasingly included in a literary-based societal discourse.

We can also see a change in the readership for agricultural literature as literate groups, both in the nobility/upper class and a growing middle class, became more interested in improvement. This can be followed both in the core regions where there had been a small but steady production of such books for centuries and which was now expanding (England, France, Germany, Spain, Italy) and in the outermost periphery where this literature had begun to appear and had then gradually expanded

(Scotland, Scandinavia, North America, etc.). The next step is to deepen the analysis by turning to different topics covered by the literature.

Topics discussed in the literature

To study how different subjects attracted the attention of writers over a length of time is easier to do when journal articles are included. A book often includes a wide spectrum of topics. The content in a number of books taken together can be analysed, which give interesting results about the relative distribution of topics, but the research involved is very time consuming.[47] Moreover, articles are more topical than books. I have focused on the Swedish bibliography, but a similar study could be done for Denmark.

I start with the more general categories where book titles can be used as an indicator, and it is thus possible to compare the English books included in the ESTC) with Hebbe (Swedish, all texts). As might be expected, forestry was just as important as gardening in Sweden (and relatively more important than in England), but the number of texts in both these categories stagnated, as in Britain. In Sweden, from the early 1740s, on average about two texts per year were published in each category. This meant a decrease from *c.*0.4 per cent of the total to *c.*0.2 per cent by the end of the century. It seems that gardening, in much of north-western Europe, was not a part of the expansion of intellectual endeavour focused on food production during the eighteenth century.

Hebbe's bibliography has organized the entries into more than a hundred categories, and we can delve deeper into the material. As a first rough grading I used the following criteria: topics being discussed over several consecutive years, and with around at least two texts per year. This resulted in about 20 topics. The problem with this method is that Hebbe's categories are often so small that they tend to hide the waves of discussion. Several of these topics concerned crop rotation and manuring and, among tools discussed in them, ploughs stood out. With respect to livestock, horses were a constant topic of discussion, while sheep were the leading topic, especially in connection with attempts to import better breeds.

From this first selection I chose three areas for closer analysis: crop rotation and soil improvement; tools and machinery; different crops. These were areas where major changes occurred. I will compare the number of texts with what we know actually happened, based on research in agrarian history.

Table 2.1 shows that crop rotation, together with manuring, was of major interest during the 1770s and 1780s. This was not a period of dramatic change in crop systems. The discussion instead stemmed from

---

47 I have done this for some of the earliest agricultural treatises, see Myrdal, 'Agricultural treatises', pp. 17–19.

a crisis where land clearance had caused an imbalance between animal husbandry and arable farming.[48] During the 1770s and 1780s, interest in crop rotation continued to be high, but in the early nineteenth century the number of texts on manuring and soil improvement expanded quickly. There was intense debate on the use of new types of manure, as well as the pros and cons of marling. It was well known in the countryside of southern Sweden that marling could increase production, but it was not generally adopted until around 1850.[49]

TABLE 2.1 Texts specifically on crop rotation and soil improvement, 1710–1849.

	Crop rotation	Manuring	Soil improvement
1710–1719	1		
1720–1729	2	1	1
1730–1739	3		
1740–1749	20	6	14
1750–1759	19	7	15
1760–1769	11	5	10
1770–1779	29	19	37
1780–1789	40	8	24
1790–1799	19	7	21
1800–1809	56	14	31
1810–1819	40	19	54
1820–1829	12	12	27
1830–1839	36	24	33
1840–1849	28	30	59

Source: Hebbe, Section D11, D3.

Table 2.2 can be compared with the research on implements and technical change. Interest in ploughs first peaked during the 1770s and 1780s, and they were then a continuous focus of interest.[50] The iron plough was

48 C.-J. Gadd, 'The Agricultural Revolution in Sweden, 1700–1870', in J. Myrdal and M. Morell (eds), *The Agrarian History of Sweden* (Lund, 2011), pp. 144–5.
49 P. Wiking-Faria, *Freden, friköpen och järnplogarna: Drivkrafter och förändringsprocesser under den agrara revolutionen i Halland, 1700–1900* (Göteborg, 2010), pp. 221–9.
50 Morell, 'Den agrara', p. 455; M. Legnér, *Fäderneslandets rätta beskrivning: mötet mellan antikvarisk forskning och ekonomisk nyttokult i 1700-talets Sverige* (Helsingfors, 2004), p. 94.

introduced in parts of northern Sweden just after the middle of the eighteenth century, and then gradually spread to the rest of Sweden until the second half of the nineteenth century.[51] The harrow was the subject of much attention during the early 1800s, according to Table 2.2, and this was also a time of innovation when new types were introduced across Sweden.[52]

A primitive threshing machine had begun to replace the flail in parts of northern Sweden during the late eighteenth century, and the topic was discussed at length.[53] Winnowing had been largely solved, at least as a first step, thanks to the introduction of the Chinese winnowing machine during the middle of the eighteenth century, where a hand-powered fan created wind, and again this was described in texts.[54]

TABLE 2.2 Texts specifically on tools and machinery, 1740–1849.

	Plough	Harrow	Seed	Thresh	Winnow
1740–1749	1		6		
1750–1759	2		1	2	4
1760–1769			2	2	1
1770–1779	9	5		4	2
1780–1789	8	1		2	
1790–1799	1	1		5	
1800–1809		2	4	5	
1810–1819	4	2	3	2	1
1820–1829			1		1
1830–1839	3	5		1	1
1840–1849	5	2		2	1

Source: Hebbe, Section K2.

Another topic concerns different crops. Buckwheat was primarily culti-vated in southern Sweden on poor soil, and its cultivation continued at least into the middle of the nineteenth century. The small upsurge in texts in the middle of the eighteenth century was caused by an article written

---

51 C.-J. Gadd, *Det svenska jordbrukets historia III: Den agrara revolutionen, 1700–1870* (Stockholm, 2000), pp. 245–6; Gadd, 'Agricultural Revolution', pp. 146–7; Wiking-Faria, *Freden*, pp. 84–106.

52 Gadd, *Det svenska*, pp. 246–7; Wiking-Faria, *Freden*, 107–16.

53 Gadd, *Det svenska*, pp. 246–7; Morell, 'Den agrara', p. 456.

54 G. Berg, 'The Introduction of the Winnowing Machine in Europe in the Eighteenth Century', *Tools and Tillage* 3 (1976), pp. 25–46.

by Linnaeus in 1747 in which he discussed Siberian Buckwheat (his article was translated into German, French, Latin and Danish.) The discussion in Sweden was concerned with whether this crop variety was suitable for Finland and northern Sweden. It was a discussion that did not reflect any kind of reality, nor did it lead to much practical change.

A major development in the late eighteenth and early nineteenth century was potato farming, which was the focus of exhaustive discussion during that period.[55] Texts on wheat and rye formed a part of the debate on crop rotation, and thus references to them increased in tandem.

TABLE 2.3 Texts specifically on different crops, 1700–1849.

	Rye and wheat	Buckwheat	Potato
1700–1709	1		
1710–1719			
1720–1729			1
1730–1739	1		1
1740–1749	7	4	5
1750–1759	2	1	3
1760–1769	2		4
1770–1779	11	1	8
1780–1789	11		6
1790–1799	3	1	2
1800–1809	5		10
1810–1819	2		9
1820–1829	3		3
1830–1839	4		10
1840–1849	3		8

Source: Hebbe, Section D12.

There is a general, though not complete, correlation between what was discussed in the literature and the changes that actually took place. The waves of interest concerning the variety of topics is, as such, a sign of an appreciation of innovation and can be connected to two other developments.

One was that the publishing of the works from Antiquity (Columella, Palladius, etc.) on how agriculture should be conducted largely ceased.

---

55   Gadd, 'Agricultural Revolution', pp. 148–9.

This change took place during the sixteenth and early seventeenth centuries. The second new pattern was the publishing of revised editions of books with amendments and corrections. This became increasingly common during the first half of the eighteenth century and is a pattern that had already been anticipated in England.

With the great variety of topics developing, and with the increasing role of printed articles, no stone was left unturned: everything could be discussed and improved. This generated wave after wave of interest from the second half of the eighteenth century and, as already mentioned, those waves often (though of course not always) reflected contemporary concerns, resulting in real change in agricultural methods.

This was the gradual establishment of what can be referred to as an 'innovation mentality', where new ways of farming methods were sought out and valued, and that can clearly be seen as an aspect of the Economic Enlightenment: the systematic promotion of innovations. Tradition certainly maintained its role, and a lot of the texts concerning agrarian topics continued to be descriptions of existing habits and methods in different regions. It is also well known that in an economy with only a small margin between success and failure, there will be an intrinsic tendency towards caution.

Conclusion

The hypothesis that the literature was very much a consequence of the actual changes occurring in agriculture can be sustained with a two-step argument.

Firstly, literature was not a major driving force as most change in Europe actually took place without any parallel expansion in the number of publications – and, besides, the print runs were so small that the vast majority of the population probably never came across them. Secondly, the literature, when the texts did increase in number, often reflected the major changes in agriculture that had transpired –we can identify a parallel between topics discussed and real changes in agriculture.

We suggest that that the expanding literature on agriculture described changes already underway, and was a reflection of a debate on how to develop food production taking place in the countryside. This is of course reasoning that does not provide an absolute certainty.

Other indicators point to the same conclusion. Many agricultural writers emphasized their own experience. Indeed, this has been typical of the genre from its very beginning, going right back to Antiquity. However, during the eighteenth century this proclamation of practical knowledge (and experiments) reached new levels. Another indicator is topographical literature. This genre, typical of the eighteenth century, has only been included in the dataset when it primarily concerns agriculture.

In fact, most of the texts about regions and parishes, even those that mainly concerned other topics, also included substantial accounts of farming practice.[56] The knowledge revolution in biology, medicine etc. began with detailed descriptions, and agriculture was no exception. Agricultural societies had an important role in this descriptive work (for instance the Board of Agriculture in Britain), as had individuals (Arthur Young is typical in his descriptions of England and France). Much of the literature was marked by a desire to reform, but also an effort to understand and take advantage of the best of the methods already existing.

A further indication is found in the written sources produced by the farmers themselves: diaries and account books. These became an important source during the eighteenth century all over north-western Europe. I have already mentioned that the agricultural literature is not very visible in these texts – however, this source, as such, can be regarded as a sign of a new attitude emerging. Not only farmers with larger farms, but also ordinary peasants began to plan their lives and their work, based on a conceptualizing of their own work efforts and economy, as both diaries and account books were used in planning. Such planning is, in itself, an endeavour for improvement and development. Research on diaries also reveals long-term strategies for expansion and change at farm level.

If we thus accept the hypothesis that the agricultural literature was, to a high degree, an effect of change in agriculture, two further conclusions can be drawn – and I will only outline them here in brief.

First, if the literature reflects the ongoing broader societal discussion, a deeper analysis of the arguments presented in the literature could possibly give us insights into the arguments used in broader, popular discussions. An additional observation can be made. It is sometimes claimed that many of the suggestions made by eighteenth-century agricultural writers were inappropriate. However, this merely reflects one aspect of the ongoing change in mentality. The 'wrong' ideas were those that questioned tradition, and we can assume that such 'wrong' ideas did exist, and were tested and discarded by peasants.

Second, the Economic Enlightenment involves a rapprochement between oral and peasant-based culture on the one hand, and written and scholarly culture on the other. Here I will try to be brief. In other areas of historical research, there has been debate on scholarly and popular culture of the late Middle Ages. The former was written, clerical

---

56   Richard Hoyle, in a personal communication, pointed out that this is concomitant to the way Arthur Young worked. He gave detailed accounts of improving farmers, but in his tours he would pass over what he considered as backward areas without much comment – so he (and their other writers) publicized advanced agricultural practices of which they approved and their practitioners. See also Goddard, 'Agricultural Literature', p. 363.

and city-centred, while the latter was oral, dominated by folklore, and anchored among the peasants. During the late Middle Ages, there was a flow between these two cultures, among other things expressed in the burlesque we encounter in art and literature. This was a phenomenon that had its counterpart in the High Middle Ages, though not to the same extent. This flow diminished with the intellectual leap and purge during the Renaissance. A new and more intellectually distinct high culture was developed, which certainly paved the way for the seventeenth-century scientific revolution. The eighteenth century can be viewed as a new rapprochement between popular and scholarly culture. The tendency to communicate innovation now had a greater level of ambition, as the learned culture became characterized by a more scientific approach in its pursuit of the truth while, at the same time, it found itself bound less by authority. One could speak of a new synthesis, but on higher level.

I shall not develop this idea of a long historical wave further on this occasion as it requires its own study, but will note that an important factor was that the educated classes were seeking to understand and influence people in general. However, the reverse is also true as there was an increasing gradual acceptance of scholarly culture among the broader masses (which certainly also came to include a critical attitude).

Coming back to my main hypothesis, that agricultural literature merely reflected the change taking place in the countryside, a counter-hypothesis should at least be acknowledged, namely that the literature did play a role in the changes occurring in agriculture and the countryside. This hypothesis cannot be rejected; in fact it may actually be complementary to the main hypothesis. Some texts certainly did have some impact on technological change in the countryside.

An observation already emphasized numerous times is the expansion of the European periphery (and we take North America to be a part of this periphery). The countries that would go on to take the lead in agrarian development, such as Denmark and Scotland, also witnessed an early and extensive increase in this type of literature. It is also striking that countries on the periphery had a greater share of such 'practically-focused' publications. Even if agricultural literature did not have any great immediate practical impact on agricultural methods, it does nonetheless act as an indicator that there was an increasing interest among scholars in practical questions of production.

Returning now to Jan Luiten van Zanden and Joel Mokyr, it is evident that my study does generally support their conclusions: a more knowledge-based society was established, and knowledge – new knowledge – became more appreciated. I have delved deeper into the agricultural literature and the main contribution is that this literature seems to mirror the change taking place in societal attitudes, even among the peasants, as we can only assume that popular discussion was indeed taking place in local networks within villages and parishes.

To summarize. Literature on agriculture certainly did instigate a measure of change at that time, but even more it reflected an ongoing and expanding discussion within the countryside. We get the sense of a deep, underlying current transforming eighteenth-century rural Europe, with a critical dialogue combined with a greater communication between different social strata.

3

Peasant Eyes: A Critique of the Agricultural Enlightenment[1]

Verena Lehmbrock

In 1831, Michael Irlbeck from Liebenstein near Kötzing in Bavaria (1786–1869) submitted a manuscript to the Bavarian Agricultural Association, the Landwirtschaftlicher Verein, with a request for its evaluation of his text. His inquiry was supported by the county court judge of Kötzing, with the association's commendation being intended to facilitate the printing of Irlbeck's debut work, a three-volume treatise on agriculture. His book was addressed to state officials as well as to farmers and, as Irlbeck proclaimed, was the 'only one of its kind', a reference to the quality and depth of his knowledge on the one hand, and to his social status on the other.[2] He was neither a wealthy landlord nor a scholarly economist, and he had received no university education. As a matter of fact, Irlbeck had worked as a farm hand before taking over his parents' farm, and his ability to write in a scholarly manner would later be recognized by

---

[1] My special thanks to Olga Thierbach-McLean and Aram McLean for the English-language translation. Where German-language sources are referenced, the quotes have been translated directly from the original text.

[2] M. Irlbeck, *Das Wichtigste der dermaligen Landwirthschaft um sie zur höchsten Vollkommenheit zu bringen; besonders in der jetzigen unglücklichen Zeit. Ein unentbehrliches Hülfsbuch für Staatsmänner, Landwirthe, Gärtner und Gewerbsleute. Bisher das einzige in seiner Art. In drei Bändchen. Nach achtundzwanzigjährigen Beobachtungen und Erfahrungen bearbeitet von Michael Irlbeck, wirklichem, und wegen glücklichen Kulturen auf das Ausgezeichnetste gerichtlich attestirtem Bauer und Mitglied der praktischen Gartenbau-Gesellschaft in Bayern* (3 vols, Augsburg 1834), title page. It is thanks to Reinhart Siegert that I became aware of Michael Irlbeck, about whom otherwise little is known. However, his dates of birth and death could be established through regional museums as a part of the project database on *Volksaufklärung* literature compiled by Siegert and Holger Böning.

reviewers as exceptional. Irlbeck, who as a *Halbbauer* possessed half of what was considered to be a full farm, sufficient to make him a member of his village's social elite, had temporarily been the village headman. Presumably, he farmed a minimum of 10 hectares of land, owned draft cattle, and had hired day labourers. For a time, Irlbeck experimented with seven-field as well as four-field rotations, but ultimately returned to a three-field system. His farm, which was at a high altitude and so cool, is reported to have been stony, with a clayey, sandy soil low in humus and not especially fertile, yielding four times the seed only in a good year. And yet Irlbeck was able to achieve remarkable economic success as a result of his intensive work and numerous improvements. Over 23 summers he brought barren land into cultivation, during which time he cleared trees and bushes, dug up two thousand cartloads (*Fuhren*) of stones, levelled hills, planted fruit trees to border the edges of his fields, drained swamps, and created artificially irrigated meadows on dry mountain slopes. It seems like no corner of his property remained untouched in the years of his activities. The Landwirtschaftlicher Verein (hereafter: Verein) had already honoured him for his many accomplishments.[3]

So what new insights into rural knowledge networks does Michael Irlbeck's book convey, and what implications can be drawn from an analysis of this exceptional source? I will argue that it is those passages that made it hard for his reviewers to recommend the book, which contain valuable information that reveal to us new perspectives on the knowledge networks of the Agricultural Enlightenment. Forming the core of the next section is a discussion of Irlbeck's perspective as I discuss the possible contribution that his position may have for research into the history of the Enlightenment and the social and cultural history of knowledge. So, what transpires when our perspective is informed by the commentary of a peasant? Being aware of Irlbeck, do we take a different outlook on the reform movements of the later eighteenth century as espoused by clergymen, wealthy landlords, state officials, university scholars and others? Here, I will offer brief asides on the chroniclers of these various historical sources and standpoints. By taking a broader view of the history of knowledge in agriculture, I seek to show that it is precisely the interplay of the different historical and historiographic perspectives that offers a rich field of inspiration. In the conclusion, I will recapitulate some aspects that seem to be important. I will also consider some concepts that can be helpful for analysing the interaction *between* knowledge networks.

[3]   Irlbeck, *Landwirthschaft*, I, pp. x, xv; II, pp. 2–5, 49–55, 90–7. A detailed account of the Bavarian Landwirtschaftlicher Verein is provided in S. Harrecker, *Der Landwirtschaftliche Verein in Bayern 1810–1870/71* (München, 2006).

Irlbeck's perspective

What was the outcome of Irlbeck's request? His book, while praised for its subject-specific content, contained polemic passages that were considered highly imprudent. For, while asserting his own expertise and experience in the field of agriculture, Irlbeck refused to concede the same competence to scholarly authors.[4] Therefore, it can be considered a stroke of luck that this extraordinary book, along with its accompanying letter and certificates, was printed in Augsburg 250 kilometres away, despite the reservations of its reviewers.[5] According to a study by Stefanie Harrecker, this may also have been due to the intellectual culture within the Verein in its early liberal phase from 1810 to 1835. Its periodical *Landwirtschaftliches Wochenblatt*, which also published Irlbeck's contributions, endorsed controversial debates and initially exercised almost no censorship. However, with a membership roster comprised of civil servants of the royal court, as well as of noble and academic circles, the Verein could not (or did not wish to) overcome its distance from the simple rural population. (It was only from 1869 onwards that smaller agricultural producers, whose interests the Verein was not able to represent, organized themselves into so-called patriotic Bauernvereine.[6]) And yet, the Verein and the public institutions it created became the central precondition for the book's publication in Augsburg – and for Irlbeck's emergence into history. Having been published as an author in the Verein's journal, it can be safely assumed that Irlbeck was at least loosely connected to the network constituted by the Verein. And as far as we know, the county court judge was a crucial link between Irlbeck's personal network and that of the Verein. It was indeed thanks to the appraisal of this academically trained judge that Irlbeck succeeded in publishing his manuscript, and thus in participating in a public

---

4   Irlbeck uses the term 'scholarly' to include all (in most cases university-) educated individuals who were active as agricultural writers. On the transformation and broadening of the concept of the scholar in the eighteenth century, see H. Bosse, 'Gelehrte und Gebildete. Die Kinder des 1. Standes', *Das achtzehnte Jahrhundert: Zeitschrift der Deutschen Gesellschaft für die Erforschung des Achtzehnten Jahrhunderts* 32 (2008), pp. 13–37.

5   The Karlsruhe Meta Catalogue locates copies of the book at Augsburg, Munich and Rostock, and it has also been digitalized by Google Books. In addition to the base text, it contains Irlbeck's letter accompanying the manuscript, the 'examination certificate' with the critique by the Verein, Irlbeck's response to this critique, as well as the report by the Kötzing country judge. Two other monographs by the Irlbeck – one on flax cultivation (1836), the other on the *'zeitgeist'* of agriculture (1838) – have been catalogued. Regarding the accusation of 'hubris', 'vain glory', 'scorn of others', etc. made in the advisors' letter, see Irlbeck, *Landwirthschaft*, I, pp. xix–xxiii.

6   See in the synopsis of the Verein's history in Harrecker, *Verein*, pp. 335–44.

conversation from which members of his social group had been habitually excluded up until this point.[7]

The reproaches of being presumptuous did little to shake Irlbeck's healthy self-confidence. As he affirmed in his thank you note to the Verein:

> To my knowledge, the world has not yet seen a peasant who produced a textbook of his trade. If this has indeed been accomplished, it can be said without any vain-glory that I have delivered something extraordinary by any account.[8]

In his text, Irlbeck retrospectively criticized the 'Agricultural Enlightenment' of the eighteenth century, a term that he uses verbatim. He even went so far as to claim that the 'blinding spirit of the times' as propagated by agricultural writers had brought on a much greater degree of misery and poverty than had 10 wars against France,[9] his criticisms being particularly directed at the propagation of new field systems. Indeed, the Agricultural Enlightenment, understood as an eighteenth-century reform movement directed to the improvement of agriculture, had seen a veritable wave of publications regarding new practices and crop rotations that were promised to be superior to the time-proven three-field system.[10] According to Irlbeck, it was specifically the recommendation to grow red clover, based on the so-called English or Schubart system (named after the agricultural entrepreneur Johann Christian Schubart), which had been advocated by the state, that had inspired thousands of young people:

[7] Regarding the paternalistic self-image of local officials in the eighteenth century and for an overview of the spectrum of their activities in the early modern age and 'saddle period' (*Sattelzeit*, a term coined by Reinhart Koselleck referring to 1750–1850), see S. Brakensiek, 'Lokale Amtsträger in deutschen Territorien der Frühen Neuzeit. Institutionelle Grundlagen, akzeptanzorientierte Herrschaftspraxis und obrigkeitliche Identität', in R. G. Asch and D. Feist (eds), *Staatsbildung als kultureller Prozess. Strukturwandel und Legitimation von Herrschaft in der Frühen Neuzeit* (Köln/Weimar/Wien, 2005), pp. 49–67.

[8] Irlbeck, *Landwirthschaft*, I, p. xxxvii. In his subsequent treatise on flax growing, Irlbeck no longer emphasizes his peasant status and instead confidently calls himself an 'economist and author': see M. Irlbeck, *Vollständiger Unterricht über Flachsbau und Leinwandfabrikation. Nach den neuesten Verbesserungen und [...] Erfahrungen, mit besonderer Rücksicht auf Bayern* (Augsburg, 1836).

[9] Irlbeck, *Landwirthschaft*, II, p. 75.

[10] For fundamental considerations concerning the Agricultural or 'Economic Enlightenment', see M. Popplow, 'Economizing Agricultural Resources in the German Economic Enlightenment', in U. Klein and E. C. Spary (eds), *Materials and Expertise in Early Modern Europe. Between Market and Laboratory* (Chicago, 2010), pp. 261–87 and P. M. Jones, *Agricultural Enlightenment. Knowledge, Technology, and Nature, 1750–1840* (Oxford, 2016).

We shall grow clover! Keep splendid cattle! This will yield fertilizer aplenty! Crops in abundance! Money will be plentiful!! – Even more clover! Even more cattle! Even more crops! Even more money!! – Oh Lord! – 'Tis stupendous! [*Ist das wahr!!*] — A dream!!'[11]

Irlbeck himself had been one of these young people. Immediately after taking over his parents' farm in 1808, he planted mostly clover as fodder plant on the fallow fields, sold half the livestock, and kept the rest of the animals in the barn. But unexpectedly, the clover grew only two inches, thus merely returning the seed – and drawing the ridicule of his neighbours. Four oxen ate the whole green fodder without getting fat. The hungry animals roared with 'high-pitched voices demanding freedom'.[12] Irlbeck was left with little straw, only a small quantity of inferior-quality fertilizer, and the clover fields became covered in weeds. Despite all this, he went on to sow clover again the following year. In the second winter he was barely able to feed the livestock and had to sell even more animals before the third winter came around.[13] Finally, he tried one last time with a heavy fertilization of his clover fields, depriving his grain fields of manure. This brought him to the brink of financial ruin, at which point he released the livestock to roam free again to graze on the stubble fields, the 'measly' clover fields, and the mountains and the woodlands. It then took him a whole 10 years to attain the same number of livestock as his father had kept.[14] Why, wondered Irlbeck, is the cultivation of clover still propagated by all publications despite the fact that on his soil it grew only with the most intensive fertilization, if at all? 'Where has one erred?! – Hark! For I am speaking from experience!'[15]

As an agricultural pioneer, Irlbeck showed a pronounced interest in the progression of agronomical practices, and certainly never questioned that improvements were necessary. Rather, he was preoccupied with the qualitative question of *how* this was to be achieved.[16] In his experience, the highly socially esteemed – enlightened – knowledge of the agricultural

---

[11] Irlbeck, *Landwirthschaft*, pp. 74–84. With regards to the spreading of red clover by state and societal initiatives in the Electorate of Hanover, Baden and Prussia, see Ulbricht, *Englische Landwirtschaft*, pp. 282–307. Johann Christian Schubart 'Edler vom Kleefelde' (1734–1787) was not only a committed promoter of clover cultivation, but also an exceptional revolutionary political author of the time. For a short biography see B. Märtin, 'Schubart von dem Kleefelde, Johann Christian', in *Neue Deutsche Biographie* 23 (2007), pp. 603–4.

[12] Irlbeck, *Landwirthschaft*, II, p. 77.

[13] *Ibid.*, II, p. 78.

[14] *Ibid.*, II, p. 79.

[15] *Ibid.*, II, p. 80.

[16] On the scientific concept of the 'agricultural pioneer', see H. Kaak, 'Agrarpionier/in', in *Enzyklopädie der Neuzeit* (16 vols, Stuttgart-Weimar 2005), I, p. 117–19.

authors, on which he had relied in his desire to pursue reform, had failed. The knowledge they had given had dashed his expectations and betrayed his earlier trust, as it had failed to address the question of soil quality, and had also barely touched upon the issue of the costs.[17] In his text, Irlbeck repeatedly stressed that his experience was representative of the rural society in which he lived, with 'thousands' having failed just like him, and numerous of his fellow farmers having been ruined. As he pointed out, after a 20-year period of failed experiments undertaken by small agricultural producers in all surrounding villages, the good intentions of Enlightenment writers had turned into an object of mockery, being ridiculed as their 'scholarly ignorance'.[18] Irlbeck, who was an enthusiast for technological innovation and yield increase, utilized the vocabulary of a profit-oriented economy, thus drawing on the progressive argumentative patterns available at that time. But in contrast to the agricultural literature he caricatured, he did so without stigmatizing as backwards the conventional forms of fallow land and pasture farming. To the contrary, he asserted that the experiences of village farmers in regions with poor soil and fertilizer shortages made them 'all too aware' of pastures being intractable (*unvermeidlich*). After all, he argued, any other method (such as cumbersome fertilization) costs twice as much as the 'value' returned by fallow land and pasture. According to Irlbeck, everybody knew that fallow pasture was 'pure profit'. For if fallow land is cultivated, the product must 'already in advance compensate for the relative damage of winter planting, deterioration of the fallow field, as well as one's own expenses'.[19] This passage provides an example of how deftly Irlbeck utilized novel vocabulary for the purpose of defending tried and trusted methods. *Improvement*, the catchword of agricultural reformers in the second half of the eighteenth century, stands out as a leitmotif in all three of his volumes.

Irlbeck regularly speaks of 'knowledge' and 'knowing' when speaking of small agricultural producers. By placing progress and the improvement of his own economy (as well as of general economic practices) at the centre of his work and argument, he positioned himself as an agricultural reformer or late participant in the Agricultural Enlightenment.[20]

---

17 Irlbeck, *Landwirthschaft*, I, pp. xxviii, xli. Based on this experience, Irlbeck came up with his own improvement suggestion, this time concerning 'the business of authorship', by suggesting that governments should ascertain that each agricultural publication is examined prior to its release as part of an 'agricultural examination' process. Irlbeck, *Landwirthschaft*, II, p. 84.

18 Irlbeck, *Landwirthschaft*, II, p. 76 and I, p. vi.

19 Irlbeck, *Landwirthschaft*, II, p. 72.

20 In the first of Irlbeck's volumes, Bavarian agriculture is discussed with an 'intention aimed at public economy' (*in staatswirthschaftlicher Absicht*); the other two volumes, labelled 'practical economy', are concerned with how

He explicitly perceived his work as a contribution to an agricultural
science that was still in the making and, as he went on to stress, up until
that point had been without 'fundamental principles' in Bavaria.[21] He
anticipated that the establishment of such fundamental guidelines would
ultimately lead agriculture to perfection. In that sense, he had produced
a typical Agricultural Enlightenment text based on which he implicitly
claimed membership to the epistemic community of enlightened economists – even if, chronologically speaking, in the 1830s such a membership
could hardly be understood in a concrete sense. Irlbeck thus made
a late contribution to the debates of the Agricultural Enlightenment.
The economists of the eighteenth century had been engaged in a lively
negotiation as to what could be legitimately deemed *scientific agriculture*,
with the debate continuing into the first two decades of the nineteenth
century up to the establishment and general acceptance of Albrecht
Thaer's agricultural teachings and his agrarian academy in northern
Germany.[22] Irlbeck's work reads like a report on how the suggestions
for improvement that had been circulating for decades in the milieu of
the Agricultural Enlightenment and in its subset of *Volksaufklärung*, the
Popular Enlightenment, had been tested and found wanting. Drawing on
his 28 years' experience of implementing improvements, Irlbeck parodied
the *Volksaufklärung* mindset:

> The peasant shall be forced! By force he shall be made to obey! He
> must keep his cattle in the barn! Cultivate all his uncultivated land!
> Build new, more beautiful villages! Unless forced to, he will not move
> a single foot! The native must be instructed about culture by foreigners,

---

to run an individual farm. Occasionally, Irlbeck also takes to the style of the
Volksaufklärung, for example when urging: 'Now just think about it!', see
Irlbeck, *Landwirthschaft*, II, p. 26.

21 *Ibid.*, pp. 6–7, 70. Cf. by contrast the writings of the 'peasant poet' Isaak
Maus as interpreted by Gunter Mahlerwein, which may be perceived as a
critique from *outside* the economic reform discourse, namely as seen from
the vantage point of a peasant subsistence economy: G. Mahlerwein, *Die
Herren im Dorf. Bäuerliche Oberschicht und ländliche Elitenbildung in Rheinhessen
1700–1850* (Mainz, 2001), pp. 242–4. Werner Trossbach stresses that, from
the sixteenth century on, hybrid forms of subsistence and market-oriented
peasant economies were continuously present: see W. Trossbach, *Bauern,
1648–1806* (München, 1993), pp. 64–70.

22 Tellingly, Irlbeck fails to mention the agricultural academies which had been
established around 1800 and, within the framework of model farms, were
generating experience-based knowledge of the very kind that Irlbeck criticizes
as lacking in agricultural writers; for a list of academies, see S. Reichrath,
*Entstehung, Entwicklung und Stand der Agrarwissenschaften in Deutschland und
Frankreich* (Frankfurt am Main, 1991), pp. 63, 68.

otherwise he would eternally keep sticking to his old rut, as he has seen it in his grandfather! The country is underpopulated![23]

Irlbeck painted a negative image of *Volksaufklärung* actors who, although outwardly motivated by philanthropy, in actuality were only attempting to rehabilitate their own failed existence through their agricultural writings:

> We always see [...] such great scholars, and at times the most illustrious men on whom emperors and kings bestow distinctions and rewards [like Johann Christian Schubart who was raised into the imperial nobility with the title 'noble of the clover field' by Joseph II] as they pass through the countryside like trade sample riders after their estates have become impoverished and subjected to forced sale, swarming hither and thither in the villages as they seek to make a living not unlike mountebanks and quack doctors, peddling the products of their mind or orders on subscriptions, preferring advance payment, and putting on airs of being great men by whatever means conceivable!! It is with pity that the peasant looks upon these grandiose pilgrims who sacrifice themselves for the improvement of husbandry purely for reasons of general philanthropy so as to make the peasant rich and prosperous!! – And it is to these very same great model economists, who in most instances also had all the advantages in life such as good soil, breweries, tithes, and the like, the peasant is referred to!!![24]

As Irlbeck noted, none of these individuals had ever successfully made a living from agriculture or managed a farm under the conditions of peasant economy. Consequently, he rejected as absurd not only their written advice, but also the notion that small agricultural producers should be instructed in schools by men who usually only appeared as 'unhelpful observers' of the rural population.[25] Moreover, Irlbeck revealed that some of the practices they urged the peasantry to adopt were not new or unfamiliar to them. For example, he complained that there was no need for the Bavarian peasant to be told about stable feeding, given the fact that it had been practised 'from time out of mind' depending on the supply of fodder.[26] Ultimately, Irlbeck not was prepared to accept as 'authorized experts' either gentlemen farmers or scholars, but only experienced agricultural producers; landowners who lived exclusively off agriculture.[27] He speculated that they could have advanced the ongoing transformation of the economic system much further, had

---

23 Irlbeck, *Landwirthschaft*, II, p. 75.
24 *Ibid.*, I, p. ix.
25 *Ibid.*, I, p. v; II, p. 75.
26 *Ibid.*, I, p. ix.
27 He does not include 'tradespersons, brewers, and manorial lords' (*Gewerbe treibende Bürger, Bräuer und Gutsherren*) on the grounds that, even as they

this process not been unnecessarily delayed by the interventions of enlightenment-minded men and the governments influenced by them. Irlbeck's call for the peasant to be given unconditional expert status regarding agricultural questions culminates in the remarkable demand for political participation. Peasants should be consulted in agricultural matters and paid for passing on their knowledge and expertise just like other scholars. According to Irlbeck, the economy can only be sustained on the national scale if small agricultural producers were represented in local associations such as the Landwirtschaftlicher Verein, as well as at the government level by a number of privy councillors and at least one minister.[28]

Irlbeck's demand for symmetry and its historiographic significance

How is Irlbeck's negative perception of the Agricultural Enlightenment and its subset of *Volksaufklärung* to be seen in a historiographical perspective, and in what style was it constructed? On a literary plane, Irlbeck's text represents the breaking of a silence. The mismatch between the published works of the *Volksaufklärung* and the peasantry could not have been greater. Thanks to the continually updated bibliography compiled by Reinhart Siegert and Holger Böning, to date more than 27,000 German-language *Volksaufklärung* publications have been identified dating from between approximately 1750 and 1860.[29] In contrast, small agricultural producers writing about their own profession are rare. Historians rarely encounter agricultural knowledge from the perspective of peasants, maids, day labourers, or village craftsmen.[30] By writing about agriculture,

---

often owned large farms, they knew little about running them: see Irlbeck, *Landwirthschaft*, I, p. xii.

28 Irlbeck maintained that, were peasants to put their advice in written form, the 'expensive notions of agriculture' would swiftly vanish from the market: see Irlbeck, *Landwirthschaft*, I, pp. xxxviii, 114. In this context, see also Ursula Schlude's fundamental considerations regarding agricultural expertise and literacy, in U. Schlude, 'Naturwissen und Schriftlichkeit. Warum eine Fürstin des 16. Jahrhunderts nicht auf den Mont Ventoux steigt und die Natur exakter begreift als die "philologischen" Landwirte', in S. Ruppel and A. Steinbrecher (eds), *'Die Natur ist überall bey uns'. Mensch und Natur in der Frühen Neuzeit* (Zürich, 2009), pp. 95–108.

29 H. Böning and R. Siegert, *Volksaufklärung. Biobibliographisches Handbuch zur Popularisierung aufklärerischen Denkens im deutschen Sprachraum von den Anfängen bis 1850 [1860/1861ff.]* (3 vols, Stuttgart-Bad Cannstatt 1990, 2001, 2016). The project database with more than 27,000 titles is even more comprehensive than the published volumes; online access is being planned.

30 However, there are some publications known in the historiography as sources, mostly autobiographies by peasants such as Ulrich Bräker, Jacob Gujer-Kleinjogg, Johann Georg Pahlitzsch, among others, as well as peasant

Irlbeck challenges this pronounced disparity in the transmitted sources. His case is remarkable, not least because he employed the same language devices as the Agricultural Enlightenment writers had done before him, and therefore represents a participant in the discourse, when seen from a historiographical perspective.[31]

Here, Irlbeck was not the only one to conduct the negotiation of knowledge claims in a polemical mode; all voices of the Agricultural Enlightenment affirmed their sometimes competing knowledge claims by making claims for their own learning, while at the same time discrediting that of their opponents.[32] While illiterate members of rural society were typically objectified in the image of the 'common peasant', Irlbeck in his turn took to casting the representatives of the Agricultural Enlightenment in generalized terms by applying to them the generic label of the 'agricultural writer'. In general, he did not criticize named authors. His reviewers justifiably charged him with failing to differentiate between good and bad books, even as they conceded that many of the latter did indeed exist. It was Irlbeck's own fault that he had taken superficial learning (*Halbwissen*) and 'wretched products of these scribblers' at face value.[33]

From today's perspective, Irlbeck's counterattack by the same means takes on an ethical dimension in that his polemical entry into the conversation can also be read as a general claim for equal status, which was by no means conceded within the German territories in the 1830s. As if schooled in twentieth-century cultural anthropology or the sociology of knowledge, he consistently established symmetries between his own position and that of conventionally academically-trained Agricultural Enlightenment thinkers. In Irlbeck's time, these social groups were considered fundamentally unequal, one may even say incomparable,

---

account books and diaries: see Böning/Siegert, *Volksaufklärung*, II, pp. xxxiv–xxxv. A compilation of peasant diary sources can be found in J. Peters, *Mit Pflug und Gänsekiel, Selbstzeugnisse schreibender Bauern. Eine Anthologie* (Köln, 2003); research on account books and diaries in K.-J. Lorenzen-Schmidt and B. Poulsen (eds), *Writing peasants. Studies on Peasant Literacy in Early Modern Northern Europe* (Kerteminde, 2002). For an overview see K.-J. Lorenzen-Schmidt, 'Verbreitung und Überlieferung bäuerlicher Schreibebücher', in H. Böning, H. Schmitt and R. Siegert, *Volksaufklärung. Eine praktische Reformbewegung des 18. und 19. Jahrhunderts* (Bremen, 2007), pp. 361–6.

31 An introduction to the various schools of opinion within the Agricultural Enlightenment can be found in S. Brakensiek, 'Das Feld der Agrarreformen um 1800', in E. J. Engstrom, V. Hess and U. Thoms (eds), *Figurationen des Experten. Ambivalenzen der wissenschaftlichen Expertise im ausgehenden 18. und frühen 19. Jahrhundert* (Frankfurt am Main, 2005), pp. 101–22 and is outlined in detail in V. Lehmbrock, *Der denkende Landwirt. Agrarwissen und Aufklärung in Deutschland, 1750–1820* (Weimar/Köln/Wien, forthcoming).

32 For polemics in the Agricultural Enlightenment, see Lehmbrock, *Der denkende Landwirt*.

33 Irlbeck, *Landwirthschaft*, I, xvii, xxi.

since they belonged to different social groups that were hierarchically either superior or inferior to one another. This means that Irlbeck's text in the field of economic expertise – and thus within the sphere of knowledge – even dared to reverse the political and cultural status quo.[34] The following comparison taken from his writings may serve as an example in this context. If state officials, incorrectly informed by agricultural literature, indiscriminately advise villagers to grow clover, then this can be compared to peasants advising salaried civil servants, discontented with their meagre income, to keep investing their yearly pay and refrain from touching it until the accumulated capital generates an interest high enough to be lived off conveniently. This counsel could also be declared to be very useful, if it were not for those 'stubborn civil servants' failing to realize its value.[35] It becomes obvious what Irlbeck was striving to convey: when it came to agriculture, small agricultural practitioners, not civil servants, must be regarded as the designated experts.[36]

If one proceeds from the assumption that for a knowledge network to exist its members must be of at least approximately equal status, Irlbeck can hardly be considered a regular member of the network of the Agricultural Enlightenment or the network of the Landwirtschaftlicher Verein. With the members of such organs being recruited from the ranks of the nobility and the civil servants of the royal administration, the Verein's membership structure was entirely in the tradition of the economic societies of the eighteenth century. The most remarkable aspect of Irlbeck's book was that it contributes to a conversation in which the common rural population, although ubiquitously discussed as a subject, had scarcely had any opportunity to participate. Here, Irlbeck rhetorically breached the social boundaries that were still very much in place after the turn of the century. At least two preconditions for his agency have already been identified: Irlbeck's competence in the written language and the support he received from a member of the educated social strata, or the *gebildete Stände*, as they were referred to at that time.[37] Another precondition that facilitated Irlbeck's agency was social change. New

---

34 Regarding the postulation of symmetry in the *strong programme* as used in the sociology of knowledge, see D. Bloor, *Knowledge and Social Imagery* (Chicago, 1998).

35 Irlbeck, *Landwirthschaft*, I, pp. xi–xii.

36 With resignation, he noted: 'Any cobbler has to pay his dues in years of apprenticeship, and so does the chimney sweeper, but in the great science of husbandry any miserable bungler seeks to be an authority': Irlbeck, *Landwirthschaft*, II, p. 90.

37 For an overview of the educated classes, see H. E. Bödeker, 'Die 'gebildeten Stände' im späten 18. und frühen 19. Jahrhundert: Zugehörigkeit und Abgrenzungen. Mentalitäten und Handlungspotentiale', in J. Kocka (ed.), *Bildungsbürgertum im 19. Jahrhundert. Teil IV. Politischer Einfluß und gesellschaftliche Formation* (Stuttgart, 1989), pp. 21–52.

ideas were emerging, claiming that in principle all individuals had the same capacity for education, which in turn opened up the possibility of social mobility through the acquisition of knowledge.[38] This may have been a premise for Irlbeck's self-confidence, as well as for the fact that the role of public critic had become conceivable for him in the first place.

Even though the *Volksaufklärung* has now been intensively researched from the side of its producers, namely regarding its actors, literary strategies, intended effects, or publication and distribution practices,[39] the reception side remains a desideratum that has lead *Volksaufklärung* historians to the question of whether the knowledge actually reached the peasants.[40] Even as Irlbeck's undifferentiated and polemical view can hardly be generalized, it still represents a valuable corrective to the considerably stronger Enlightenment-minded invectives towards small agricultural producers and a peasant economy. Irlbeck challenges the knowledge of the representatives of the *Volksaufklärung* instead. For Irlbeck, the main issue is not whether economic advice has been success-fully conveyed to small agricultural producers, but rather whether the advice was worth being conveyed at all. Thus, even where not completely reducing it to absurdity, he at least considerably qualified the question that was so pervasive in the metadiscourse of the Enlightenment, namely why it was that common rural populations insisted on their convictions in spite of being offered purportedly better knowledge about agriculture by educated men. After all, his text clearly affirms that reform-minded villagers were certainly willing to put the suggestions of agricultural liter-ature into practice. And so, with a view to the Agricultural Enlightenment *en gros*, Irlbeck's position causes fundamental astonishment: why and under what circumstances did protagonists of the *Volksaufklärung* – especially those without deep agricultural expertise – even conceive of the notion that they were in the position to offer advice in a domain that was not theirs? Research inspired by Irlbeck would therefore, firstly, have to explore more deeply the quality and origin of the Agricultural Enlightenment. Where did the knowledge, which was circulated in economic texts and reproduced *en masse*, originate? Secondly, Irlbeck particularly points to disruptions and boundaries in the circulation of

---

[38] See H. Alzheimer-Haller, *Handbuch zur narrativen Volksaufklärung. Moralische Geschichten 1780–1848* (Berlin, 2004), pp. 47–53.

[39] For a summary, see H. Böning, 'Das Forschungsprojekt Biobibliographisches Handbuch Volksaufklärung. Seine Geschichte samt einigen Bemerkungen zur Bedeutung von Periodika im Aufklärungsprozess', in H. Boning (ed.), *Volksaufklärung ohne Ende? Vom Fortwirken der Aufklärung im 19. Jahrhundert* (Bremen, 2018), pp. 13–42.

[40] W. Greiling, 'Gemeinnützigkeit als Argument. Zur Publikationsstrategie der Volksaufklärung', in H. Böning, W. Greiling and R. Siegert (eds), *Die Entdeckung von Volk, Erziehung und Ökonomie im europäischen Netzwerk der Aufklärung* (Bremen, 2011), pp. 239–58.

knowledge within the societal structures of the early modern period, which may have continued far into the nineteenth century. At least in Irlbeck's region (and to a much greater degree than in modern society), the societal knowledge system was apparently lacking ways of providing feedback between hierarchical social groups that were separated from one another. In Irlbeck's time, differences in social status could not only entail massive disparities in education and prosperity, but were also the expression of a fundamental political inequality. The question as to why it was barely feasible for feedback from the rural population to be effectively circulated back into the educated knowledge networks of the Late Enlightenment thirdly suggests that an analysis of the social structures of the pre-modern social order should be considered as a key aspect in each respective explanatory approach.

Dialectics of historical and historiographical perspectives

How much can we rely on Irlbeck's statement that he was not the only peasant who ran his farm in a reform-minded manner? After all, his progressive self-image stands in sharp contrast to established images of the peasantry during the Enlightenment, describing a tradition-fixated, 'superstitious', and resistant peasantry.[41] The body of work from the *Volksaufklärung* in particular offers a rich stock of negative portrayals of the peasantry, the significance and function of which for the Agricultural Enlightenment will be discussed subsequently. The agricultural literature of the eighteenth century spawned a more positive image of peasants, particularly when it came to the category of virtue. For instance, Gerendina Gerber-Visser has identified idealized images of the rural population in the topographical descriptions of the Oekonomische Gesellschaft Bern, which primarily referred to the Bernese Oberland: The 'healthy, simple and happy mountain dweller', the 'peaceable and unspoilt shepherd' or the 'honest old Swiss' are figures that sprang from poetry and travel literature and were conceived in the context of the civilization-critical discourses of the time.[42] For example, the Swiss Jakob Gujer (1716–1785), alias Kleinjogg, was stylized as the model peasant and unspoiled human being in the Rousseauian sense, and was correspondingly received as such by urban readers.[43] By contrast, it was only in isolated cases

41 See the conference proceedings, D. Münkel and F. Uekötter (eds), *Das Bild des Bauern. Selbst- und Fremdwahrnehmungen vom Mittelalter bis ins 21. Jahrhundert* (Göttingen, 2012).

42 See G. Gerber-Visser, *Die Ressourcen des Landes. Der ökonomisch-patriotische Blick in den topographischen Beschreibungen der Oekonomischen Gesellschaft Bern (1759–1855)* (Baden, 2012), pp. 237–8, 240.

43 See H. C. Hirzel, *Kleinjogg oder Tun und Denken eines naturnahen glückseligen Bauern. Aufgezeichnet durch Hans Caspar Hirzel* (Zürich, 1980). On Hirzel and the

that educated authors attributed qualities decidedly associated with the category of knowledge to the figure of the ordinary peasant. Even Hans Caspar Hirzel (1725–1803), who marvelled at Kleinjogg's 'natural genius' as possessing the 'best qualities of an observing mind', immediately conceded that Kleinjogg's rather clear concepts still remained 'dark and fragmentary' when communicated to other peasants, since he either did not make the effort or was unable to express knowledge in a verbally-differentiated manner.[44] While there are undoubtedly individual cases (such as Hirzel's) where the cognitive skills of peasant actors were acknowledged and positively assessed, a serial analysis of *Volksaufklärung* statements reveals a distinctly contrasting evaluation pattern.[45] Usually, there is the basic assumption that the so-called 'simple peasant' has to be taught how to use their intellect directly. Put more pointedly, from the Enlightenment perspective, the 'simple peasant' may well have experience, but did not have knowledge. What is striking about the *Volksaufklärung* texts is that their authors seldom address agrarian conditions, whether it be at the place of the work's publication, the author's place of domicile, or on a more general level. Consequently, peasant economies appear all but detached from manorial and municipal ownership, as well as juridical and regulatory conditions, so that these structures are rarely perceived as an obstacle for improving agriculture. The entire literature of the Agricultural Enlightenment is characterized by the tendency to omit structures and problems related to agricultural policy, so that, in the words of Marcus Popplow, it can 'not least be considered as an early example of attempts to solve societal issues through technological innovation without having to touch upon conflict-laden social constellations'.[46] Incidentally, the polemical political writings of the well-known Schubart, who raged against the privileges of the Saxon landed gentry, represent an exception to this rule.[47] According to *Volksaufklärung* literature, it is typically the people, or more precisely the

---

function of Kleinjogg as a figure, see R. Graber, 'Die Zürcher Bauerngespräche: Innovation der Volksaufklärung oder Instrument der Herrschaftssicherung?', in Böning, Greiling and Siegert (eds), *Die Entdeckung von Volk, Erziehung und Ökonomie*, pp. 43–58.

44 H. C. Hirzel, *Die Wirthschaft eines philosophischen Bauers. Entworfen von H.C. Hirzel, M. D. und Stadtarzt in Zürich* (Zürich, 1774), pp. 54–6.

45 Lehmbrock, *Der denkende Landwirt*.

46 M. Popplow, 'Die Ökonomische Aufklärung als Innovationskultur des 18. Jahrhunderts zur optimierten Nutzung natürlicher Ressourcen', in M. Popplow (ed.), *Landschaften agrarisch-ökonomischen Wissens. Strategien innovativer Ressourcennutzung in Zeitschriften und Sozietäten des 18. Jahrhunderts* (Münster, 2010), p. 19.

47 See J. C. Schubart, 'Hutung, Trift und Brache; die grösten Gebrechen und die Pest der Landwirthschaft', in J. C. Schubart (ed.), *Hofrats J. C. Schubart ökonomisch-kameralistische Schriften* (Leipzig, 1784), pp. 1–48.

character, of the small agricultural producers, that was standing in the way of improving agriculture by means of innovative technology. For example, in one of the first recorded periodicals of the *Volksaufklärung* entitled *Der Wirth und die Wirthin* (The Farm-man and Farm-woman), it is bemoaned that the 'foolish attachment to old customs, superstition, ignorance and indolence' exhibited by the peasants represent the 'most common obstacles' to agricultural development. Apart from the charge of laziness and lack of discipline, it is usually the sensory organs and mental capacities of the rural population that came under suspicion. It was lamented that the 'truths of the sciences' were not 'respected and much less put into practice' by the 'brutish peasants' (*Sudelwirthe*). The peasant, who lived 'only sensually' and was 'shallow' and 'somnolent', perceived 'everything through faulty eyes', displaying 'bad reasoning' and 'recalcitrance against all good advice and instruction'. Generally, it was assumed that the peasant strove 'to remain dumb' by refusing to shed his 'distorting goggles' (*Vexierbrillen*).[48] And such a fundamentally flawed view of things in turn engendered economically detrimental behaviour:

> Because of these distorting goggles, our peasants may indeed lack in land and in time to grow and collect food, even though they would still have enough time, enough land, enough feed crops [...] [if only they would refrain from] seeing their entire husbandry through the goggles of old customs and deliberate ignorance, or dull-witted simple-mindedness, or even the sloppiness, and stubbornness against any instruction.[49]

This self-image of *Volksaufklärung* actors, and hence also a certain disdain for the peasant economy and epistemology, has been at least implicitly reinforced by *Volksaufklärung* scholarship. By contrast, agrarian history indirectly emerges as an advocate for rural society and its small actors, taking a critical stance towards Enlightenment invectives and negative images of the peasantry.[50] In other words, both fields of research

48 *Braunschweigische Sammlungen von Oekonomischen Sachen als des einzeln heraus-gekommenen Wochenblatts der Wirth und die Wirthin, nebst einer Vorrede und Register* (Braunschweig-Hildesheim, 1757), pp. 35, 117, 123, 130–1, 135, 137, 141.
49 *Ibid.*, pp. 34–5.
50 Werner Trossbach lists a number of studies in W. Trossbach, 'Beharrung und Wandel 'als Argument'. Bauern in der Agrargesellschaft des 18. Jahrhunderts', in W. Trossbach and C. Zimmermann (eds), *Agrargeschichte. Positionen und Perspektiven* (Stuttgart, 1998), pp. 128–9. Regarding the clash of Enlightenment-minded accusations of traditionalism with the findings of agrarian history, see also C. Zimmermann, 'Bäuerlicher Traditionalismus und agrarischer Fortschritt in der frühen Neuzeit', in J. Peters (ed.), *Gutsherrschaft als soziales Modell. Vergleichende Betrachtungen zur Funktionsweise frühneuzeitlicher Agrargesellschaften* (München, 1995), pp. 219–38. A fundamental criticism of

stand in a positive, affirmative relationship to their respective subject matter and, consequently, in a certain contradiction to each other. A prominent agrarian-historical hypothesis that seems relevant with regard to Irlbeck has been worded particularly clearly by Michael Kopsidis, when he argued that growth and progress, that is yield and productivity gains of agriculture in the pre-industrial period up to 1850, can be attributed only marginally (if at all) to intellectual or administrative interventions. This is to say that, where they came from the outside, the endeavours of the Agricultural Enlightenment had no effect on agrarian development given the fact that up until the late nineteenth century all 'resources for agricultural growth, from the labour to the knowledge [...] still originated in the agricultural sector itself' and were achieved by means of traditional pre-industrial technology.[51] Seen from an imagined vantage point of historical Enlightenment figures, this formulation would appear to be completely counterintuitive. As far as they were concerned, it was inconceivable that the knowledge that promised progress could be found in the rural society itself. In keeping with a commonly encountered explanatory pattern, it was first and foremost the peasants' behavioural disposition, that is, their alleged irrationality as described above, that stood in the way of agronomic progress. Thus, what Böning and Siegert identify as the self-imposed programme of *Volksaufklärung* actors was focussed on 'fighting against common superstition' by seeking to make an impact on the 'mentality' of the population with the goal of

assisting the disadvantaged in successfully advancing their character and realizing the human possibilities potentially present therein, whilst on the other hand contributing to solving burning issues of the time (in particular tackling the food and energy shortages caused by a population explosion) by changing their behaviour.[52]

---

the image of the peasant as ascription has been put forward by M. Kearney, *Reconceptualizing the Peasantry. Anthropology in Global Perspective* (Boulder, CO, 1996).

51 M. Kopsidis, *Agrarentwicklung. Historische Agrarrevolutionen und Entwicklungsökonomie* (Stuttgart, 2006), p. 9.

52 Böning/Siegert, *Volksaufklärung*, p. xxvii. While these core topics continued to be discussed, according to Siegert the thematic spectrum was expanded with legal, historical, political and, at times, also emancipatory offers of knowledge from the 1780s onwards. *Ibid.*, pp. xxviii–xxix. With regards to the core corpus of knowledge transfer, Alzheimer-Haller also states that representatives of the *Volksaufklärung* 'were primarily concerned with influencing and altering mentality: the people as well were to be put into a position where they would be able to influence and ameliorate their living conditions in keeping with reasonable principles, and namely as a result of gaining a deeper understanding of the interests of society as a whole'. Alzheimer-Haller, *Narrative Volksaufklärung*, p. 28. Böning, Siegert and Schmitt take a more critical stance when reflecting on the principles that 'Enlightenment figures accepted as

Agrarian historians would object that this *Volksaufklärung* perspective fails to take into account socio-economic structures such as ownership and legal conditions, which could vary considerably from one region to another, or even within one village. Among other factors, these are crucially important for whether an agricultural producer benefited from any additional income or whether they had to surrender it to another party, which is an important difference that influenced economic behaviour.

There is a notable contradiction between the opinions of the *Volksaufklärung* and Enlightenment historians on the one hand, and Irlbeck and agrarian historians on the other, with these divergent inter-pretations respectively drawing on disparate sources of knowledge. Unlike the sources of Enlightenment research, those of economic history-oriented agrarian history are usually not sourced through a narrative, but rather result from quantitative sources such as tax registers, land registries and harvest statistics. Based on the volumes of empirical data acquired from such documents, agrarian historians respectively recon-struct and interpret the historical development for concrete cases, from individual regions down to individual villages. Through the process of referencing these regional studies, negative Enlightenment-informed images of the peasantry have been widely challenged and dismissed by agrarian history, particularly with regard to the charge of traditionalism. The accumulative conclusion from these individual studies is that – depending on the agricultural system and market access of the region – it was more often peasants, small farmers and members of the sub-peasant social strata with insignificant acreages who perceived innovative agricul-tural practices as offering an opportunity.[53] It is therefore uncertain

> whether there are any indications that economy-external goals of peasant economies came into conflict with economic rationality, hampered economic growth, and thus had an impact as an economic factor. So far, no example can be found for Europe in the eighteenth and nineteenth centuries that 'market attitudes' obstructed the detection of market opportunities and delayed the process of market integration.[54]

Indeed, when regarded more closely, it is possible to identify different groups in every region, and sometimes even in every village, that

---

reasonable': see H. Böning, H. Schmitt and R. Siegert, *Volksaufklärung. Eine praktische Reformbewegung des 18. und 19. Jahrhunderts* (Bremen, 2007), p. 9.

53 One such case is described by Niels Grüne for the Baden Rhenish Palatinate: see N. Grüne, *Dorfgesellschaft – Konflikerfahrung – Partizipationskultur. Sozialer Wandel und politische Kommunikation in Landgemeinden der badischen Rheinpfalz (1720–1850)* (Stuttgart, 2011).

54 M. Kopsidis, *Marktintegration und Entwicklung der westfälischen Landwirtschaft, 1780–1880. Marktorientierte ökonomische Entwicklung eines bäuerlich strukturi-erten Agrarsektors* (Münster, 1996), p. 73.

were particularly eager for innovation. By way of example, Gunter Mahlerwein has shown that in the case of Rhine Hesse, some agricultural innovations such as fertilization with gypsum or brandy distilling were initially pioneered by Mennonite families, and subsequently adopted by the village upper classes. By contrast, the ending of collective land use by enclosure found stronger support among the lower classes of the village.[55] Agrarian history notably differs from *Volksaufklärung* research in that it explains historical economic practices by completely foregoing the category of mentality. Instead, progressive as well as conservative outlooks are described as advantage-seeking behaviour based exclusively on demographic and market economic factors.[56] Thus, agrarian historians employ the *homo economicus*, which, in turn, should be extremely susceptible to accusations of anachronism, since the model of *homo economicus* let alone a theory of the market economy was far from in sight.[57] The point seems to be that agrarian historians do identify practices that can be interpreted as market-orientated or market-integrated in a modern sense, irrespective of the historical semantics. The outlined scepticism of agrarian history towards intellectual interventions into peasant economy is more amplified than mitigated by the distinctly negative representations of the peasantry in the *Volksaufklärung* texts. As Irlbeck deplored,

agricultural scholars [...] have gone so far in their science as to flatly deny to the peasant any powers of the soul for observation and judgement in his own trade, and find him to be no more than a mechanical apparatus driven solely by the rut of old customs.[58]

---

55 Mahlerwein, *Herren im Dorf*, pp. 246–62. Stefan Brakensiek arrived at a different conclusion for north-western Germany, where farmers profited from the elimination of the commons while the village's lower classes did not. S. Brakensiek, *Agrarreform und ländliche Gesellschaft. Die Privatisierung der Marken in Nordwestdeutschland, 1750–1850* (Paderborn, 1991), pp. 432–3.

56 An overview of older and more recent theoretical explanatory approaches to agricultural development is also provided in Kopsidis, *Agrarentwicklung*, pp. 65–6. The economic historian Werner Plumpe calls into question an economic history that makes its argument strictly from a neoclassic stance by alleging *homo economicus* is incapable of capturing the complexity of economic developments. Plumpe instead calls for a triple perspective based on practices, semantics and institutions: W. Plumpe, 'Ökonomisches Denken und wirtschaftliche Entwicklung. Zum Zusammenhang von Wirtschaftsgeschichte und historischer Semantik der Ökonomie', *Jahrbuch für Wirtschaftsgeschichte* 1 (2009), pp. 27–52.

57 L. Roberts, 'Practicing oeconomy during the second half of the long eighteenth century. An introduction', *History and Technology* 30 (2014), pp. 133–48.

58 Irlbeck lunges into his counterattack by demurring that this 'single account' reveals the 'utter ignorance' of these men 'in a subject in which they seek to act as being learned'. Irlbeck, *Landwirthschaft*, I, p. iv.

Is it possible that, ultimately, *Volksaufklärung* entirely ignored one of its essential subject matters (agriculture) as well as its intended audience (small agricultural producers), and instead engaged in processing quite different concerns relating to its protagonists own social networks? Indeed, forms of self-reference, passages in which authors comment either directly or indirectly on their own affairs, can be encountered on many different levels. For one thing, they are contained in the numerous meta-discursive parts of texts in which authors speak *about* small agricultural producers in the third person instead of addressing them directly. The peasant, as an explicitly stated addressee, takes the backseat to other implied reader groups, which consisted of those from like-minded *Volksaufklärung* circles, potential mediators, and also possibly an interested non-peasant reading public who stood as prospective buyers of *Volksaufklärung* literature.[59] Additionally, those passages in which authors urged the rural population to adopt a different cognitive attitude towards the subject matter of agriculture can also be considered to be self-referential. One author who charged small agricultural producers with a 'fleeting, heedless view upon the works of nature' explicitly cited natural history as the best 'aid' for a better approach to contemplating nature. Not only would it acquaint the farmer with the 'results of an attentive observation of nature' and benefit him economically, but also 'lift from his eyes that veil through which he could hitherto see the beauty of his environment, namely nature, only as if in the dark'.[60] There are good reasons to assume that such descriptions were modelled on the contemporary image of a *Naturliebhaber,* an educated nature lover, which served as a source for the authors' narrative. The following example illustrates this assumption even more vividly. An author expressed his incomprehension as to why, even where they had the space, people living in the countryside would not set up a *Denkerstube,* a thinking parlour, to pursue serene contemplation undisturbed by children and servants. He is at a loss to understand

> how one is supposed to think if one cannot find some solitude at least for a few hours? I know many thousands of farmers who have sufficient means and opportunity to set up their own little room apart from the general sitting room. And yet, they do not even express a desire to do so because they lack the mental cultivation [*Geistesbildung*] which teaches us to find expedient comfort.[61]

---

59 In addition to farmers, *Der Wirth und die Wirthin* is also addressed to what are referred to therein as '*Stadtwirte*', i.e. urban 'artisans, manufacturers, craftsmen, and common citizens', see *Wirth und Wirthin,* p. 10.

60 *Wirthschaftsmann,* II, pp. 1513–14. Already Böning and Siegert have pointed out the outstanding importance of the emerging natural sciences in the context of *Volksaufklärung: Volksaufklärung,* pp. xxii–xxiii.

61 *Wirthschaftsmann,* I, p. 627.

The assumption of a complete absence of epistemic practices is questionable, especially since peasant writing and account books have survived.[62] Nevertheless, this insinuation (which, read strongly enough, could also be taken as an imputation of *irrationality*) is contained in many *Volksaufklärung* articles. Among other things, it is conveyed by how much ink has been spilled in the text to establish an allegedly different cognitive attitude. While the author of the above quote identifies the lack of 'mental culture' as the reason why somebody would make do without the thinking parlour, he fails to address other reasons why setting up a thinking parlour might make little sense under the conditions of a peasant economy – even where 'mental culture' is present. Regarded from the angle of a retrospective critique as informed by a culture-anthropological view, the author was ready to evaluate a finding (no thinking parlour) based exclusively on his own assumptions (due to a lack of mental cultivation) since he ignored information about the actual environment of the people he judged. It seems like this mode of non-knowing, the failure to include any information obtained from small agricultural producers and their rational reasons, often leads to a short circuit in *Volksaufklärung* articles, whereby those actors who did not act in accordance with the author's ideas were readily cast as irrational.[63] The negative image of the peasantry that dominated *Volksaufklärung* can be interpreted as a clear indication of a factual, social and lifeworld distance by its authors from the peasant economy.[64] What conclusions can be drawn from all this,

---

62 Various studies have demonstrated the extent to which practices of nature observation and manipulation in European artist's and craftsman's workshops inspired the natural sciences in the sixteenth and seventeenth centuries. See for instance P. H. Smith, *The Body of the Artisan. Art and Experience in the Scientific Revolution* (Chicago, 2004) and P. O. Long, *Artisan/Practitioners and the Rise of the New Sciences, 1400–1600* (Corvallis, 2011). Conceptual approaches to such intertwining phenomena in the field of agriculture can be found in Schlude, *Naturwissen*.

63 See the known adaption of cultural anthropology for Science and Technology Studies in B. Latour, *Science in Action. How to Follow Scientists and Engineers Through society* (Cambridge, MA, 1987). Latour concludes that '[a]ll questions of irrationality are merely *artefacts* produced by the place from which they are raised'. *Ibid.*, p. 185.

64 However, Gerber-Visser's study suggests that, in the late eighteenth century and later, authors who were living permanently in the vicinity of the rural population they described could sometimes also come to more nuanced evaluations, thus beginning to relativize negative as well as idealized generalizations as brought forth by their contemporaries: Gerber-Visser, *Ressourcen*, pp. 241, 309, 313. Cf., by contrast, the results of research by Regula Wyss according to which questions of social distinction and belongingness (to the Enlightenment networks) were dominant in representatives of the *Volksaufklärung* also in the direct vicinity of small agricultural practitioners: R. Wyss, *Pfarrer als Vermittler ökonomischen Wissens? Die Rolle der Pfarrer in der*

with regards to the role of the *Volksaufklärung* in the broader context of the Agricultural Enlightenment that formed a cross-regional knowledge network of an educated middle class?

Othering the 'simple peasant' within the Agricultural Enlightenment

The devaluation or non-recognition of the knowledge of small agricultural producers within *Volksaufklärung* does not necessarily have to be indicative only of the frustrating communication problems between the educated actors and the rural population. As I have shown, the figure of the simple peasant was an important silhouette target in the broader arena of Agricultural Enlightenment.[65] As we know, one aim of its noble and civic protagonists was to confer the dignity of a science to the area of agricultural practice, which had traditionally been conceptualized as an *ars mechanica*. Agriculture had been, in other words, categorically excluded from the realm of erudition and learned subjects. The ambition to change this is also ubiquitous in texts of the *Volksaufklärung*. In a certain sense, the recurring attempts to enable small agricultural producers to convey a new cognitive position towards agriculture reflect the notions of Agricultural Enlightenment circles about how agriculture could be practised differently, namely in a scientific manner. It is obvious that this transformation was not merely an epistemic challenge but – in view of the social stigma of agriculture as the trade of an inferior class or estate (*Stand*) – it was also, above all else, a social one. The lowest common denominator of all middle-class protagonists remained that the 'simple peasant' was no scientist and was not allowed to be one. Against the background of contemporaneous conceptions of social rank and honour, the stigmatized peasant economy represented a taboo sphere up until the end of the century, the border of which no member of the Agricultural Enlightenment circles dared to officially cross. The *Volksaufklärung* texts particularly contributed to conceptualizing the expertise of small agricultural producers as a purely mechanical matter, and therefore as mindless. Within the Agricultural Enlightenment, the 'simple peasant' became the symbolic figure of non-knowledge. By taking recourse to this figure, civic actors set themselves apart from the unsophisticated country population socially as well as epistemically, which was an inevitable social-historic precondition for them to be able to fully dedicate themselves to agriculture. As a landowner reported in the 1770s, in the 1740s it had still been considered 'infra dignitatem' for young noblemen to personally engage in agricultural activities. In the meantime, he

---

Oekonomischen Gesellschaft Bern im 18. Jahrhundert (Nordhausen, 2007). On this point, also Alzheimer-Haller, *Narrative Volksaufklärung*, pp. 86–7.
65   Lehmbrock, *Der denkende Landwirt*.

argued, it was high time for agriculture to go back to being 'pursued and directed by noblemen predominantly as a science', like in ancient Rome.[66] Another author argued that inventions in agriculture required 'mostly sour and hard work', and for that reason could not be realized by 'scholars' or 'statesmen', but only by 'sturdy country folk' and 'persons of intermediate social standing' (*mittlere Standespersonen*).[67] These statements are obviously situated in the pre-modern period, when not all activities were considered suitable for everyone, and literally everything could become a question of honour or its potential loss.

Conclusion: Pre-modern inequality and the (non-)circulation of knowledge

Irlbeck's case suggests that a considerable communication problem existed between the trans-territorial knowledge networks of the Agricultural Enlightenment and *Volksaufklärung* and the village-based networks of knowledge of which actors such as Irlbeck were a part. As a result, while the advice contained in circulating agricultural writings did indeed reach peasant society, the experience of the local population – above all reports about failures with new practices – did not necessarily find their way back into the public discourse, or either failed to do so in a timely manner, or were simply ignored. With this situation in mind, it appears worth examining closely the conditions that facilitated or restricted the circulation of knowledge content *between* networks, and particularly between networks of different social classes. It thus seems a useful project to further develop instruments to detect and to analyse knowledge transfers across social borders. A comprehensive history of knowledge networks in the early modern period should put a stronger focus on the

66 J. G. von Schönfeld, *Die Landwirthschaft und deren Verbesserung nach eigenen Erfahrungen beschrieben* (Leipzig, 1791), pp. xliv, xlvi. John Shovlin puts forward the hypothesis that in the course of the eighteenth century it was increasingly considered honourable to earn money by agriculture: see J. Shovlin, *The Political Economy of Virtue. Luxury, Patriotism, and the Origins of the French Revolution* (Ithaca, NY, 2007), pp. 51, 75–9 and 161–8. The reference to the status of agriculture in antiquity is ubiquitous and formulaic in prologues or dedicated chapters in agricultural literature: 'History, that teacher of mankind, shows that already for the Romans, field cultivation and gardening was a pursuit of great, educated and famous men. Princes were shepherds, heroes planted trees and ploughed the fields; having bravely fought battles and achieved victory, they went to the plough; and from the plough to conducting war and state business': see *Nützliche und praktische Vorschläge die Landeskultur in Baiern zu befördern. Nebst Beantwortung der im baierischen Landboten aufgeworfenen ökonomischen Fragen* (München, 1791), p. 1.

67 J. G. von Eckhart, *Johann Gottlieb von Eckharts Geheimbden Hof- und Cammerraths Vollständige Experimental Oeconomie über das vegetabilische, animalische und mineralische Reich [...]* (Jena, 1754), p. 2.

social inequality among people and the ensuing diversity of forms of living, which was taken for granted in the societal structure of the early modern period. In this context, Regina Dauser *et al.* have suggested the term *gekammertes Wissen*, i.e. chambered knowledge, for such structural barriers to knowledge circulation, arguing that knowledge remained socially 'chambered' to the same significant extent that knowledge appropriation was influenced by social factors such as class, legal status, ideas of honour or habitus, right up until the mid-nineteenth century.[68] The concept of chambered knowledge may, for example, provide a partial explanation as to why, despite its philanthropic intention, the project of *Volksaufklärung* produced a negative vision of peasant (ir)rationality, leading to the exclusion of peasant experts from the sphere of knowledge. From a historiographical perspective, the writings of the Agricultural Enlightenment and the *Volksaufklärung* can thus be analysed predominantly as self-referential sources that, rather than containing information about the rural population and their economy, primarily provide information on the perceptions and notions of its authors.

In this case, an interesting follow-up question would be by which channels was it possible for knowledge to jump from one chamber and from one network to another? More recently, promising concepts for analysing such leaps in the early modern period have been developed in the history of science and technology, among them the concept of *trading zones* understood as specific locations where exchanges of knowledge took place between scholars on the one hand, and high-status artisans on the other, for example in the field of architecture or goldsmithery.[69] Moreover, the second half of the century saw the establishment of technical schools and the first technical colleges, and concurrently of what researchers have identified as the first 'hybrid experts', namely individuals whose activities, for instance, combined work in academic geology as well as in the princely mines.[70] Albrecht Thaer, who is generally credited with being the founding figure of agricultural science in Germany, can certainly be regarded as such a hybrid expert, combining his roles as a university professor, academy founder and a farmer. This process went hand in hand with an emerging image of the scholar as an 'all around useful member of society'.[71] Monika Mommertz even identifies

---

[68] R. Dauser, P. Fassl and L. Schilling (eds), *Wissenszirkulation auf dem Land vor der Industrialisierung* (Augsburg, 2016), pp. 8–9.

[69] See for instance L. Roberts, S. Schaffer and P. Dear (eds), *The Mindful Hand. Inquiry and Invention from Late Renaissance to Early Industrialisation* (Amsterdam, 2007) and Long, *Artisan/Practitioners*.

[70] U. Klein, 'Savant officials in the Prussian mining administration', *Annals of Science* 69 (2012), pp. 349–74.

[71] M. Mommertz, 'Das Wissen "auslocken". Eine Skizze zur Geschichte der epistemischen Produktivität von Grenzüberschreitung, Transfer und Grenzziehung zwischen Universität und Gesellschaft', in Y. Nakamura

'learning' from practice as a key aspect for the epistemic productivity of the new sciences in the early modern period, arguing that the formation of modern sciences was characterized by a crossing of boundaries from the traditionally contemplative university learning into areas of practical knowledge.[72] In addition to these possibilities – isolated trading zones or the institutionalization of technical knowledge – Irlbeck's case also points to a context that opened up the possibility for low-status experts, such as simple agricultural producers, to make an impact even in a high-status knowledge network. Especially in rural networks, the local officials of territorial administrations can be assumed to have been of major significance for the circulation of knowledge between different social classes. Just as in the case of the county court judge of Kötzingen, they could appear in the role of mediators. After all, they too can be regarded as hybrid figures, belonging to Enlightened Society by virtue of their education and to rural society based on their place of residence. Research on local officials already provides a wealth of interesting results that show how far the exercise of power in the countryside was not a one-way street, but rather included complex negotiations with villagers.[73]

Research on rural knowledge networks can draw from a broad knowledge base of different historiographies, which it seems worthwhile to bring together into a cross-fertilizing dialogue. For instance, ethnology can be a valuable partner for knowledge networks in villages in the early modern period. Depending on the subject matter, agrarian history, Enlightenment scholarship, administrative history, and the history of science and technology may then reconstruct other aspects and perspectives of social groups: What could Enlightenment figures such as peasants, natural scientists, clergy, administrative officials and other people involved in agriculture know in light of their professional experience? Supported by agrarian history, Irlbeck's criticism could cast some doubts on the claims of the *Volksaufklärung* actors that they were the only true carriers of agricultural knowledge. Conversely, the assumption that the Agricultural Enlightenment was nothing more than an ivory-tower project, without any resonance in rural society, also seems implausible when considered in the case of Irlbeck. He, and many others it seems, accepted the recommendation urged on them to grow clover: the point was that the advice they implemented did not produce the promised rewards. Looking at the various audiences that had been created by the Bavarian Landwirtschaftlicher Verein as an institution and

---

(ed.), *Theorie versus Praxis? Perspektiven auf ein Missverständnis* (Zürich, 2006), pp. 19–51.

[72] *Ibid.*, p. 46.

[73] See e.g. S. Brakensiek, 'Akzeptanzorientierte Herrschaft. Überlegungen zur politischen Kultur der Frühen Neuzeit', in H. Neuhaus (ed.), *Die Frühe Neuzeit als Epoche* (München, 2009), pp. 395–406.

into which Irlbeck would ultimately force his way with his publication, as well as the manner in which he adopted the vocabulary of agricultural literature, show in at least two respects how far he was affected by and engaged with the Agricultural Enlightenment. Finally, research into rural knowledge networks is inevitably confronted by diachronic boundaries of knowledge circulation; namely the limits that undoubtedly hamper the work of historiography and that must always be taken into account. Here, a mixture of perspectives may also be helpful. It is indeed conceivable that the ambitions of state officials, wealthy landowners or other enlightened economists were vividly discussed and mocked by villagers, just as Irlbeck reported. Unfortunately, these sections of the overall panorama of historical communication are simply unrecoverable.

4

Fighting the Angoumois Grain Moth: Henri-Louis Duhamel du Monceau and his Network of Entomological Observers[1]

Pierre-Etienne Stockland

In the spring of 1760, the controller-general of finances of the kingdom of France, Henri Léonard Jean-Baptiste Bertin (1720–1792) received an alarming report on the devastation caused by an infestation of insect pests in the wheat fields of the western province of Angoumois.[2] Christophe Pajot de Marcheval (1724–1792), the intendant of the généralité of Limoges, informed Bertin that the crops in Angoumois had been devastated for several successive years by an insect that consumed the grain on the stalk before the harvest, leaving the inhabitants of the province without sustenance and unable to pay their taxes.[3] Even more cause for alarm was that these insects were 'spreading with fury in neighbouring jurisdictions', and had already begun to advance upon the neighbouring provinces of Poitou, Aunis and Saintonge. Fearing that this 'contagion might spread throughout the kingdom', Bertin summoned two naturalists from the Académie Royale des Sciences, Henri-Louis Duhamel du Monceau

[1] This chapter is a substantially revised version of an article previously published as E. Stockland, 'La Guerre aux Insectes: Pest Control and Agricultural Reform in the French Enlightenment', Annals of Science 70 (2013), pp. 435–60. This chapter was written with financial support from the Social Sciences and Humanities Research Council of Canada and the Social Science Research Council.

[2] Archives de l'Académie des Sciences (hereafter AAS), Pochettes de Séances, Henri-Leonard Jean-Baptiste Bertin, 'À propos d'une récolte d'Angoumois attaquée par un insecte', Versailles, 28 June 1760.

[3] The généralité of Limoges was an administrative district in ancien régime France composed of the three provinces of Limousin, Angoumois and La Marche.

(1700–1782) and Mathieu Tillet (1714–1791), both of whom had prior experience of the study of agricultural blights, and instructed them to travel to Angoumois in order to 'conduct the investigations necessary for putting an end to this calamity'.[4]

Often described as poor, isolated and backward by historians of ancien régime France, in fact the province of Angoumois underwent a period of accelerated economic development and integration in the period that preceded the mid-century reforms of the intendant Anne-Robert-Jacques Turgot (1727–1781).[5] Farmers in Angoumois devoted an increasing proportion of their labour to the commercial cultivation of wheat. The construction of a dense network of roads between 1715 and 1760 connected rural settlements in the province to other localities within the *généralité* of Limoges and beyond, spurring the development of a carefully regulated, but brisk trade with the surrounding cereal-deficient provinces.[6] Yet the extension of commercial wheat cultivation and the multiplication of trade networks, as Duhamel du Monceau and Mathieu Tillet came to recognize, provided favourable material conditions for the proliferation and spread of invasive insects like the Angoumois grain moth (*Sitotroga cerealella*).[7]

---

4   Mathieu Tillet was awarded a prize from the Académie des Sciences, Belles-Lettres et Arts de Bordeaux for his work on wheat smut, while Duhamel du Monceau was elected to the Académie des Sciences in the 1720s following his research on parasitic weeds that destroyed saffron crops: *Couronnes académiques ou Recueil des prix proposés par les sociétés savantes, avec les noms de ceux qui les ont obtenus* (Paris, 1787), p. 320; H.-L. Duhamel du Monceau, *Histoire d'un insecte qui dévore les grains de l'Angoumois avec les moyens que l'on peut employer pour le détruire* (Paris, 1762), pp. 6–7.

5   This image was cultivated by Turgot himself, and then by his nineteenth- and twentieth-century hagiographers: G. D'Hugues, *Essai sur l'administration de Turgot dans la généralité de Limoges* (Paris, 1859), pp. 6–24; M. C. Kiener and J.-C. Peyronnet, *Quand Turgot régnait en Limousin: un tremplin vers le pouvoir* (Paris, 1979), pp. 117–38.

6   R. Lafarge, *L'agriculture en Limousin au XVIIIe siècle et l'intendance de Turgot* (Paris, 1902), pp. 69–70, 234–9; P. Boissonade, 'La Province de l'Angoumois au XVIIIe siècle', *Bulletin de la Société archéologique et historique de la Charente* (Angoulême, 1889), pp. 33–84; M. Boiron, *L'action des intendants de la généralité de Limoges de 1683 à 1715* (Limoges, 2006), pp. 393–400. On the general proliferation of road networks in France between 1730 and 1780, see G. Arbellot, 'La Grande Mutation des Routes en France au XVIIIe siècle', *Annales, Économies, Sociétés, Civilizations* 28 (1973), pp. 765–90; J.-P. Pousson, 'Sur le rôle des transports terrestres dans l'économie du Sud-Ouest au XVIIIe siècle', *Annales du Midi: Revue de la France Méridionale* 90 (1978), pp. 389–412; N. Verdier, 'Le réseau technique est-il un impensé du XVIIIe siècle? Le cas de la poste aux Chevaux', *Flux* 68 (2007), pp. 7–21.

7   J. D. Sedlacek, P. A. Weston and R. J. Barney, 'Lepidoptera and Pscocoptera', in B. Subramanyam (ed.), *Integrated Management of Insects in Stored Products* (New York, 1996), pp. 44–7.

Denser farm settlements and the conversion of wasteland to wheat production facilitated the reproduction of the insect as the moths could, before the end of their brief lifespan, flutter from field to field and lay their eggs on unripened grains of wheat still on the stalk or in granaries.[8] Above all, it was the extensive circulation of infected grain that accounted for the rapid geographical spread of the insect.[9] For Duhamel du Monceau it was clear that grain merchants were the primary vectors for the diffusion of the Angoumois moth. Grain merchants were the 'true source of this curse', unintentionally introducing this pest, either through ignorance, neglect or blind self-interest, into neighbouring provinces by exporting grain that contained the insect either in its larval or adult stage.[10]

The Angoumois grain moth epidemic exposed the biological risks associated with an intensified, but poorly regulated commercial trade in grain. As the royal administration attempted to liberalize the grain train in the 1760s, lifting restrictions on the inter- and intra-provincial trade in wheat, it became clear to observers like Duhamel du Monceau that the increased circulation of grain might also be accompanied by the unwanted circulation of harmful crop pathogens.[11] Nightmares of a generalized insect epidemic across the kingdom were the opposite to liberal reformers' euphoric visions of an agricultural sector regenerated by an unfettered trade in grain.

For Duhamel du Monceau, the vigilance of public authorities was of the utmost necessity for containing and putting an end to the scourge afflicting the provinces of western France, especially in the context of the liberalization of the grain trade in the 1760s.[12] Only the imposition of strict regulations over the production, storage and sale of wheat by state administrators and public officials could prevent the spread of this epidemic to the entire kingdom. It was just as imperative that such administrative measures be based on a proper understanding of the life cycle of these insects. This natural knowledge, in turn, could only be gained through the disciplined regimes of patient observation and repeated experimentation that characterized the expanding field of

---

8   H.-L. Duhamel du Monceau, *Histoire d'un insecte*, pp. 14, 90–1, 93; Duhamel du Monceau and Mathieu Tillet, 'Sur l'insecte qui dévore les grains de l'Angoumois', *Histoire de l'Académie royale des sciences* (Paris, Imprimerie Royale, 1763), p. 289.

9   Duhamel du Monceau, *Histoire d'un insecte*, pp. 16, 78, 173; Duhamel du Monceau and Tillet, 'Sur l'insecte qui dévore les grains de l'Angoumois', p. 289.

10   Duhamel du Monceau, *Histoire d'un insecte*, p. 78.

11   On the liberalization of the grain trade see S. Kaplan, *Bread, Politics and Political Economy in the Reign of Louis XV* (The Hague, 1976), chs 2 and 3.

12   Duhamel du Monceau was probably the author of an anonymous political tract on the issue: L.-P. Abeille, *Réflexions sur la police des grains en France et en Angleterre* (Paris, 1764).

eighteenth-century natural history.[13] Histories of insect metamorphosis and reproduction could be more than 'amusements' for curious readers, Duhamel du Monceau and Mathieu Tillet wrote, as they provided the foundation for the development of effective measures for eradicating agricultural pests.[14]

The widely publicized expeditions of these two *académiciens* in the summers of 1760 and 1761 sparked a flurry of interest in the natural history of insect pests among agricultural improvers throughout the kingdom.[15] As one of the most emblematic public figures of the royally-sponsored agronomic movement, already known for his translation and commentary on the writings of the English agricultural improver Jethro Tull in the 1750s, Henri-Louis Duhamel du Monceau became the centre of an informal network of geographically-dispersed entomological observers made up of noblemen, farmers, clergymen and enlightened state officials.[16] These 'philosopher-citizens', as Duhamel du Monceau referred to his correspondents, supplied him with useful observations, experimental reports, and insect and plant specimens, which were to act as the raw materials for a comprehensive natural history of crop-eating insects.[17] By contributing in this manner to the improvement of agricultural production, civic-minded amateur naturalists accomplished a 'patriotic' duty, while also fulfilling more self-interested aspirations of gaining public credit for their efforts in Duhamel du Monceau's agronomic publications.[18]

---

13 On the emergence of observation as an epistemic genre and as a set of embodied practices, see L. Daston, 'The Empire of Observation, 1600–1800', in L. Daston and E. Lunbeck (eds), *Histories of Scientific Observation* (Chicago, 2011), pp. 81–113; M. Terrall, *Catching Nature in the Act: Réaumur and the Practice of Natural History in the Eighteenth Century* (Chicago, 2014).

14 Duhamel du Monceau and Tillet, 'Mémoire sur l'insecte qui dévore les grains de l'Angoumois', p. 297. The two men had in mind here René-Antoine Ferchault de Réaumur's (1683–1757) highly popular *Mémoires pour servir à l'histoire des insectes* (6 vols, 1734–42).

15 The Economic society of Bern also launched an investigation into agricultural pests in 1762. M. Stuber and R. Wyss, 'Useful Natural History? Pest Control in the Focus of the Economic Society of Bern', in A. Holenstein, H. Steinke and M. Stuber (eds), *Scholars in Action: The Practice of Knowledge and the Figure of the Savant in the eighteenth century* (Leiden, 2013), pp. 891–920.

16 On Duhamel du Monceau's role in the agronomic movement, see A. Bourde, *The Influence of England on the French Agronomes* (Cambridge, 1953); A. Bourde, *Agronomie et agronomes en France au XVIIIe siècle* (Paris, 1967); B. Dupont de Dinechin, *Duhamel du Monceau: un savant exemplaire au siècle des lumières* (Paris, 1999).

17 Duhamel du Monceau first used the term 'philosophe-citoyen' in his *La physique des arbres où il est traité de l'anatomie des plantes et de l'économie végétale* (Paris, 1758), p. x.

18 H.-L. Duhamel du Monceau, *Éléments d'agriculture* (2 vols, Paris, 1761),

In this chapter, I reconstruct the web of exchanges that connected amateur naturalists in the French provinces to Duhamel du Monceau, in order to show how natural historical and agricultural knowledge about insect pests was created, debated and refuted through the circulation of written observations and natural specimens between Paris and rural localities in the kingdom of France. I will also demonstrate how similar dynamics were at play in Duhamel du Monceau's efforts to disseminate material technologies for exterminating insect pests. By examining these associations between agricultural improvers, state officials and academic naturalists, I show how insect pests came to be configured as a highly consequential field of knowledge in the Enlightenment, and how natural history came to provide the foundation for administrative strategies of agricultural and environmental management.

More broadly, my aim is to examine how knowledge networks were elaborated within the countryside, and between the countryside and urban areas, in the kingdom of France during the Enlightenment. How did agricultural knowledge circulate within and between epistolary networks, scientific academies, agricultural societies and the world of print? What kinds of relationships did *savants* maintain with actors outside scientific academies that were vital to the production of agricultural knowledge, such as state administrators, clergymen, farmers and noble agricultural improvers? In what ways did this collectively-produced natural knowledge impact or fail to impact on actual agricultural practices? The case of the Angoumois grain moth provides a point of departure for answering the questions that lie at the heart of this book.

The expedition to Angoumois: Combating pests and provincial prejudices

After arriving in Angoumois in July 1760, Duhamel du Monceau and Tillet quickly identified the *chenille d'Angoumois* as a *phalena* briefly described in the second volume of René-Antoine Ferchault de Réaumur's *Mémoires pour servir à l'histoire des insectes*.[19] In order to 'see more than M. Réaumur had been able to', the two naturalists travelled throughout the province, collecting specimens and conducting observations in fields and barns infested with these insects. During these expeditions, they made the home of M. Marantin, the subdelegate of the intendant of Limoges, their principal seat of residence. Marantin's house was ideally suited for the two naturalists' investigations. Situated near La Rochefoucauld, in

---

Duhamel du Monceau, *Expériences et réflections sur la culture des terres: faites pendant l'annee 1752* (Paris, 1753), p. viii.

19 Archives Nationales de France, Paris (hereafter ANF), 127AP/6, 'Note de M. Fougeroux sur le papillon d'Angoumois', 28 Aug. 1760; R. A. Ferchault de Réaumur, *Mémoires pour servir à l'histoire des insectes*, II, p. 490.

proximity to the parishes that were hit hardest by the outbreak, it offered ready access to an inexhaustible supply of insect specimens.[20] For several weeks, the house acted as an observational and experimental laboratory. The house was equipped with microscopes, which both men used to observe insects, caterpillar excrement and moth eggs, and to dissect grains containing live larvae. Moth specimens were kept in glasses of crystal in a darkened room in the basement, where both men were able to observe the nocturnal coupling of these insects.[21] Tillet, who possessed 'piercing eyesight', counted the eggs laid by the Angoumois moths to estimate their rate of reproduction.[22] Specimens of larvae and moths were also kept with stalks of wheat in large glass cases, in order to observe their growth, feeding habits and metamorphosis in controlled environments.

The two men also paid close attention to local beliefs about the physical causes of insect generation among the inhabitants of the province. Duhamel du Monceau pored over a 'great number of memoirs and instructive letters' made available to him by the intendant, and conversed with property owners, local officials and peasants, finding a plethora of opinions and 'contradictory observations' on the matter. Of all the 'foolish' ideas he surveyed, Duhamel du Monceau singled out the theory of spontaneous generation, 'which had so many partisans in Angoumois', as being particularly worthy of censure. He objected to the widespread belief among farmers in the province that the larvae they found in their wheat stalks were generated from the corruption of the grain partly on philosophical grounds, noting that eggs were the 'primitive principle' of all living organisms and maintaining that matter could not be generated from putrefaction. Yet it was imperative that these 'unfounded ideas be suppressed' primarily because they gave rise to ineffective, and even harmful techniques of pest control.[23] The belief that the cause of the insect epidemic was a 'noxious sap' in the soil of Angoumois that corrupted the grain on the stalk, for example, had led to fruitless attempts to clear 'healthful soil' in which to plant wheat crops. Even more damaging were attempts to obtain an ordinance to ban maize from Angoumois, on the grounds that the insects were generated from its putrefying roots and stems. This measure, Duhamel du Monceau warned, would not only fail to halt the epidemic, but it would also lead to the 'total loss of Angoumois', as maize, relatively unaffected by the epidemic of cater-pillars, formed the staple of the peasants' diet in the region during times of famine and shortages of wheat.[24]

---

20   Duhamel du Monceau, *Histoire d'un insecte*, p. 291.

21   *Ibid.*, pp. 10, 31, 41, 48, 52.

22   AAS, Pochettes de séances, Duhamel du Monceau and Tillet, 'Observations sur les Papillons', 3 Sept. 1760.

23   Duhamel du Monceau, *Histoire d'un insecte*, pp. 13, 67, 152, 159, 171, 292.

24   *Ibid.*, pp. 111–12, 149–50, 160, 161.

For Duhamel du Monceau, the 'pseudo-scientific reasoning' of ignorant locals who 'lacked even the first principles of natural philosophy', could not provide the basis for practical efforts to exterminate these insects. In order to rid the region of these pests, Duhamel du Monceau quickly came to the conclusion that it was first necessary to 'destroy all the ideas which have been formed in Angoumois on the efficient and distant causes of this calamity'. To convince the farmers of Angoumois to 'abandon all talk of spontaneous generation ... and form more truthful ideas of the multiplication of these insects', the two naturalists staged public displays of the insect's life cycle in Marantin's household, which Duhamel du Monceau tellingly referred to as the 'theatre of our experiments'.[25] Marantin's home was a hive of activity in the summers of 1760 and 1761, as locals eagerly came to witness the two naturalists' investigations. The observation of the process by which freshly hatched larvae burrowed themselves into stalks of grain in order to feed on the endosperm, for instance, attracted a great number of spectators. Even the stable boys of Marantin's household became familiar with this fact, 'amusing themselves by finding stalks of wheat containing miniscule caterpillars and showing them to their friends, for whom it was a novel spectacle'.[26] Through these acts of collective witnessing, Duhamel du Monceau and Tillet were able to turn their private observations of the various stages of the insect's life cycle, from conception to metamorphosis and reproduction, into publicly-attested facts.[27] The presence of 'so many witnesses' at these observational trials, Duhamel du Monceau wrote, had made it a well-proven fact, one that it was 'no longer possible to doubt', that the larvae found by farmers in their stalks of wheat were the progeny of the moths that periodically swarmed over their fields and in their barns.[28]

These public demonstrations, and the widely disseminated circulars, printed publications and engravings that verbally and visually recorded the life cycle of the Angoumois moth, formed part of a carefully elaborated strategy of rural enlightenment, aimed at reforming provincial prejudices and ill-informed agricultural practices.[29] (And see Figure 4.1.) Duhamel du Monceau hoped that this project would be carried on by enlightened farmers in Angoumois, whom he encouraged to publicly

---

25   *Ibid.*, pp. 146, 148–9, 159.
26   Duhamel du Monceau, *Histoire d'un insecte*, pp. 35–6.
27   On collective witnessing as a crucial feature of early modern experimental science see S. Shapin, *A Social History of Truth: Civility and Science in Seventeenth-Century England* (Chicago, 1995).
28   Duhamel du Monceau, *Histoire d'un insecte*, pp. 28–9.
29   Abridged pamphlets of the *Histoire d'un insecte* were distributed throughout the généralité of Limoges by the intendant and his subdelegates: ANF, AP 127/6, 'Expériences faites en Angoumois d'une méthode à la portée de tous les cultivateurs pour mettre les blés en état d'être bien conservés, et même pour faire périr jusqu'aux moindres insectes'.

reproduce his observations in order to 'sensibly demonstrate' the true principles of insect generation.[30] As Duhamel du Monceau recalled, the expedition to Angoumois had kindled great enthusiasm among local officials and farmers for the natural historical observation of insect pests:

> Everywhere we went [...] the desire to converse with us on a subject which was of such great importance to the province attracted several learned persons who brought us samples of their damaged grains, and they informed us of what they believed they had observed [...] when we discovered something interesting, we informed those who were present. One can imagine that this exchange of knowledge was very useful: it excited a great deal of emulation; everyone proposed to try out more exact and decisive experiments than the vague observations that had been conducted up to that point.[31]

While Duhamel du Monceau lamented that the local enthusiasm for entomological investigation had subsided after his departure from Angoumois, he consoled himself that this 'ardour' had remained alive among a 'few zealous and enlightened citizens' like Madame de Chasseneuil, a local noblewoman who continued to send him observations on insects 'conducted [...] with all the intelligence of a consummate natural philosopher'.[32] Correspondence with these *bon citoyens*, as we will now see, would prove crucial to the generalized programme of entomological observation that Duhamel du Monceau pursued in the 1760s.

Observing insects: Duhamel du Monceau's entomological network

Shortly after returning from his expedition to Angoumois, Duhamel du Monceau began to collect and collate observational and experimental reports that would allow him to write a comprehensive natural history of crop-eating insects.[33] To this end, he corresponded with amateur naturalists and agricultural improvers throughout France who provided him with observations, insect specimens and diseased plants from fields beyond his reach. Duhamel du Monceau became the centre of an expansive network of entomological observers, who acted at once as eyes with which he could see at a distance, and as suppliers of materials for his own investigations.[34]

---

30 Duhamel du Monceau, *Histoire d'un insecte*, p. 42.
31 *Ibid.*, p. 10.
32 *Ibid.*, pp. 11, 12, 90, 117, 207.
33 H.-L. Duhamel du Monceau, *Supplément au traité de la conservation des grains, contenant plusieurs nouvelles expériences* (Paris, 1765), p. 26; American Philosophical Society, Philadelphia (hereafter APS), Papers of Henri-Louis Duhamel du Monceau, BD87 group 14, 'Notes sur les insectes qui dévorent les grains de froment'.
34 On 'seeing at a distance', the obligatory reference point is B. Latour, *Science*

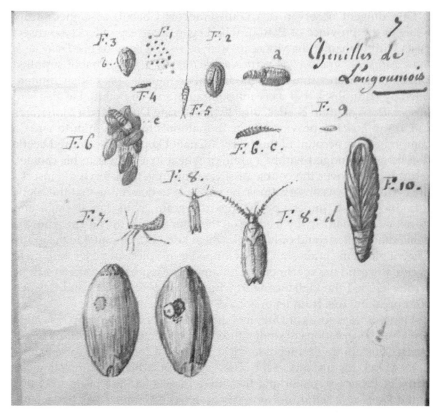

Figure 4.1 Sketches of the different life stages of the *chenille d'Angoumois*. American Philosophical Society, Philadelphia B D87 Henri Louis-Duhamel du Monceau Papers, Group no. 8. Courtesy of the American Philosophical Society Library.

These circuits of exchange were constituted and maintained through the strategic use of his printed publications. Duhamel du Monceau used his highly popular agronomic texts to mobilize entomological observers, by soliciting his readership to send him specimens and observations of insects that they might find in their fields, and then by reciprocating their favours through the publication of their experimental and observational accounts in subsequent editions of his works.[35]

---

in Action: How to Follow Scientists and Engineers Through Society (Cambridge, 1987).

[35] A strategy that Réaumur used to great effect in writing his *Histoire des insects*. See M. Terrall, 'Following insects around: tools and techniques of

One diligent observer was Louis-François Chabot, a seigneur from Niort in the province of Poitou, who began a correspondence on insect pests with Duhamel du Monceau after he read a copy of his *Traité de la conservation des grains et en particulier de fromont* (1753). Chabot supplied Duhamel du Monceau with 'a good number of gnats', previously unidentified by naturalists, that were infesting granaries in Poitou. He also sent observations of grain beetles, directly answering Duhamel du Monceau's call in the *Traité* to provide him with materials to enable him to write a comprehensive account of this insect.[36] Chabot kept a red-coloured beetle that he found lodged within a grain of wheat in a drawer in his cabinet, returning to it over the course of several months to observe the insect's life cycle. From his observations, he was able to determine that the beetle introduced itself imperceptibly into the grain in its larval stage and developed to maturity by feeding on the flour within, thus disproving the belief that beetles could only attack wheat kernels from outside the grain. Chabot glued the grain shut and wrapped it in a piece of paper, hoping to eventually send the specimen to Duhamel du Monceau. But the insect, he wrote, 'eluded the vigilance with which I had observed it', and escaped after breaking free from its prison.[37]

Many other readers of Duhamel du Monceau's texts took up his call to send him observations of understudied or previously unidentified insect pests. Toustain de Frontebosse, vicar general of the Ordre Notre-Dame-de-la-Merci, for instance, sent observations of a black fly infesting the barns of Provence, remarking that these insects had not been described in the *Traité de la culture des terres* (1753–1761).[38] Madame de Chasseneuil, one of Duhamel du Monceau's most assiduous collaborators, began to send observations of grain-eating caterpillars having read one of the early editions of the *Traité de la conservation des grains et en particulier du froment* several years before to the expedition to Angoumois.[39] Duhamel du Monceau filled his agronomic treatises with the entomological observations of his correspondents, which, as he observed with satisfaction in 1757, 'are continuously increasing in their number and zeal'.[40] Duhamel

eighteenth-century natural history', *British Journal for the History of Science* 43 (2010), pp. 573–88.

36 APS, BD87 group 8, Chabot to Duhamel du Monceau, 21 May 1762; Chabot to Duhamel du Monceau, 5 Jan. 1763.

37 APS, BD87 group 8, Chabot to Duhamel du Monceau, 5 Jan. 1763.

38 APS, BD87 group 8, Toustain de Frontebosse to Duhamel du Monceau, n.d.

39 H.-L. Duhamel du Monceau, *Traité de la Culture des Terres, suivant les principes de M. Tull* (6 vols, Paris, 1750–1761), VI, p. 482.

40 Duhamel du Monceau, *Traité de la Culture des Terres*, VI, p. v; id., *Traité de la conservation des grains* (Paris, 1753), pp. 84–100; Duhamel du Monceau, *Traité de la culture des terres*, V, pp. 296–313; Duhamel du Monceau, *Éléments d'agriculture*, I, pp. 288–302, 413–21; H.-L. Duhamel du Monceau, *Supplément au traité de la conservation des grains*, pp. 26–48; J.-L. Duhamel du Monceau,

du Monceau presented himself as an arbiter in this expanding network of 'philosopher-citizens', collecting, collating and publishing the reports that he deemed worthy of approval. This moral economy of credit, in which amateur naturalists were rewarded with public acknowledgment of their efforts through print, was the glue that held together Duhamel du Monceau's observational network and ensured the continued circulation of specimens and observations.

Some observers went beyond descriptive histories of insect pests and ventured into the territory of *physique*, or natural philosophy, by making causal claims about the physiological relationship between insects and plants. In August 1761, M. Bruté, a manufacturing inspector from Montauban, sent Duhamel du Monceau a letter in which he claimed to have proven that microscopic insects were the causes of all diseases afflicting wheat and millet crops.[41] Duhamel du Monceau had himself raised the possibility in the second volume of his *Traité de la Culture des Terres* (1753) that wheat rust and smut might be caused by the stings of insects. However, given the absence of conclusive evidence, he left the question open to 'agricultural enthusiasts' (*amateurs d'agriculture*) who might resolve the question through the 'multiplication of observations and experiments'.[42] Bruté obligingly responded to the call for such experiments, examining droplets of water infused with rusted and smutted wheat under a solar microscope that revealed an innumerable quantity of imperceptible insects and insect eggs.[43] He then sent Duhamel du Monceau a descriptive account of the shape, size and movement of these insects and eggs, along with stalks of rusted and smutted wheat so that he himself might repeat these observations. For Bruté, who at the time was preparing a manuscript on the subject of plant diseases, a correspondence with Duhamel du Monceau provided the possibility of gaining powerful epistemic validation from an eminent naturalist whose approval could transform his private conjectures into publicly-attested facts.

While Duhamel displayed a moderate scepticism towards Bruté's claims, noting that they were 'conjectures deserving more observations', he could be outright dismissive of other correspondents who, in his view, proceeded on the basis of mistaken premises. Such was the case with M. Thazeau, a parish priest from the village of Solomé in Poitou and member of the Société d'Agriculture d'Angoulême, who took an active

---

Mémoires d'agriculture adressés à M. Duhamel du Monceau, par plusieurs agriculteurs (Paris, 1765), *passim*.

41 APS, BD87 group no. 8, Bruté to Duhamel du Monceau, 3 Aug. 1761; Bruté appears as *inspecteur de manufactures* in Montauban in *Almanach Royal* (Le Breton, Paris, 1764), p. 436.

42 J.-L. Duhamel du Monceau, *Traité de la Culture des Terres*, II, p. 176.

43 APS, BD87 group no. 8, Bruté to Duhamel du Monceau, 3 Aug. 1761.

role in efforts to combat the Angoumois moth.[44] Thazeau determined that the 'qualities' communicated to wheat plants by the soil in which they were planted, and by the seeds from which they developed, had a determining impact on the reproductive cycles of this insect. The Angoumois moth proliferated especially on wheat planted in 'warm earth' (*terre chaude*), as the 'heat' of the soil caused a fermentation of the plant that accelerated the hatching of eggs laid on the stalk.[45] The seeds of wheat planted in 'cold earth' (*terre froide*) should be reserved for sowing, as they retained freshness from the soil that prevented the mature plant from fermenting and imparting a generative heat to insect eggs. This insight, Thazeau wrote, was the 'the key that opens the door to the path that leads to the annihilation of these insects', as it followed that the proper selection of soils and seeds for planting wheat would rid Angoumois of this pest.[46]

Duhamel du Monceau categorically rejected these conclusions, remarking in a series of observations on Thazeau's manuscript that his specious distinction between warm and cold soils made clear that 'the very first principles of this system are false'.[47] Thazeau was distressed by this response, expressing surprise that Duhamel du Monceau could attempt, with a 'single stroke of the pen', to 'erase the work of a man who has spent more than three months meditating on the means to completely destroy these moths'. To convince his correspondent, Thazeau sent two packages containing seeds from wheat planted in cold and hot soil, and implored him to carry out experiments that, he was certain, would validate his purportedly 'illusory system'.[48] That these seeds have remained ever since in unopened packages in Duhamel du Monceau's private papers is indicative of how seriously he took Thazeau's observations. Nevertheless, the episode demonstrates that provincial naturalists and agricultural enthusiasts were not simply passive actors mobilized in the service of Duhamel du Monceau's observational programme. That some of Duhamel du Monceau's correspondents pursued independent observational programmes, and came to conclusions that clashed with his own, reveals how the dynamics of his network could be at once centripetal and centrifugal.

---

44 ANF, H/1503, 'Mémoire de Thazeau sur les Papillons de Blé', 1766.
45 *Terre chaude* or *terre brulante* corresponded to dry, light and sandy soils while *terre froide* corresponded to heavier, humid soils like clay: A.-C. Aviler, *Dictionnaire d'architecture civile et hydraulique et des arts qui en dépendent* (Paris, 1755), p. 344.
46 ANF, AP 127/6, Thazeau, 'Mémoire instructif pour venir à la destruction totale des insectes qui dévorent les bleds des provinces', 1766.
47 ANF, AP 127/6, 'Observations sur le mémoire de M. Thazeau', 1766.
48 ANF, AP 127/6, Thazeau to Duhamel du Monceau, 16 Apr. 1766.

Disseminating pest-control technologies

If Duhamel du Monceau's publications were partially intended to create a geographically dispersed community of observers, they were also meant to be used in the field as practical manuals for exterminating insects. These printed treatises were supposed to cultivate and satisfy the demands of provincial officials and cultivators with a body of useful knowledge that would assist them in the management of agricultural crises caused by insect pests.[49] Duhamel du Monceau's correspondents were effective proselytizers for his proposed techniques of pest-control. Chabot wrote in May 1762 to ask for a copy of the forthcoming *Histoire d'un insecte qui dévore les grains d'Angoumois*, remarking that this book, 'distributed into the hands of every farmer', would 'bolster the public's confidence and encourage them to carry out your remedies in practice'.[50] The following year, Chabot informed his correspondent that 'the communication of your book and my exhortations', had allowed certain farmers in Niort to successfully protect their stored wheat from grain-eating caterpillars.[51] Unfortunately, the majority of farmers in the area had refused to follow the techniques contained in this book. As we will see, it was easy enough for Duhamel du Monceau to disseminate printed instructions for controlling pests, but it proved to be much more difficult to convince farmers in rural France to adopt his solutions when they believed them to be a threat to the marketability of their crops.

Insect-repelling plants, homemade chemical remedies and combustible substances had a long-established place in the canon of pre-modern techniques of agricultural pest-control.[52] In the second half of the eighteenth century, these substances received increasing public attention from French agricultural improvers, *savants* and royal administrators.[53] Recipes for insecticide liquors circulated widely in economic periodicals, as agricultural improvers made the insecticidal properties of various plants and nostrums that they tested in their fields public. Duhamel du Monceau's correspondents did not fail to alert him to plants and treatments

---

49 Duhamel du Monceau tried to have four to five hundred copies of a five-page pamphlet extract of this book distributed in Angoumois through the intendant. He also hoped to have a copy of the book in its entirety distributed to all the agricultural societies in France: ANF, H/1503, 'Conservation des Grains', 19 Sept. 1767.

50 APS, BD87, group 8, Chabot to Duhamel du Monceau, 21 May 1762.

51 APS, BD87, group 8, Chabot to Duhamel du Monceau, 5 Jan. 1763.

52 K. H. Dannenfeldt, 'The Control of Vertebrate Pests in in Renaissance Agriculture', *Agricultural Hist.* 56 (1982), pp. 542–59; H. A. Beecham and J. Brown, 'Crop Pests and Diseases' in G. E. Mingay (ed.), *The Agrarian History of England and Wales*, VI, *1750–1850* (Cambridge, 1989), pp. 311–13.

53 P.-E. Stockland, 'Statecraft and Insect Oeconomies in the Global French Enlightenment (1670–1815)' (Ph.D., Columbia University, 2018), ch. 7.

that had proved effective in keeping their fields and granaries free from insect pests. Toustaint de Frontebosse informed Duhamel du Monceau that the strong odour of a species of hay from Provence protected stored wheat from the mites that often infested barns in the region.[54] A parish priest from Angoumois sent him a report of a remedy that he acquired from a nobleman from Poitiers, and that was claimed to completely expel mites from granaries within 24 hours.[55] Chabot also reported that farmers in Niort succeeded in expelling caterpillars from infested stalks of wheat by burning sulphur and tobacco around their fields.[56]

Duhamel du Monceau himself tested the efficacy of various fumigations and insect-repellent substances, but he was highly sceptical of the value of 'those many recipes that are held as infallible'.[57] Other traditional conservation techniques used by farmers (constantly working the stored wheat with shovels, submerging the grain in boiling water and letting it dry in the sun) were too labour intensive and failed to kill insects lodged inside grain.[58] For Duhamel du Monceau, the most economic and effective solution to the problem of wheat pests was the *étuve*, a thermally insulated chamber connected to an oven that could be used to dry wheat and exterminate burrowed insects. The heat from the kilns would kill the eggs and larvae contained in infected grain, allowing farmers to safely preserve their crops in granaries.[59] It would also halt the metamorphosis of larvae and caterpillars into egg-laying moths, thereby preventing further outbreaks of insects in fields during harvest season. Finally, the kilns would make wheat safe for long-distance transport, ensuring that insect pests did not spread throughout the kingdom by being surreptitiously carried into neighbouring provinces. The provincial administration, Duhamel du Monceau wrote, ought to insist that all wheat shipped out of the province be processed in public *étuves*, it being the only means to 'prevent the dispersal of the moths' to the rest of the country.[60] If these kilns were disseminated throughout the countryside, Duhamel du Monceau hoped, it might even be possible to 'annihilate this entire race of grain-eating insects'.[61]

---

54 APS, BD87, group 8, Toustain de Frontebosse to Duhamel du Monceau, 'Moyens pour détruire les mites dans les greniers', n.d.
55 ANF, H/1503, 'Insecte du bled en Angoumois', 1766, fo. 13.
56 APS, BD87, group 8, Chabot to Duhamel du Monceau, 5 Jan. 1763.
57 Duhamel du Monceau, *Traité de la conservation des grains*, p. 92; Duhamel du Monceau, *Histoire d'un insecte*, pp. 203–4.
58 Duhamel du Monceau, *Histoire d'un insecte*, pp. 184–210; for an overview of contemporary granary practice, see F. Sigaut, *Les réserves de grains à long terme. Techniques de conservation et fonctions sociales dans l'histoire* (Paris, 1978).
59 Duhamel du Monceau, *Traité de la conservation des grains*, p. 160; *Supplément au traité de la conservation des grains*, pp. 26–48, 58–9.
60 Duhamel du Monceau, *Histoire d'un insecte*, p. 299.
61 *Ibid.*, pp. 17, 194.

The Angoumois grain moth epidemic provided Duhamel du Monceau with the ideal opportunity to promote the model kiln that he had developed in the 1750s with his nephew Fougeroux de Bondaroy (1732–1789).[62] In this effort, he was assisted by royal administrators, who saw the *étuve* as a valuable means of containing the spread of the insect. The intendants and subdelegates in the généralité of Limoges distributed pamphlets calling upon wealthy farmers to establish public kilns on their estates.[63] At the insistence of the controller-general Bertin, members of the Société d'Agriculture d'Angoulême built a public kiln based on Duhamel du Monceau's model.[64] The intendant of Limoges, Anne-Robert-Jacques Turgot (1727–1781), oversaw the construction of these kilns in his généralité and promoted its use by staging public experiments that demonstrated the instrument's utility and ease of use.[65] Duhamel du Monceau praised the 'tremendous patriotic zeal' of the lieutenant general of Beauvais, who had built a desiccation oven on his property that was open to all inhabitants of the town.[66] Agricultural improvers and amateur naturalists who had collaborated with Duhamel du Monceau in his study of the Angoumois grain moth were also useful allies. Montalembert de Cers, who Duhamel du Monceau described as 'one of the good *physiciens* of Angoumois', sent the royal administration several reports of experiments aimed at determining the ideal temperature at which insects burrowed in grains of wheat at different life stages could be killed in the *étuve*, without altering the taste of the flour or destroying the germinative property of the seed.[67]

Beyond Angoumois, numerous correspondents and readers of Duhamel du Monceau's agricultural treatises installed kilns on their estates. Duhamel du Monceau kept a model of the instrument that he had built at Denainvilliers in his lodgings in Paris, hoping to court landowners

---

62 Duhamel and Fougeroux spent several years making technical improvements to the kiln in order to dry large quantities of grain more effectively: ANF, 127AP/6 'Expériences d'étuves à Pithiviers en juillet et août 1754'; 127AP/6 'Expériences d'étuve à blé à Corbeil', 1766. For an overview of conservation technologies in eighteenth-century France. S. L. Kaplan, *Provisioning Paris: Merchants and Millers in the Grain and Flour Trade During the Eighteenth Century* (Ithaca, NY, 1984), pp. 66–79.

63 ANF, H/1503, fo. 21, 'Expériences faites en Angoumois d'une méthode à la portée de tous les cultivateurs, pour mettre les blés en état d'être bien conservés, et même pour en faire périr jusqu'aux moindres insectes', 1763.

64 ANF, AP 127/6, Bertin to Boisbedeuil, 30 July 1765.

65 ANF, H/1503, fo. 23, Duhamel du Monceau to M. Parent, 14 Oct. 1761.

66 Duhamel du Monceau, *Supplément au traité sur la conservation des grains*, p. 136.

67 ANF, H/1503, 'Mémoire de M. de Montalembert de Cers, Major de la Ville et Château d'Angoulême et Directeur du Bureau d'agriculture de la ditte ville, touchant la manière de passer le froment au four pour y faire périr les papillons et chrisalydes en conservant le germe du bled'.

and royal officials who resided in the capital.[68] When the administrators of the royal granary in the Faubourg Saint-Denis came to see the model kiln in the 1760s, they acquired the plans for this instrument and had one constructed in their building. The financier and military administrator Joseph Paris du Verney (1684–1770) was likewise convinced by Duhamel du Monceau to establish a desiccating oven in the storehouses of the royal military academy in Paris.[69] Public demonstrations of the instrument's effectiveness in exterminating grain-eating insects were then staged at the military academy, in the presence of a number of high-ranking royal officials.[70] The Abbé de Monbourg, director of the Hôtel-Dieu in Paris, had an *étuve* built in the granary of the hospital after reading a copy of the *Traité sur la conservation des grains*.[71] Monbourg reported that he had been able to exterminate the insects that had previously infested the granaries of the hospital, and that the archbishop and many bakers of the city had approved the bread baked from wheat passed through the *étuve*.[72]

Such favourable testimonies, which Duhamel judiciously reprinted in successive editions of his works, were valuable for deflecting the scepticism of those who opposed the use of kilns for processing grain. In fact, Duhamel du Monceau was to be thoroughly disappointed in his hopes that property owners and administrators would unanimously adopt the *étuve* as a technique for grain conservation. In Lyon, 'entrenched prejudices' and 'private interests' had led to attempts to remove Duhamel's *étuve* installed in the city's public granary at Bertin's request.[73] Duhamel du Monceau was troubled to hear that opposition to his kilns was mounted not only in Lyon, but also in Angoulême:

> What is utterly mortifying to me, is that there are people who were present [in Angoumois] at my investigations and who cannot call into doubt the exactness and truth of the facts which I have put forward [...] and who nevertheless try, in the agricultural assemblies of Angoulême, to prevent that the means that I have proposed to remedy this evil be put into practice: it is very easy to gain proselytes when one is a partisan of laziness and indolence. Nevertheless, I myself have carried out my mission as a true patriot.[74]

---

68 Duhamel du Monceau, *Supplément au traité sur la conservation des grains*, p. 68.
69 *Ibid.*, pp. 49–50.
70 *Ibid.*, pp. 49–67.
71 *Ibid.*, pp. 127–8.
72 *Ibid.*, pp. 131.
73 ANF, AP 127/6, Monlong to Duhamel du Monceau, Lyon, 6 Aug. 1762; Monlong to Duhamel du Monceau, Lyon, 13 Sept. 1764; Bertin to Duhamel du Monceau, Compiègne, 4 Aug. 1765.
74 Duhamel du Monceau, *Supplément au traité de la conservation des grains*, pp. 41–2.

Duhamel du Monceau fumed that the unfounded objections to the kiln by local noblemen like the Marquis d'Argens, 'who produces no experiments, but only fine words', could only act as an encouragement to 'lazy and pig-headed farmers' in Angoumois who neglected the 'public good' and brought ruin to their neighbours by refusing to carry out operations necessary to prevent the spread of the epidemic.[75]

On what grounds were Duhamel du Monceau's kilns opposed? The cost of the instrument and the losses in weight that the grain suffered after being passed through it were frequent objections.[76] An even more serious objection was that the flour from desiccated grain was of poor quality. Concern for the quality of the wheat was fundamental for Duhamel du Monceau, as it was for most consumers and state officials in eighteenth-century France. As Steven Kaplan has shown, eighteenth-century Parisians 'insisted not merely that their bread be not defective or noxious; it must be good, even delicious'.[77] It was thus crucial for Duhamel du Monceau to convince this discriminating public that the taste of the flour was unaffected by his oven. In public demonstrations in Angoumois and elsewhere, collective taste-tests by 'grain connoisseurs' had been organized to attest to the ocular, gustatory and olfactory quality of the wheat passed through the kiln.[78] In Angoumois, local officials conducted collective taste-tests of bread baked from wheat passed through the ovens – which were all deemed 'excellent'.[79]

Nevertheless, Duhamel du Monceau found that the 'prejudice' against the instrument remained strong, and was difficult to 'destroy'.[80] Chabot found a 'great repugnance' for the kilns by the *petits gens* of Niort, who claimed that bread made with this wheat was 'worthless'.[81] Jacques-Donatien Leray de Chaumont (1726–1803), who had a kiln installed on his domain near Blois after reading Duhamel's *Supplément au traité de la conservation des grains*, complained that wheat passed through the kilns often yielded darkened flour.[82] Similar complaints about the 'offensive

---

75 ANF, H/1503, 'Conservation des Grains', 19 Sept. 1762; Duhamel du Monceau, *Histoire d'un insecte*, p. 297.

76 Duhamel du Monceau, *Histoire d'un insecte*, pp. 247–51; Duhamel du Monceau, *Traité de la conservation des grains*, pp. 139–40; Duhamel du Monceau, *Supplément au traité de la conservation des grains*, p. xxiv; A. F. L. Lapostolle, *Traité de la carie ou bled noir* (Amiens, 1787), pp. 20–1.

77 Kaplan, *Provisioning Paris*, p. 58.

78 Duhamel du Monceau, *Supplément au traité de la conservation des grains*, pp. 62–5; Duhamel du Monceau, *Histoire d'un insecte*, p. 266.

79 *Ibid.*, p. 266.

80 *Ibid.*, p. 247.

81 APS, BD87, group 8, Chabot to Duhamel du Monceau, 5 Jan. 1763.

82 ANF, 127 AP/6, 'Étuve construite à Chaumont pour seicher les bleds'; 'Lettre de Leray de Chaumont à Duhamel du Monceau sur son nouveau traité de la conservation des grains'.

taste' acquired by wheat passed through the kiln were reported by Montalembert de Cers, and Turgot's subdelegate in Limoges.[83] As Steven Kaplan has suggested,

> doubts about the feel of the wheat, the colour of the flour, and the taste of bread are perhaps sufficient to explain why the kiln process did not become standard practice in the eighteenth century.[84]

Thus, Duhamel du Monceau may have won the hearts and minds of improving landowners and enlightened officials throughout France, but his inability to win the palates of consumers, grain merchants and bakers was a serious impediment to the success of his programme.

Conclusion

In the 1760s, French naturalists and agricultural improvers turned in great numbers to the study of insect pests. The tools and techniques of natural history became connected to a generalized programme of patriotic agricultural improvement. Duhamel Du Monceau was a central node in the networks of entomological observation that were formed across France in this period, although interest in the natural history of insect pests far exceeded his limited circle of correspondents. When the Rouergue farmer Jean Mouret kept detailed notes on the parasitic insects that attacked his wheat crops on his property in Saint-Jean-du-Bruel in the province of Languedoc in the 1760s, he submitted them not to Duhamel du Monceau, but to the naturalist Jean-Baptiste Romieu (1723–1766) of the Académie Royale des Sciences de Montpellier.[85] Nevertheless, Mouret noted in the prefatory remarks of the report read to the Société that it was his reading of the *Traité de la culture des terres* that had motivated him to embark on a series of agronomic experiments on his property in Saint-Jean-du-Bruel.

Duhamel du Monceau succeeded in convincing his contemporaries that a socio-epistemic alliance between administrators, scientific experts and enlightened rural elites provided the surest means to develop effective administrative and technical solutions to the problem of insect pests and their diffusion. Administrators like the intendant Anne-Robert-Jacques Turgot used their authority to forge such alliances at the local level by sending out questionnaires on the subject of insect pests and holding prize competitions, thus encouraging provincial elites to turn

---

83 ANF, H/1503, fos. 14, 25, 'Conservation des Grains'.
84 Kaplan, *Provisioning Paris*, p. 75.
85 Archives Départmentales de l'Hérault, Montpellier, D 182, fos. 34–5, 'Expériences d'agriculture et description de plantes et d'insectes par M. Mouret correspondant de la Société Royale des Sciences à Saint-Jean-du-Burel, diocèse de Vabres en Rouergue'.

their attention to the vermin that consumed their crops.[86] In this chapter, by reconstructing the networks in which natural knowledge and technologies of pest control were created and debated through the circulation of observations, specimens and materials, I have demonstrated how such alliances worked in practice. *Savants* like Duhamel du Monceau occupied an important role in these scientific and administrative networks, although they often failed to obtain the cooperation that they sought from farmers in the provinces.

The collective practices of observation and experimentation utilized by Duhamel du Monceau and his collaborators were at the heart of the Enlightenment project. The encyclopaedic movement epitomized their conviction that the reform of artisanal and industrial practices could only be achieved through the union of theory and practice, of savants and practitioners.[87] Socially heterogeneous epistemic networks that crossed urban sites of knowledge and commodity production were formed across Enlightenment France. Epistemic communities were also formed in rural areas, as this chapter has shown, although historians have largely neglected them. These rural networks of knowledge production deserve further attention, as they provide a way of bridging the divergent historiographical fields, namely the history of science, agricultural history, economic history, and the history of Enlightenment France more generally. Attention to these networks will also provide a way of 'ruralizing' the Enlightenment, that is to show how this movement was limited not only to small urban enclaves, but encompassed the vast agrarian spaces that were, after all, central to the French economy in this period.

---

86 'vis sur l'imposition dans la généralité de Limoges pour l'année 1762'; 'Lettre à l'Intendant de Poitiers, de Labourdonnaye, de Blossac'; 'Concours Ouverts par la Société d'Agriculture', in G. Schelle (ed.) *Oeuvres de Turgot et Documents le Concernant* (5 vols, Paris, 1913–1923), II, 115–17, 433.

87 See P. Bertucci, *Artisanal Enlightenment: Science and the Mechanical Arts in Old Regime France* (New Haven, CT, 2017).

5

'Promoting and Accelerating the Progress of Agriculture': A Case Study of Agricultural Societies in the Doncaster District, South Yorkshire, England

Sarah Holland

The generation, communication and acquisition of agricultural knowledge were important during the mid-nineteenth century.[1] 'High farming' – the pursuit of more efficient, productive and profitable agriculture as characterized by capital-intensive practices and innovation – promoted the advancement of agricultural knowledge. A growing awareness that knowledge, ability and skill were as crucial as capital in successfully implementing new practices, underpinned advancements in agriculture. Agricultural societies were therefore significant conduits in the creation, transmission and reception of knowledge, and accordingly flourished in mid-nineteenth century England.[2] Their collective objective was to encourage innovation and experimentation in order to improve or advance agriculture.[3] This chapter examines the function of village and town farmers' clubs and agricultural associations in this process. It demonstrates their intrinsic role in stimulating and transmitting knowledge and their contribution to complex mechanisms of knowledge production and diffusion.

Previous studies have highlighted the importance of national agricultural organizations in the conveyance of knowledge. Nicholas Goddard's

---

[1] N. Goddard, *Harvests of Change: The Royal Agricultural Society of England, 1838–1988* (London, 1988), p. 11.

[2] N. Goddard, 'Agricultural Institutions: Societies, Associations and the Press', in E. J. T. Collins (ed.), *The Agrarian History of England and Wales*, VII, *1850–1914* (ii) (Cambridge, 2000), pp. 650–5.

[3] Goddard, *Harvests of Change*, p. 1; Goddard, 'Agricultural Institutions', p. 655.

influential work on the Royal Agricultural Society of England (RASE) demonstrated the institutional circulation of agricultural knowledge at a national level.[4] The RASE, founded in 1838 (as the Agricultural Society of England), aimed to promote the application of science in agriculture, stimulate agricultural progress and development, and generate and communicate agricultural information. To a certain extent it shaped the purpose and organization of the many regional and local agricultural organizations that emerged during the 1840s and 1850s. Goddard positioned the RASE within a hierarchical typology of agricultural associations, which categorized them by scale (national, regional, county or district, and local) and by their purpose and objectives (educational, social, political and commercial).[5] Naturally, enthusiasm for agricultural improvements and information on advancements predated the RASE – with the Board of Agriculture (established in 1793 and dissolved in 1822) leading the institutional promotion of agriculture, accompanied by local agricultural societies from the late eighteenth century. It was within this context that Stuart Macdonald, in a study that evaluated the diffusion of knowledge among Northumberland farmers, made reference to regional agricultural societies between 1780 and 1815.[6] Both Goddard and Macdonald highlight that agricultural associations were an important way in which knowledge was created and circulated.

Nevertheless, few studies provide detailed analysis of the role of local and regional agricultural associations during the mid-nineteenth century. The tendency to interpret the numerous regional and local agricultural associations within a hierarchical framework that emphasizes the role of the RASE, underestimates the complex dynamics and inter-connections in operation.[7] Closer analysis of village farmers' clubs and town-based agricultural societies provides new perspectives about how knowledge was created, circulated and accessed. This chapter uses a case study of a northern English town, Doncaster, and the surrounding agricultural district to explore the role of agricultural societies, and analyses these complex dynamics in more depth. It provides a comparison of the national RASE with the locally-based knowledge networks centred on Doncaster. It emphasizes the importance of the relationship between town and country and the urban world and the countryside. The chapter is divided into three main parts, each one exploring the key components

---

4   N. Goddard, 'Agricultural Societies', in G. E. Mingay (ed.) *The Victorian Countryside* (2 vols, London, 1981), I, pp. 245–59; Goddard, *Harvests of Change*, p. 1, 77; S. Wade Martins, *Farmers, Landlords and Landscapes: Rural Britain, 1720 to 1870* (Macclesfield, 2004), pp. 13, 88.

5   Goddard, 'Agricultural Institutions', pp. 651, 684.

6   S. Macdonald, 'The Diffusion of Knowledge among Northumberland Farmers, 1780–1815', *Agricultural History Rev.* 27 (1979), pp. 30–9.

7   Goddard, 'Agricultural Institutions', p. 684.

of agricultural societies in the facilitation of knowledge networks: agency, sites of agricultural knowledge and geographical reach, and the nature of agricultural knowledge. It demonstrates the importance of village and town agricultural societies, as vital channels for the transmission of knowledge within locales, and the interconnectivity between agency, societies and other vehicles for creating and communicating agricultural knowledge.

Drawing upon original research of the Doncaster district (located in the old West Riding of Yorkshire and now in South Yorkshire), this chapter contributes a new regional perspective on knowledge networks. Doncaster was a vibrant market town serving a thriving rural hinterland, and home to what Goddard defined as local and district organizations, striving to achieve social and educational objectives.[8] During the mid-nineteenth century, Doncaster was a country market town on the cusp of change. The population of the town, including its suburbs, grew from 12,967 in 1851 to 39,404 in 1901.[9] Yet despite significant growth in terms of the population and urban development, Doncaster and the surrounding countryside were not heavily industrialized in this period. The Great Northern Railway engineering works was the largest industry, with other smaller firms clustering around the railway. Agriculture continued to be an important part of the local economy. The intersection of different geological areas – upper and lower magnesian limestone, low lying marshland with clay soils, and sandy land – and contrasting patterns of landownership resulted in large estate and small freeholder villages in close proximity, equated to both arable and mixed farming.[10] Local knowledge networks had to respond to this geological and agricultural diversity, and adapt to the changing infrastructure and evolving economy of the district and region.

The records of village and town-based farmers' clubs and agricultural societies in the Doncaster district are fragmentary in coverage and dispersed between different archival collections. For instance, no records of the Sprotbrough Farmers' Club exist in the Doncaster Archives, despite other records pertaining to the village and the Copley family who owned the estate being deposited here. A copy of the club's rules does survive in the papers of Miss Copley, a relative of the Sprotbrough Copleys, in the University of Durham Special Collections, where her family papers are held. Similarly, printed ephemera relating to the Doncaster Agricultural Society (DAS) can be found in the papers of local landowners. Local newspaper reports, however, published detailed

---

8   Ibid., 650–2, 684.
9   D. Holland and E. M. Holland, *A Yorkshire Town: The Making of Doncaster* (iBook edition, 2012), p. 27.
10 Sarah Holland, *Communities in Contrast: Doncaster and Its Rural Hinterland, c.1830–1870* (Hatfield, 2019).

accounts of the activities, meetings and shows of these clubs and societies, often printing verbatim their minutes, proceedings, speeches and prize winners, as well as commentary pieces. The local media was also a vehicle for encouraging participation in the clubs and societies, and for the diffusion of agricultural knowledge and ideas, and were thus vital in terms of stimulating the complex mechanisms of knowledge networks. The *Doncaster Chronicle* published a feature on local farmers' clubs in 1845, arguing that such organizations were an important means by which farmers could exchange opinions, discuss ideas and profit from the experience of their neighbours, and accordingly praised the work of local clubs.[11] The *Doncaster Gazette* also supported local organizations and encouraged wider participation in them. Its proprietors gave a silver cup, worth £5 5s., to be awarded at the DAS show in 1872 for 'the best shorthorn heifer which, previous to the day of entry, has never obtained a prize of £3 or upwards'.[12] This strong interconnection between the media and these agricultural associations means that local newspapers diffused agricultural knowledge and the work of agricultural associations to a broader audience, and are a vital source in studying the societies and the construct of knowledge networks within the district.

Agency

Agency is a concept that allows us to examine those who shaped the creation and distribution of agricultural knowledge, the extent to which the recipients of this knowledge were active or passive, and the way in which people responded to it and were influenced by it. Such a concept should not be restricted to individual agents and their respective roles, but also embrace the links between different agents and their position within wider knowledge networks. The majority of agricultural societies in the nineteenth century were characterized by hierarchical membership, with landed elites, local notables and large farmers occupying prominent committee positions and maintaining control. In this respect, agency gave structure and direction to knowledge networks, and was evident at national, regional and local level. The RASE was the product of a small group of landowners, agricultural writers and farming enthusiasts, who determined the society would be run by a committee comprised of an elected president, vice presidents and 50 subscribers.[13] This structure is reflected in the village and town farmers' associations in the Doncaster district, and an example of both, Doncaster Agricultural Society (town) and Sprotbrough Farmers' Club (village), are used here to explore this in more depth.

11   *Doncaster Chronicle*, 24 Oct. 1845, p. 5.
12   *Sheffield Independent*, 28 June 1872, p. 4.
13   Goddard, *Harvests of Change*, p. 1.

The Doncaster Corporation, local landowners and leading agricul-turalists in the district collectively supported the formation of a local agricultural society during the 1840s. The matter of establishing a town-based agricultural society, with an accompanying show, was initially raised in October 1844 at a dinner to celebrate the completion of the first covered corn market in the town.[14] Thomas Dyson, an owner-occupier farmer, argued that with

> so many conveniences for an Agricultural show in Doncaster, and such a body of men to support it, that he must say it would be a disgrace to them if they did not come forward and establish one.[15]

He referred specifically to the local farmers who attended the Doncaster markets, who had been awarded prizes at the Royal and/or Yorkshire Agricultural Societies' shows. Indeed, he believed it to be the duty of all agriculturalists to establish such a society with the support of the corporation. The mayor and the Doncaster Corporation assumed shared responsibility in the creation of a local agricultural society and show. The mayor agreed to lend support to such a venture, with a view to ensuring it being both 'beneficial and important'.[16] Edmund Denison, MP, declared that he would take the liberty of initiating a society for 'the exhibition and improvement of stock, and cattle, and implements'.[17] A 'considerable sum' was raised by subscription for this purpose, further evidence of the rural elites supporting this venture. News of the formation of an agricultural society in the town was also reported further afield. The *York Herald* expressed surprise that 'such an institution was not established in that town long ago, considering the advantages that have been derived from agricultural associations, all over the country'. Its report asserted:

> These are not times in which farmers can be backward in the race of improvement, if they wish to retain their position, or to realise a fair return for the outlay of their capital.[18]

The opening of the new corn market and the promotion of an agricul-tural society for the town and its surroundings coincided with the

---

14 S. Holland, 'Doncaster and its Environs: Town and Countryside – A Reciprocal Relationship?', in M. Hammond and B. Sloan (eds), *Rural–Urban Relationships in the Nineteenth Century: Uneasy Neighbours?* (London, 2016); S. Holland, 'The Evolution of a Northern Corn Market: Doncaster, 1843–1873', *Northern Hist.* 52 (2015), pp. 233–49.
15 *Doncaster Chronicle*, 18 Oct. 1844, p. 5.
16 *Ibid.*
17 *Ibid.*
18 *York Herald*, 26 Oct. 1844, p. 5.

national campaign to repeal the corn laws, which unsettled farmers and provoked anxiety for the future.[19] 'High farming', it was argued, served to strengthen agriculture, where protection weakened it.[20] The impetus for the DAS therefore came from the rural elites, and in response to economic and agricultural circumstances.

The collaboration between the town and country elites, which had been instrumental in the foundation of the DAS, was embodied in its governance and leadership. The president of the DAS was Sir W. B. Cooke, a landowner in the Doncaster district, while the vice chair was the mayor of Doncaster.[21] Following the first show, staged in October 1845, about 150 agriculturalists attended a dinner for the society held at Mansion House, which suggested that, at least in principle, it was supported.[22] Reports of the second annual meeting of the society in 1846 emphasized the considerable growth in membership, while also acknowledging that a smaller number of people had attended the annual show. Again, the presence of landowners from the district was highlighted. Interestingly, despite the overwhelming role of the rural elites in supporting the DAS, a report regarding its third annual meeting in 1847 noted that, in addition to Cooke as president and the illustrious list of vice presidents and patrons, 'the society originated with, and is almost wholly supported by the tenant farmers of the district'.[23] Despite such eclectic agency providing impetus, and the presumed support of farmers, the society appeared to falter within a few years of its inception. By 1847, it was reported that 'the funds are not in the most flourishing condition this year, owing to extraordinary expenditure last year, which will not again occur for a long time'.[24] Even in what was an auspicious year for the DAS, the agricultural committee of the town council met for 'the purpose of taking into consideration the best means of inducing the Royal Agricultural Society to hold their meeting in Doncaster in 1848'.[25] It was proposed that the corporation should contribute £250 and that the town clerk approach the president of the DAS to request their cooperation in effecting this. It was perhaps precisely because of the elite leadership and the ambitious plans of landowners and the corporation alike that resulted in the society overstretching itself financially and going into abeyance for 25 years.

19 Holland, 'Doncaster and its Environs', pp. 80–1.
20 J. Caird, *High Farming under Liberal Covenants, the Best Substitute for Protection* (Edinburgh, 1849), pp. 5–7.
21 *Hull Packet*, 25 July 1845, p. 1; *York Herald*, 4 Oct. 1845, p. 5; *Yorkshire Gazette*, 11 Oct. 1845, p. 8.
22 *Yorkshire Gazette*, 11 Oct. 1845, p. 8.
23 *Derby Mercury*, 22 Sept. 1847, p. 3.
24 *Derby Mercury*, 22 Sept. 1847, p. 3.
25 *York Herald*, 20 Feb. 1847, p. 5.

A fully-fledged Doncaster Agricultural Society and Show was therefore not established until 1872.[26] Reports of the re-formation of the society made reference to its earlier incarnation. The *Sheffield Independent* noted:

> Lest the general public should think that the people of Doncaster and the neighbourhood have only just awoken to the importance of agricultural societies, it should be stated that they could boast of such an institution more than thirty years ago.

Motivation and encouragement for the re-establishment of the DAS again came from the rural elites, with £1,100 subscribed including '£50 from Earl Fitzwilliam, the patron of the society, and £50 from J. Brown, Esq., of Rossington, the president of the Society, and similar handsome sums from other gentlemen'.[27] The hierarchical structure of the society is evident from the list of eminent figures displayed inside their annual show leaflets.[28] In 1876, the patron was none other than the Earl Fitzwilliam who, despite his main residence being Wentworth Woodhouse, retained links with the Doncaster area; and the president was James Brown, landowner and lord of the manor of Rossington. The society simultaneously had approximately 35 vice presidents, the majority of whom were large landowners in the district.[29] The management of the DAS was vested in its committee, including the president, vice presidents and the highest paying subscribers, which cultivated elitism.[30] The committee wielded influence and power over the agriculturalists of the local area, taking decisions on their behalf. In patronizing the DAS, landowners were socially motivated by the prestige bestowed upon them as a consequence, and perpetuated the idea, advanced by the local newspapers, that it was the responsibility of landowners to be engaged with such matters.[31]

The notion of elitism, which the society could be argued to have cultivated, can be seen in the reports of annual shows through the 1870s. Prizes were frequently awarded to landowners for their livestock, and the admission fee of half a crown was considered a 'deterrent' to attending the show.[32] The rapid growth and success of both the society and its shows

---

26 Cusworth Hall Museum, Doncaster, uncatalogued papers, DAS leaflet, 1876.
27 *Sheffield Independent*, 28 June 1872, p. 4.
28 Cusworth Hall Museum, uncatalogued papers, DAS leaflet, 1876.
29 *Ibid.*
30 *Doncaster Chronicle* as follows, 5 Dec. 1840, pp. 7–8; 2 May 1845, p. 8; 3 July 1846, p. 5; 21 Aug. 1846, p. 1; 4 July 1851, 5; 2 Mar. 1855, p. 5; *The Farmer's Magazine*, 17 (1860), p. 477; *Doncaster Gazette* as follows,10 Oct. 1845, p. 6; 27 June 1873, p. 8; 12 Nov. 1875, p. 5; Doncaster Archives (hereafter DA), DD/ BW/E11/126, 'Miscellaneous Papers', Doncaster Agricultural Society Leaflets; Cusworth Hall Museum, uncatalogued papers, DAS leaflet, 1886.
31 *Doncaster Chronicle*, 1 Oct. 1847, p. 8.
32 *York Herald*, 29 June 1872, p. 7.

was attributed to the rural elites that supported them. With regards the fifth annual show of the DAS in 1876, it was reported:

> There are probably few societies whose progress has been as rapid as the one under whose auspices this show is held. Various causes have produced this satisfactory state of things, and not the least among them is the liberal support the Society has received from its promoters.[33]

Also in 1876, it was reported:

> With an energetic committee and a strong list of subscribers, it has passed all the other agricultural shows held in the district, and holds a second position only to the Yorkshire show.[34]

Nevertheless, despite the hierarchical nature of the DAS, a combination of inclusive membership policies and the recognition of the importance of small farmers and agricultural labourers promoted active participation. The objective of the DAS was stated to be 'the advancement of pursuits connected with the farm and all its varied departments'.[35] This necessitated the participation of farmers from the surrounding countryside. The committee was well aware that many of the farms in the Doncaster district were less than 100 acres (*c.*40 hectare) in size, and consistent with their aims and objectives were anxious not to exclude any farmers who could help improve local agriculture in a practical way.[36] They therefore reduced the membership rate to half a guinea (it was usually a guinea) with equal privileges for farmers of smaller acreages, and sought to reward and encourage 'the agricultural ploughmen, and other labourers, shepherds, outdoor labourers [...]'.[37] Inclusive membership policies such as this were intended to facilitate knowledge networks based on the exchange of experience, ideas and knowledge rather than simply prestige and status. Through active participation, knowledge could be both constructed and received by the wider agricultural community.

The extent of participation was varied, and to a large extent is difficult to discern from the available evidence. Membership lists or accounts of the general visitors who attended the shows do not survive. Reports of the exhibitors and prize winners offer some insight into who contributed to the construction or reception of knowledge. In addition to landowners and rural elites, tenant farmers exhibited and won prizes at the annual shows of the DAS. The DAS also credited the role of the cottager and

---

33 *York Herald*, 29 June 1876, p. 7
34 *Sheffield Independent*, 29 June 1876, p. 7.
35 DA, DD/BW/E11/126, 'Miscellaneous Papers', Doncaster Agricultural Society Leaflets.
36 *Ibid.*; *Doncaster Gazette*, 10 Oct. 1845, p. 6; Cusworth Hall Museum, uncatalogued papers, DAS leaflet, 1886.
37 *Doncaster Gazette*, 15 Nov. 1844, p. 5

labourer, to which it awarded prizes. In 1846 a prize was awarded to the 'the cottager or labourer, who shall exhibit the best fat or feeding pig', and it was reported that 'The cottagers' pigs were remarkably fine'.[38] This was similarly emphasized in 1875, when it was noted that 'The cottagers' pigs deserved attention, and were exceedingly creditable to the exhibition, both for the condition and cleanliness of the animals penned'.[39] Prizes were also awarded to

> the most meritorious farm labour who has worked at least ten years without intermission on the same farm or with the same master or mistress; who has brought up his family without parochial relief, except in cases of sickness, the amounts so received to be stated in his claim.[40]

They also noted that the cottagers' pigs would have been 'a credit to any show in the kingdom', and hoped that farmers would give their servants and labourers a holiday on such occasions so as to encourage these exhibitions.[41] This apparent inclusivity was of course shrouded in more restrictive practices. The labourers and cottagers were always in a class of their own, with an emphasis on upholding Victorian values of morality and social order. Nevertheless, agriculture in the district relied on the work of labourers and, as such, their participation played an important, though tangential role in local knowledge networks. Moreover, the wider circulation of the activities of the DAS, via the local press, meant that more people than had attended the shows could access some of the knowledge. The DAS was part of interconnected knowledge networks in the district.

At village level, landowners often provided the leadership for clubs that catered for the tenant farmer more specifically.[42] Sprotbrough Farmers' Club was founded in 1848, with support from the dominant local landowner, Sir J. W. Copley. The *Doncaster Chronicle* reported Copley's 'kindness and attention in promoting the success of the society', and his liberal contributions to the club's funds.[43] Copley was also a member of the Royal Agricultural Society of England, the Yorkshire Agricultural Society, the Doncaster Agricultural Society and the Doncaster Horticultural Society. Belonging to and patronizing different agricultural associations promoted the interconnectivity of knowledge networks. The list of 15 printed rules further emphasizes the hierarchical structure of this organization.[44] For example, the president of the club was Sir J.

---

[38] *Sheffield Independent*, 26 Sept. 1846, p. 1.
[39] *Sheffield Daily Telegraph*, 24 June 1875, p. 3.
[40] *York Herald*, 26 Sept. 1846, p. 2.
[41] *Ibid.*
[42] Goddard, 'Agricultural Institutions', p. 668.
[43] *Doncaster Chronicle*, 16 Feb. 1848, p. 2; *Doncaster Chronicle*, 1 Feb. 1850, p. 3.
[44] Durham University Library, Archives and Special Collections, GRE/

W. Copley, and the vice presidents were William Battie-Wrightson (landowner of neighbouring Warmsworth and Cusworth) and Rev. J. G. Fardell (incumbent of Sprotbrough parish church).

In addition to the dominance of local landowners and clergy, the committee was comprised of leading tenant farmers on the Copley estate. Mr S. Vickers, Mr Clark, Mr Jenkinson and Mr Wood, the founding committee members, were the leading tenant farmers on the estate and often dominated club discussions. The committee was granted the 'power' of inviting gentlemen of the Doncaster district to become honorary members, whereas regular members of the club were forbidden by rule even to introduce friends. Members also had to be elected and pay an annual subscription of 10 shillings. Rule nine specified the expectation for courteous and respectful behaviour and outlined procedures to deal with misconduct.[45] The management structure of the club was organized in favour of the landowners, clergy and leading farmers, who dominated the decision-making processes and financial arrangements. It also culti-vated social and community cohesion and congeniality with the overall aim of maintaining control within the estate village.

The objective of the Sprotbrough Farmers Club was to promote agricul-tural improvement and to provide a forum for local farmers to meet. The club adopted an inclusive membership policy in line with that of the DAS. Rule four of the Sprotbrough Farmers' Club specified that members had to occupy 50 acres (*c.*20 hectare) of land. Younger gentlemen who were learning farming, as well as farm bailiffs, were exempt from this stipulation.[46] The majority of farmers in the vicinity of Sprotbrough tenanted larger acreages anyway (between 100 and 300 acres).[47] This rule enabled the majority of tenant farmers in the neighbourhood to contribute their experience, skills and knowledge, while excluding small farmers and landless agricultural labourers. In England, during the nineteenth century, the relative benefits of farm size were contested, but farms smaller than 200 acres were considered inhibitive to 'high farming'.[48] In this respect, the Sprotbrough Farmers' Club adopted restrained inclusivity, which in fact excluded certain groups, and could be argued only to be a form of 'paternalistic' inclusion. Nevertheless, by setting the threshold at 50 acres, the club provided recognition that tenant farmers in the neighbourhood could contribute to the advancement of

---

G18/2/193, 'Miscellaneous Box of Papers Relating to Miss Copley', Rules of the Sprotbrough Farmers' Club, 1848.

45   *Ibid.*

46   *Ibid.*

47   The National Archives, HO 107/2346; TNA, RG 9/3516; TNA, RG 10/4716.

48   J. V. Beckett, 'The Debate over Farm Sizes in Eighteenth and Nineteenth Century England', *Agricultural History* 57 (July 1983), pp. 308–13, 323; Caird, *High Farming*, pp. 5–7.

agriculture through experience, skill and knowledge, and that, in order to implement new ideas and practices, and share ideas and experience, a wide range of farmers had to be able to participate in the acquisition and distribution of knowledge.

Locations

Sites of agricultural knowledge and their geographical scope provide an important spatial perspective on knowledge networks. The inter-relationships between the farming communities and agents of agricultural knowledge on the one hand, and the sites of agricultural knowledge on the other, and the inter-connections between different locations where knowledge was created, disseminated and acquired, stimulated recip-rocal relationships. The location of agricultural societies was significant for the formation of knowledge networks in terms of access and scope. At one end of the spectrum were the village-based societies with an apparent limited geographical scope, and at the other were the district-wide organ-izations situated in nearby market towns. Leadership, membership and participation varied according to the location and locational remit of each society, which in turn shaped the identity of the knowledge networks being created.

As a national organization, the RASE had a wide geographical reach, which was reflected in its objectives, publications and annual shows. It benefitted from the expansion of a national rail network, which made it possible to hold national agricultural shows in provincial localities.[49] Large towns were increasingly competitive in agricultural matters, not only constructing new market buildings and reorganizing market places, but also competing to host regional and national agricultural shows.[50] Competition to host the RASE annual show was particularly intense.[51] Doncaster Corporation actively sought to stage the RASE show on a number of occasions during the nineteenth century. After their initial proposal in 1848, the corporation again resolved in 1860 that 'a strenuous effort should be made to obtain the holding of the meeting of the Royal Agricultural Society of England in 1861 at Doncaster'.[52] It would be a further 30 years before they fulfilled this ambition, but their desire to do so was firmly rooted in civic pride. This manifested itself through tangible outputs, such as the redevelopment of the market infrastructure in the town and successfully securing the Yorkshire Agricultural Society

---

49 Goddard, *Harvests of Change*, p. 1.
50 L. Miskell, 'Putting on a Show: the Royal Agricultural Society of England and the Market Town, c. 1840–1876', *Agricultural History Rev.* 60 (2012), pp. 37–59.
51 *Ibid.*
52 *York Herald*, 20 Feb. 1847, p. 5; Doncaster Archives, AB2/2/5, 9 May 1860.

meeting in 1865.[53] With regards the latter, a report noted that the society played an important role in 'promoting and accelerating the progress of agriculture'.[54] These activities were vital in sustaining and perpetuating knowledge networks in the district during the hiatus of the DAS.

Despite its national objectives and remit, the RASE also acknowledged the importance of interconnections between farming regions and agricultural progress.[55] Its ninth objective specifically emphasized that its annual shows should 'encourage the best and most advantageous mode in which farms may be cultivated in the neighbouring districts', and that breeders of livestock calculated to produce a profit in their respective localities be rewarded.[56] This intimate relationship with geology and land type within knowledge networks was even more evident at the local and regional level. Apparent geographical restrictions of village farmers' clubs stimulated and strengthened the development of rural knowledge networks, encompassing groups of villages on the basis of geological similarities. Residents in these communities may have shared other connections, including family ties and attendance at a common place of worship, which would facilitate the transmission of knowledge. Geology principally meant they shared a similar way of farming the land, and comparable challenges. A rule of the Sprotbrough Farmers' Club specified that members should be resident within a five-mile (*c.*8-kilometre) radius. Villages within this proximity were predominantly situated on the upper or lower magnesium limestone, and club meetings had a strong emphasis on agricultural practices relevant to that geological area. Discussions therefore took into account the role of the geology, and the suitability of crops, practices and techniques for magnesian limestone soil, which was of great relevance to both the farmers of this parish and to neighbouring villages and parishes. This included communities whose landowning and social structure was in sharp contrast to that of the estate village of Sprotbrough. For example, Thomas Dyson, an owner-occupier farmer from the freeholder village of Braithwell, attended many meetings of the Sprotbrough Farmers' Club, and was able to make a number of relevant contributions based on his experience of farming at Braithwell on account of the shared geology.

Agricultural societies based in large towns facilitated the inter-relationship of opinion 'for landowner, occupier and labourer alike'.[57] Many villages did not have their own official agricultural organizations, so the meetings and shows that took place in Doncaster potentially had broad spatial and social scope and reach. The DAS met regularly and

53 Holland, 'Doncaster and its Environs'; *Yorkshire Gazette,* 29 July 1865, p. 10.
54 *Leeds Intelligencer,* 5 Aug. 1865, p. 7; *Leeds Mercury,* 4 Aug. 1865, p. 4.
55 Goddard, *Harvests of Change,* p. 31.
56 *Ibid.,* p. 26.
57 Goddard, 'Agricultural Institutions', p. 686.

staged shows in the town, which encouraged both the acquisition of and contribution to agricultural knowledge through membership and attendance. Doncaster was therefore a nucleus for agricultural debate, through which socially and occupationally diverse groups could meet and exchange knowledge. Such ostensive centralization of knowledge in fact interconnected diverse rural communities, stimulating district-wide knowledge networks and sometimes extending beyond the district or even region. Exhibitors and visitors to the annual shows provide some indication of this, drawing people from elsewhere in Yorkshire, Lancashire, Darlington, Lincolnshire, and London.[58] As with the RASE, the railways played an important part in providing the physical infra-structure to support the work of the DAS, acting as a stimulus and impetus to effective knowledge networks. Doncaster was located on the Great Northern Railway from London to Scotland, as well as a number of smaller branch lines. The success of the re-formed DAS was partially attributed to the 'first class railway facilities' of the town, which facili-tated the conveyance of stock and implements to and from the show.[59] Moreover, the distribution of research undertaken in the locality via the agricultural press encompassed America, ensuring a town-based agricul-tural society had a global reach.[60]

The nature of agricultural knowledge

Agricultural knowledge was characterized by new ideas, innovation and experimentation, and played an important role within knowledge networks by establishing connections and promoting improvement. The promotion of agricultural knowledge was embodied in the work of agricultural associations. Principal objectives of the RASE included corre-sponding with other societies, encouraging agricultural improvement, and promoting the best cultivation of land and the breeding of livestock.[61] Strategies employed by the RASE included the hosting of agricultural shows and the awarding of prizes.[62]

Similar objectives and strategies were reflected in the agricultural societies and farmers' clubs in the Doncaster district. The aim of the DAS was to further the cause of agriculture, specifically 'the advancement of pursuits connected with the farm and all its varied departments'.[63] Reports

58 Cusworth Hall Museum, uncatalogued papers, DAS leaflet, 1876.
59 *York Herald*, 29 June 1876, p. 7.
60 *The Farmers Magazine* 1 (May–Dec. 1834), pp. 336–7; *New York Farmer and American Gardener's Magazine* 9 (1836), p. 333.
61 Goddard, *Harvests of Change*, pp. 25–6.
62 *Ibid.*, p. 31.
63 DA, DD/BW/E11/126, 'Battie-Wrightson Miscellaneous Papers', Doncaster Agricultural Society Leaflets.

in the *Doncaster Chronicle* argued that prize-giving stimulated competitiveness and productivity as well as loyalty, and that active participation in agricultural societies and shows was an integral part of agricultural improvement.[64] Prizes awarded by the DAS, and commentaries on the standard of exhibits at their shows, indicate key areas of agricultural innovation and advancement. At the first annual meeting of the DAS, the stock exhibited was considered to be 'very good', commenting on the sheep and pigs as being 'equal to any ever shown' and the 'superior character' of the bulls and cows.[65] Similarly, in 1846, it was noted that 'The show of bulls and cows was very good, comprising some of the best breeds that are to be met within the country'.[66] The quantity and quality of livestock increased when the DAS relaunched, demonstrating the central role of agricultural knowledge pertaining to livestock.[67]

The nature of agricultural knowledge being promoted also included agricultural implements. In 1875, it was noted that, although they did not compete for prizes, the exhibition of agricultural implements contributed to the success of the DAS annual show.[68] By 1881, the DAS awarded prizes for agricultural implements and machinery, including a silver medal for

> the Thrashing Machine (fitted with or without a self-feeder), which shall in the opinion of the Judges, thrash and finish ONE Cart Load of Sheaf Corn upon the Show Ground in the most perfect manner.

Silver medals were also to be awarded to the best Stand of Agricultural Implements upon the Show Ground and to

> any improvement in useful FARM IMPLEMENTS, calculated to save labour, or for any MACHINE, IMPLEMENT, or MISCELLANEOUS ARTICLE which they [the judges] may deem worthy of such recognition for this or any other merit.[69]

Local implement and machine makers, as well as those from further afield, increasingly exhibited at the DAS show.[70]

The activities of the agricultural societies and clubs in the Doncaster district, including discussions at their meetings, were closely related to land type and specific crops and livestock. Consequently, interconnections

---

64 *Doncaster Chronicle*, 31 Mar. 1871, p. 5.
65 *Yorkshire Gazette*, 11 Oct. 1845, p. 8.
66 *York Herald*, 26 Sept. 1846, p. 2.
67 *York Herald*, 29 June 1872, p. 7; Cusworth Hall Museum, uncatalogued papers, DAS schedule of prizes leaflet, 1886.
68 *Sheffield Daily Telegraph*, 24 June 1875, p. 3.
69 Cusworth Hall Museum, uncatalogued papers, DAS schedule of prizes leaflet, 1881.
70 Cusworth Hall Museum, uncatalogued papers, DAS exhibition catalogue, 1876 and DAS schedule of prizes leaflet, 1886.

based upon shared characteristics were stimulated, and knowledge networks were promoted through the nature and relevance of the knowledge being exchanged. Geology and geography affected the way in which a network operated, determining what knowledge was created and disseminated and why. The DAS conducted research into new practices and products, publishing their findings. The primary objective of this research was the advancement of local agricultural production, with the underlying motive of promoting economic prosperity. They argued that geology influenced agriculture, and that accordingly new ideas and innovative practices had varying impacts. Their evaluation of the use of new ideas and techniques therefore made specific reference to geological variations.[71] For example, a report on the use of bones as manure concluded that they were particularly beneficial on the limestone and lighter soils around Doncaster, but not on the heavy clay soils.[72] The promotion of place-specific knowledge through a centralized organization transcended distance and differences between rural communities and consolidated knowledge networks in the district. Moreover, the DAS conducted research into new practices and products, which they then published and sold. Adverts for, and references to, these reports featured in prominent farming journals such as *The Farmers' Magazine* and even the *New York Farmer* and *American Gardener's Magazine*.[73] The potential audience for this research and advice was global, although it was directly related to the concerns of local farmers.

A widely distributed and frequently cited report, researched, written, published and distributed by the DAS, addressed the problems of the turnip fly and how to prevent it.[74] Crop disease had potentially devastating economic implications, and turnip fly was a recurring problem that threatened to destroy turnip crops across England. The report was based on the returns of over one hundred farmers in England and Wales, and was advertised as being of 'immense importance to farmers in general'.[75] It recommended the use of a long-haired hearth brush and quick lime to rid

---

[71] Holland, 'Doncaster and its Environs', p. 85.

[72] *J. Royal Agricultural Society of England* 2 (1841), p. 320; *The Farmer's Magazine* 5 (July–Dec. 1836), p. 419; *New York Farmer and American Gardener's Magazine* 10 (1837), p. 278

[73] *The Farmers Magazine* 1 (May–Dec. 1834), pp. 336–7; *New York Farmer and American Gardener's Magazine* 9 (1836), p. 333.

[74] Doncaster Agricultural Association, *The Turnip Fly. Report of the Committee of the Doncaster Agricultural Association on the Turnip Fly, and the means of its prevention. Founded on returns received to the questions of the committee from 102 correspondents in different parts of England and Scotland* (London, 1834; 2nd edn, 1842).

[75] *The Farmers Magazine*, 1 (May–Dec. 1834), pp. 336–7; *J. Royal Agricultural Society of England* 2 (1841), p. 207; H. Stephens, *The Farmer's Guide to Scientific and Practical Agriculture* (2 vols, New York, 1862 edn), II, p. 74.

the plants of the turnip fly.[76] This information was particularly beneficial to local agriculturalists, as the cultivation of turnips in the Doncaster district had increased, both as a fodder crop to fatten livestock and as a cleansing crop to improve the fertility of the land and reduce the amount of fallow land.[77] The importance of the turnip crop and ability to combat turnip fly was demonstrated by the inundation of stock at the November fair in Doncaster in 1858. The failure of the turnip crop that year meant many animals could not be over-wintered and had to be offered for sale in poorer condition than usual, and with supply greater than demand, inferior beasts were sold more cheaply or not at all.[78] The ability to identify and disseminate ideas on productivity and the prevention of disease had multiple benefits for the agricultural economy.[79]

Village farmers' clubs hosted a variety of speakers, who presented ideas and information relevant to local geological and economic conditions, such as methods of ploughing and sowing.[80] Wheat and turnips were among the principal crops grown at Sprotbrough on the magnesian limestone, which meant discussions about these crops were particularly pertinent to members of the Sprotbrough Farmers Club. For example, a meeting held in their first year focused on the growth of wheat, and the advantages of thick and thin sowing.[81] The following year, in 1849, the club discussed the application of different manures, advocating that good farmyard manure was superior in the improvement of the soil and the most profitable form of cultivation. In addition, the meeting identified the use of bones as the best artificial tillage, and that a combination of natural farmyard manure and bones should be recommended to farmers.[82] Also in 1849, they discussed the best method for the improvement of inferior grass land, resolving that thin limestone soils be ploughed up and left for two rotations of the crops.[83] In each instance special reference was made to the magnesian limestone soil, and determined which of the numerous ideas and techniques being promoted would be most beneficial to them.

The Braithwell Farmers Club, which was established in 1843, hosted ploughing matches in addition to evening lectures and meetings to discuss agricultural matters. The ploughing matches were particularly successful and heralded by the local press as being admirable. The

---

76 Stephens, *Farmer's Guide*, p. 74.
77 Wade Martins, *Farmers, Landlords and Landscapes*, p. 27.
78 *Doncaster Gazette*, 19 Nov. 1858, p. 5.
79 *Doncaster Chronicle*, 2 July 1844, p. 7; *Doncaster Chronicle*, 21 Nov. 1845, p. 7; 29 May 1846, p. 6; 12 Feb. 1847, p. 7.
80 *Doncaster Chronicle*, 16 Feb. 1848, p. 2; 1 Feb. 1850, p. 3.
81 *The Farmers' Magazine*, sec. ser. 18 (July–Dec. 1848), p. 447.
82 *Doncaster Gazette*, 19 Jan. 1849, p. 3.
83 *Doncaster Gazette*, 16 Mar. 1849, p. 3.

objective was to improve efficiency among those who used ploughs, with prizes awarded for competitors who ploughed land in the best manner within a certain time. This tested the skills of labourers and stimulated competitiveness. In this respect, the nature of agricultural knowledge could be skill-orientated and actively engage the labouring class.[84]

Beyond knowledge that centred on livestock, crops, implements or skill, the intersection between agriculture and politics underpinned discussions within the DAS. Contemporary issues therefore shaped agricultural knowledge. For example, at the annual dinner of the DAS in 1846, E.B. Denison began by acknowledging that 'This was a purely agricultural meeting, and he knew he had no business to introduce politics; he would, therefore, abstain as much as possible' and yet added that

> he believed he was justified in saying there was never was a time when it was more necessary for the agriculturist to put his shoulders to the wheel if he meant to get a living.

The context to these comments was the campaign to repeal the Corn Laws, and Denison's position on this issue, and the recent election campaign he had fought and lost. Denison was opposed to free trade, arguing that:

> If the agricultural interest at home were damaged, he was quite sure they would receive no adequate compensation from foreign parts; he, for one, did not want to depend upon foreign parts, and he felt quite sure that the best customer of the English manufacturer was the English agriculturist. It was far better for the manufacturer of the West Riding to exchange his product for that of the Lincolnshire farmer than that of the farmer of Poland, because in the one case this country would derive all the profit of both transactions, in the other it would obtain only half. Therefore, he said it was in the interest of the manufacturer of this country to do all he could to promote the interest of the English agriculturist.[85]

Denison argued that organizations like the DAS could advance agriculture, highlighting that local societies benefitted from having people in close geographical proximity meeting together.[86] An emphasis was placed upon the prosperity of agriculture and the nation in response to impending free trade, and that the promotion of agricultural knowledge through agricultural societies was important in achieving this. The chairman added that the DAS 'must not stand still; they must progress, and endeavour to keep pace with the great improvements

---

84 Holland, *Communities in contrast*, pp. 46–7.
85 *York Herald*, 26 Sept. 1846, p. 2.
86 *Ibid.*

which are going on in the manufacturing districts'.[87] Similarly, in 1885, the DAS's review of the year was placed within the context of agricultural depression and the challenges faced.[88]

Conclusion

This chapter has demonstrated the fundamental role that local agricultural societies played in establishing and developing knowledge networks in nineteenth-century England. Integral to the operation and effectiveness of these networks were three key components: agency, sites of agricultural knowledge and geographical reach, and the nature of agricultural knowledge – and specifically the complex interaction between them. Through a detailed analysis of village farmers' clubs in the Doncaster district and the DAS, this chapter has explored the complex dynamics and interconnections in operation, and provided new perspectives about how knowledge was created, circulated and, to some extent accessed. Local agricultural associations were fluid and adaptable, spanning town and country, and they generated practical knowledge that was both location specific as well as having wider relevance. The ability to communicate knowledge effectively was of crucial importance for the agricultural communities in the Doncaster district in the mid-nineteenth century, as evidenced in this chapter in relation to crops and crop disease, livestock, techniques and implements. It allowed ideas and experience to be exchanged within rural communities and between town and country.

Agricultural associations, within villages and towns, were vehicles for individual and collective human agency. Their hierarchical nature meant that the Doncaster Corporation, landowners, large farmers and agriculturalists dominated these knowledge networks. They were certainly the most visible participants, as these groups belonged to the committees or were recurring names in reports of activities of these clubs and societies. Inclusive membership policies and reduced-price entry to the annual shows gave the appearance of democratizing agricultural knowledge and the knowledge networks they were part of; yet the process was largely top down. Nevertheless, agricultural knowledge was diffused through rural society via village farmers' clubs and the DAS. Farmers with smaller holdings, implement makers and even labourers could benefit from some of this knowledge. Moreover, they were not necessarily passive recipients of this knowledge. These groups could actively engage with the evaluation and adaptation of ideas and innovations at a local and practical level, which in some instances would create

---

[87] *Ibid.*
[88] Cusworth Hall Museum, uncatalogued papers, DAS Schedule of prizes and review of the year 1886.

new or at least modified knowledge. This knowledge could then be spread more informally among and between communities, extending the knowledge networks that these agricultural associations formed. Those who attended meetings, visited annual shows, read the reports of village farmers' clubs or the DAS in local newspapers, or otherwise informally engaged with this knowledge and contributed to the knowledge networks are unfortunately predominantly unknown entities. The extent to which the knowledge generated and shared through these agricultural associations was applied to the locale and/or were subsequently adapted is an area worthy of further investigation.

These knowledge networks incorporated villages and districts of differing geological differentiation and landholding character. The nature of the agricultural knowledge reflected both issues and challenges within agriculture and local circumstances. Agricultural knowledge, and certainly the practical application of this knowledge, was firmly rooted in experience and relevant to the geological and topographical conditions of a village or the district. The different people, locations and the nature of the knowledge associated with the village farmers' clubs and DAS collectively moulded the identity of the knowledge networks. The scale and relevance apparent in these organizations is important because the potential for the knowledge to be applied and for people to contribute was greater. This analysis of village farmers' clubs and the DAS has also demonstrated the importance of contextualization. These associations were social and cultural constructs that were created in response to and shaped by local circumstances, as well as within a national framework. It is therefore imperative to understand them within the context of where they were located and their geographical reach, the people who controlled and participated in them, and the nature of the agricultural knowledge created and disseminated. Moreover, these village and town-based agricultural associations were interconnected with other knowledge networks – both regional and national agricultural societies on the one hand, and other networks such as the media on the other. Agricultural societies not only stimulated and sustained the creation and acquisition of knowledge, but forged important connections between people and places, and were interactive channels through which knowledge could be exchanged – both formally as a predominantly top-down process, and informally in a much more participatory manner. They were vital channels for the transmission of knowledge within locales, and the interconnectivity between agency, societies and other vehicles for creating and communicating agricultural knowledge meant that these associations created distinct knowledge networks and shaped the networks with which they were interconnected.

6

'Proper Values' in Agriculture: The Role of Agricultural Associations in Knowledge Dissemination in Hungary, 1830–1880

Zsuzsanna Kiss

Since the time of the Renaissance, attempts to disseminate agricultural knowledge have been made throughout Europe. Agricultural texts and scientific observations on the ideal way to farm were circulated throughout the literate population. From the mid-eighteenth century onwards, meetings of educated and progressive landowners and their agents (as well as farmers to some extent) occurred from time to time to popularize agricultural innovations. It was not until the nineteenth century, however, that such initiatives became systematic and organized in the form of permanent associations that were intended to be the means by which farmers could be directly given information, advice and encouragement about their day-to-day farming activities. This chapter investigates how agricultural associations worked as disseminators of the new values that informed agriculture in nineteenth-century Hungary.

As a part of the Austrian Empire, and subsequently of Austria-Hungary, Hungary was often called the 'pantry of the empire'. Approximately a third to a half of the empire's total arable land was to be found within Hungary, while Hungary was a major exporter of agricultural goods both inside and outside the empire.[1] The government's agricultural policy encouraged agricultural improvements from the late eighteenth century onwards. By that time, the increasing domestic demand for agricultural goods – due, on the one hand, to the growth of the population and, on the other, to the expectations of a mercantilist economic policy – led to the increasing recognition of the agricultural sector as an important part of the empire's economy. Consequently, various forms of governmental

---

1   R. Sandgruber, *Österreichische Agrarstatistik, 1750–1918* (Wien, 1978), p. 28.

intervention were introduced following the logic of Cameralism[2] in order to enhance agricultural production.

The pursuit of the growth of agricultural production was furthered by such means as the managed settlement of farmers in lightly populated regions and the colonization of uncultivated lands, by encouraging the production of specific products (e.g. root crops, corn or potatoes) or by subsidizing new forms of production (pre-eminently the introduction of rotational cropping). The Habsburg state also encouraged the creation of agricultural associations from the mid-eighteenth century onwards as a concrete way of introducing, disseminating and realizing its endeavours in order to improve agricultural practice.

In this chapter, I focus on the operation of one professional association in order to show how the policy of agricultural improvement was implemented. In the first and second parts, I outline the development of agricultural associations at the national level. Third, I outline the message that was circulated at the national level regarding agriculture in the mid- and later nineteenth century. Then, I examine the activity of a single regional agricultural association involved in the process of knowledge dissemination. I see this association as part of a communication system[3] and analyse the channels that the association employed to deliver the national message at both the theoretical and practical level. Finally, I turn to the recipients of the message and analyse the membership of the association, investigating who was able to become members and who was affected by the activities of the association, as well as those who were excluded from the network of knowledge dissemination by the cost of participation.

The role of professional associations as translators and disseminators of knowledge is now commonly recognized.[4] However, it is still important

2   The discipline of Cameralism (German: *Kameralismus*) refers to the science of administration (influential in the eighteenth century and in the first half of the nineteenth century in the central and northern European states), especially that concerned with the management and administration of the financial issues of the state (originally with those of the monarch) in order to foster social well-being. See, for example, K. Tribe, 'Cameralism and the Science of Government', *Journal of Modern History* 56 (1984), pp. 263–84.

3   This concept is based on Lasswell's model of communication that describes the act of communication by answering the question 'who says what in which channel to whom and with what effect?'. See H. Lasswell, 'The Structure and Function of Communication in Society', in L. Bryson (ed.), *The Communication of Ideas* (New York, 1948), pp. 37–52. However, the effect of the messages delivered through the system of agricultural associations is too broad an issue to be analysed in detail here.

4   This idea is mentioned in innovation management handbooks but never given much weight. See the following, as an example: 'Such associations functioned like networks and their goal was the transfer of knowledge and the local introduction of innovations in agriculture'. A. Hergenröther and J. Siemes,

to reveal the trajectory by which such associations have been able to build up and develop this role. An in-depth investigation of one particular association and its workings promises to generate insights into this process.[5]

The National Society for Agriculture in Hungary

In 1764, the empress Maria Theresa ordered all provinces to establish agricultural associations to disseminate advanced knowledge about agriculture among the rural population. According to the order, the most important way in which new knowledge was to be created was by experiments carried out in the fields of landed members, the results of which were to be disseminated in printed reports. The first association was established in Klagenfurt (1764) and others followed throughout the empire, but none in Hungary where further decrees ordering the foundation of associations in 1766 and 1770 also went unanswered.[6] Though it is hard to ascertain the cause of the failure to found associations, the main reason may well be that the idea of a voluntary association of equal members drawn from differing social ranks was too alien to contemporary Hungarian society. Landowners and peasants were so far removed from each other regarding their perceived social rank, prestige, and status, as well as their very different rights and standing in social, economic and political life, that their coming together in a common, mutual action within the frame of an essentially democratic organization was simply unimaginable.

The first association that had a connection with rural life was established as late as 1826 in Pressburg (present-day Bratislava), although its constitution was never officially acknowledged by the monarch. Initially a horse racing club, this association was socially exclusive and was marked by feudal social distinctions. Horse breeding and horse riding as a pastime, as well as attending races as a spectator, were expensive activities and could only be pursued by a narrow stratum of society. Promoters of the horse racing society were thus overwhelmingly recruited from the

---

'Managing Open Innovation Networks in the Agriculture Business: The K+S Case', in A. Gerybadze, U. Hommel, H. W. Reiners and D. Tomaschewski (eds), *Innovation and International Corporate Growth* (New York, 2010), p. 251.

5 Similar research has been pursued in the British colonial environment in the form of an investigation of the agricultural periodical of the Deccan Agricultural Association. S. Baksi and T. Kamble, 'The Dissemination of Modern Agricultural Knowledge in the Colonial Period: A Review of the Marathi Monthly Shetki aani Shetkari', *Rev. of Agrarian Studies* 6 (2006), pp. 48–79.

6 V. Stampfl and E. Bruckmüller (eds), *Bauernland Oberösterreich. Entwicklungsgeschichte seiner Land- und Forstwirtschaft* (Linz, 1974), pp. 106–7.

aristocracy and the landed elite.[7] Following an intermediary preparatory step (when the association was reorganized as a general Society for Husbandry in 1830), the association was finally relocated to the capital Pest in 1835 and named the National Society for Agriculture (NSA).[8] The objectives of the original horse racing association were limited to issues narrowly related to horses (feeding, breeding, etc.) and agriculture fell outside its remit. When it was reorganized as the National Agricultural Society in 1835–1836, it was given more general objectives. The goals of the society, laid out in its founding document, were as follows: first, to promote and disseminate all kinds of useful knowledge and inventions related to agricultural practices; second, to collect information on the state of agriculture, on different forms of land use, the obstacles that impeded agricultural development and the methods for overcoming these obstacles; third, to translate and disseminate foreign work about agriculture; fourth, to introduce new instruments and methods to the Hungarian agricultural public; fifth, to hold competitions in agricultural topics, and, finally, sixth, to recognize the most outstanding farmers.[9] With the broadening of the programme, the association also expanded its membership in terms of social profile, as well as in geographical origin. The number of members grew from 498 in 1835 to 634 in 1841.

After a period when its activities were suspended following the revolution of 1848–1849, the association recommenced operations at the end of the 1850s and the number of its members peaked in 1864 at 1,285. In the subsequent decade, interest in it decreased for a time (there were 735 members in 1879) but then grew considerably until the end of the century with 2,618 members in 1895.[10] As to the social profile of its members, it is clear that the landowners remained dominant throughout the second half of the nineteenth century, but the number of aristocrats involved in the society declined, giving way to noblemen without aristocratic titles and non-noble landowners. The presence of land agents was also significant from the very beginning, as was the number of intellectuals (physicians, lawyers, priests and schoolteachers). Land agents, who joined in large numbers as early as the 1850s and who represented the largest occupational group among the membership (40 per cent of all members were agents in 1859), were a mixture of educated and qualified professionals, but the majority of them were only managers by experience. The membership included very few smallholders or tenants:

---

7   *Pesti gyepen való ló-futtatások júniusban 1827; Pesti lóversenykönyv 1829-re* (Pest).

8   A. Tasner (ed.), *Gyepkönyv. 1835-iki jelentés a Magyarországi Állatenyésztő Társaság (ezentúl Gazdasági Egyesület) munkálódásairól* (Pest, 1835).

9   K. Galgóczy, 'Országos magyar gazdasági egyesület', in S. Zoltán (ed.), *Gazdasági egyesületek monográfiái* (Budapest, 1896), pp. 53–4.

10 A. Vári, *Urak és gazdászok. Arisztokrácia, agrárértelmiség és agrárius mozgalom Magyarországon, 1821–1898* (Budapest, 2009), pp. 72, 202, 417.

the new structure of land use was slow to evolve after the abolition of serfdom in 1781, and tenant farming had not yet taken root. A final characteristic of the membership was its geographical spread. The society was established and had its offices and held its meetings in Budapest. According to records detailing the place of residence of its members in 1892, 67 per cent of members were resident in one or other county of the kingdom of Hungary (the south-eastern part of the Austro-Hungarian dual monarchy, as established in 1867), and only 25 per cent in Budapest. (The remainder either had dual residence in both the country and Budapest, or lived abroad.)[11] It is therefore apparent that the NSA had significant reach and influenced a diverse segment of the population with agricultural interests: from landowners and estate managers to intellectuals living in a rural environment. Tenants, however, seem rarely to have been members.

Agricultural societies across the country

Although the first constitution of the National Society in 1835–1836 included some vague ideas about establishing societies all over the country, there was no plan as to how an associational network should be developed, or how the branch associations should function or be related to the National Society. Later revisions of the governing statutes in 1840 and 1843 outlined a network system of one central and several regional sub-societies.[12] The 1843 statutes envisaged an institutionalized link between the National Society and regional associations in the following form: the president of each regional society would sit *ex officio* on the governing board of the National Society, and in return the National Society would nominate to the committee of each regional society a member with voting rights. The institutionalization of connections between core and peripheral groups was strengthened by later statutes. Strong connections between the county and the capital would always contribute to strengthening the National Society, while on the other hand a well-functioning network of societies was thought to be a proper means of reaching a broader public both at the national and regional level. However, the system outlined in these plans was over-centralized, making the regional associations subordinate to the National Society.

By 1847 the national network of agricultural societies consisted of 22 regional societies. However, the real 'boom' in agricultural associations took place in the 1860s and 1870s: this has already been shown by the growing number of members of the National Society, but the same trends are revealed by the number of new associations founded. By the end of the

11 *Ibid.,* 203, 417.
12 *A Magyar Gazdasági Egyesület név- s alapítványkönyve1847. május 31.-én* (Pest, 1847).

117

1870s, 38 regional associations, plus 13 associations limited to one specific town or city, as well as a further 17 agricultural associations specializing in horticulture, viticulture, forestry or apiculture, had been established in Hungary.[13] Contrary to what had been envisaged in the original plans, these associations did not have an institutionalized relationship with the National Society, nor with each other. This is because the government, both before and after the Compromise of 1867, tightly controlled and strictly monitored all forms of civil society organization. It was especially wary of networks that embraced the whole country, for it considered such networks to be a potential hotbed of political conspiracy and thus a danger to the state.[14]

At such a time of political repression, agricultural societies had a relatively favoured position, in as much as they were regarded and treated as an important means of economic development by the government. Cameralist economic thought was now revived: agriculture was again conceived of as a profitable sector that benefited the national economy and thus the establishment of agricultural associations was supported by the emperor. It is important to note, however, that taking advantage of this privileged position, many agricultural associations had become covert political meetings by the early 1860s. The background to the revival of political discussion was the less oppressive political atmosphere after the release of the October Diploma (adopted on 20 October 1860) and the February Patent of the next year (adopted on 26 February 1861).[15] Although both reforms (and especially the Patent of 1861) were finally rejected by Hungarian political representatives, they were initially welcomed by Hungarians as the beginning of a new 'constitutional'

---

13 G. Vargha (ed.), *Magyarország egyesületei és társulatai 1878-ban* (Budapest, 1880).

14 A public order of Kaiser Franz Josef (published in 1852) fixed the conditions of the establishment and functioning of all kinds of societies across the whole of the empire for the rest of the nineteenth century (*Az ausztriai birodalmat illető közönséges birodalmi törvény- és kormánylap/Allgemeines Reichs-Gesetz- und Regierungsblatt für das Kaiserthum Oesterreich* (Wien, 1852), pp. 1109–16). Two years later (1854), Archduke Albrecht (Governor General for Hungary after 1851) published a new regulation concerning Hungary that prescribed even stricter control over public societies (*Magyarországot illető Országos Kormánylap*, 1854, p. 76). According to this new regulation, societies had to present regular accounts of their activity to the political authorities of their region, and police commissioners were always to be present *ex officio* at general assemblies and at meetings of the governing board of associations.

15 The final outcome of the constitutions was favourable for Hungary because it promised wider political autonomy when compared to the previous decade by restoring the Hungarian constitution and the central political organs. According to the Diploma, the Austrian Parliament (Reichsrat) would not have any power over Hungary, except in matters that affected the whole empire (that is, in foreign and military affairs).

period of the empire. Civil society began to expect further political progress, and agricultural associations, as privileged institutions in the civil sphere, seemed to be a convenient foundation on which to build.[16] Many of the societies established in this period were thus short-lived or lost members as political optimism faded – which it had by the end of the 1860s. Those societies that survived this politically charged period and that were able to retain a considerable number of members until the end of the decade tended to develop into professional associations.

The message: 'proper values' in agriculture

General and agricultural discourse, particularly from the middle of the nineteenth century onwards, often focused on 'modernization' or 'development'.[17] But development as a motto in agriculture did not yet carry the political overtones in the sense of political unification or the mobilization of agricultural interests that it came to possess by the end of the nineteenth century. In the 1860s, modernization in agriculture was interpreted as the improvement of productivity, techniques and skills. The slogan of the National Association, as well as its journal following its launch in 1849, made the demand 'Let us bring proper values into our agriculture!'[18] This motto contained all the elements that characterized contemporary agricultural interests: 'proper' in this case could have and should have been understood in different ways: as the equivalent of 'fair', 'rational', or 'modern'. Let us explore the implicit meanings.

Firstly, the distribution of landholding after the legal abolition of the feudal tenure system in 1848 was conceived of as 'unfair' by reason of its extreme level of polarization.[19] In 1895, almost 99 per cent of all property holdings were in the hands of landholders who owned units of under

16 O. Sashegyi, *Az abszolutizmuskori levéltár* (Budapest, 1965), p. 74.
17 Not in Hungary alone. The phrase 'high farming' denotes a somewhat similar meaning (in the sense of 'modern', though not in the sense of 'fair') to that of farming according to 'proper values', which was widely used to characterize British farming from about 1840 to 1880. See P. J. Perry, 'High Farming in Victorian Britain. Prospect and Retrospect' *Agricultural Hist.* 55 (1981), p. 156.
18 The slogan was printed on the title page of *Gazdasági Lapok* from the first issue (1 Jan. 1849) until it was taken over by another journal in 1881. The issue of 'proper values' had been part of agricultural discourse since the 1840s, but the need for agricultural reforms became sharply articulated after the revolution of 1848–1849, particularly by professional actors (educated land managers) and some groups of progressive landowners. Public debates about proper agriculture and the identification of the issue as a political question requiring reform came about only in the last two decades of the century.
19 The first statistically credible report about the distribution of holdings, however, was published half a century after the redistribution of lands, in 1895. See *A magyar korona országainak mezőgazdasági statisztikája* (3 vols, Budapest, 1900), III.

100 holds (half of whom held only five holds or less). The remaining 1 per cent of the farm holdings were possessed by large property owners (that is, by owners with over 100 holds).[20] If we match these numbers with data about the proportion of the total amount of cultivated land owned by properties of different sizes, the result is more striking. One per cent of all holdings (that is, large estates of more than 100 holds) occupied 55 per cent of the cultivated territory of Hungary, while the remaining 99 per cent shared the other 45 per cent of the reclaimed agricultural area.[21] Such extreme polarization prompted demands for a redistribution of land.

Second, in addition to the uneven distribution of landholding, the structure of land use was also perceived as irrational. Livestock and livestock products dominated Hungarian exports until the middle of the nineteenth century. From the 1850s onwards, however, in response to the growing demands of the external market (especially that of the Austrian part of the empire, where Hungary had a privileged export position), there was a shift from pastoralism to grain-growing, especially wheat.[22] This is reflected in the distribution of land use (Table 6.1), which shows that the share of arable land increased, largely with land newly brought into cultivation. Despite constant warnings by agriculturists in journals and public discourse on the need to introduce 'proper values' (i.e. the need for a 'rational' system of mixed farming), the share of arable land became ever more dominant in the forthcoming decades. Professional agricultural writers emphasized the dangers posed by a reliance on an unbalanced arable farming system. Even in the late 1870s, when the so-called grain crisis shocked the European markets, the share of arable land was still growing in Hungary. By comparison, it is apparent that the tendency for arable acreage to increase had ended in Austria by the middle of the century.[23] In Hungary, where at the beginning of the century the source of new arable was mostly uncultivated wasteland, the expansion in the later decades of the century was, to some extent, fuelled by the conversion of grasslands and pastures to arable land. The long-term disruption of balanced land use this produced proved difficult to rectify when the downsides of a one-sided farming system based solely on arable cultivation became widely apparent.[24]

---

[20] One 'hold' is 0.57 hectares. G. Kövér, 'Distribution of wealth and income', in G. Gyáni, G. Kövér and T. Valuch (eds), *Social History of Hungary from the Reform Era to the End of the Twentieth Century* (New York, 2004), p. 116.

[21] J. Puskás, 'A magyarországi mezőgazdaság tőkés fejlődésének vizsgálata az 1895. évi üzemstatisztika adatai alapján', *Történelmi Szemle* 4 (1960), pp. 446–79.

[22] I. Orosz, *Szerkezeti változások a XIX. századi magyar mezőgazdaságban* (Budapest, 1988).

[23] Sandgruber, *Österreichische Agrarstatistik*, p. 37.

[24] Regarding aspects of the grain crisis see, Z. Kiss, 'Gesellschaftshistorische Aspekte der Getreidekrise gegen Ende des 19. Jahrhunderts', in M. Keller,

TABLE 6.1 Land use in Austria and Hungary from 1830/1850 to 1895/1897 (as percentage of total territory).

	Austria (Cisleithanian territories), 1830/1850	Hungary, 1850	Hungary, 1873	Austria, 1883	Hungary, 1883	Austria, 1897	Hungary, 1895
Arable	33.7	31.0	34.7	35.5	41.0	35.4	42.8
Orchards		13.0	13.3		1.2		1.3
Grassland	11.6			11.5	10.6	11.5	10.2
Vineyard	0.7	1.2	1.2	0.8	1.3	0.8	1.0
Pasture	15.3	13.3	14.8	13.5	13.1	13.5	13.0
Woodland	31.5	25.7	28.2	32.6	26.9	32.6	26.6
Reeds		0.8	0.5		0.3		0.3
Cultivated Area	92.8	85.0	92.7	93.9	94.4	93.8	95.2
Uncultivated Area	7.2	15.0	7.3	6.1	5.6	6.2	4.8

Source: M. Szuhay, 'A szántóföldi termelés fejlődése a magyar mezőgazdaságban, 1867–1914 között', *Agrártörténeti Szemle* 1–2 (1971). p. 39 and Sandgruber, *Österreichische Agrarstatistik*, p. 37.

Third, besides fair land distribution and rational land use, the need for 'proper values' in agriculture referred to the need for a 'modern spirit of economy'. Because of their dominant position in the inland agricultural market of Austria-Hungary, Hungarian farmers were not encouraged to become more efficient and were thus increasingly unable to compete in international markets. Attempts to enhance production were largely based on extensive (and exploitative) farming methods and on the use of cheap manpower, even after the middle of the century. Advocates of 'proper values', however, recognized and emphasized the necessity of making thorough calculations about financial and human resources, as these were conceived of as the basis of rational management and as a starting point for further development and investment.

In terms of knowledge dissemination, I examine below how the message of 'proper values', which was formulated on a theoretical level in professional and public discourse, was transformed into practical action by an agricultural association from Zala County. I focus my attention on local channels of knowledge dissemination: the professional journal that was published and events organized by the association and the various forms of agricultural schooling initiated in the county.

The Agricultural Association of Zala County

The Agricultural Association of Zala County was officially established in 1861, proposals having been made some years before.[25] Its statutes,[26] like those of the National Society, emphasized that one of its most important aims was the dissemination of knowledge among its members; indeed, among all the inhabitants of the county. Ideally, this would have included a permanent survey of the agricultural conditions of the county; the elaboration of various methods for eliminating all obstacles to further development; the publication of specialist and practical guide books to all branches of agriculture; the organization of exhibitions of crops, products,

---

G. Kövér and C. Sasfi (eds), *Krisen/Geschichten in mitteleuropäischem Kontext: Sozial- und wirtschaftsgeschichtliche Studien zum 19./20. Jahrhundert* (Wien, 2015), pp. 143–66.

25 Zala County was situated in the south-western part of the kingdom of Hungary, in proximity to the Austrian Empire, next to the border with Croatia-Slavonia. From 1862 to 1870 the total population of the county grew from approximately 270,000 to 320,000. In 1870, approximately 55 per cent of its active (above 14 years old) population was occupied in agriculture: 45 per cent as owners or tenants and 55 per cent as wage-earners such as estate-managers and agricultural labourers (on an annual, seasonal or daily basis).

26 National Archives of Hungary (hereafter, 'NAH'), Archive of the Absolutist Period, 1848–67, D2 Section, K. K. Ministerium des Innern. Akten 'Ungarn' und 'Woiwodina', Box No. 205.

animals and machinery to introduce them to rural people; and the establishment of model farms where experiments could be carried out.

The National Society provided a model for the association's structure: various membership types (founders, regular members and yearly subscribers), the organization of committees and sections dedicated to particular fields of agriculture or to special tasks, and a schedule for regular assemblies. As prominent members of the Zala County Association were also members of the National Society, they were familiar with its modes of operation. Apart from personal contacts, journals and periodicals were the principal means of communication between associations, as well as between the association and its members.

Most county associations had a printed form of communication: either their own periodical or a special supplement in a popular regional journal compiled by association members. Such printed material furthered communication in three ways. First, it provided a means for facilitating the flow of information among the membership and between the governing boards and members of different societies. In many instances, members of the same society lived a significant distance from each other, which impeded regular personal meetings. Accordingly, the opportunities for knowledge exchange provided by the correspondence columns was realized early on and they played an important role throughout the period as the forum where opinions could be shared and farming discussed with geographically-distant fellow farmers. Also, associations used such periodicals for publishing official announcements, such as invitations to meetings or notifications about financial reports. Second, journals also created a direct link between the National Society and rural associations. In many instances, county journals reprinted short news or even longer articles from *Gazdasági Lapok* (Acta Ruralis/Oeconomica), the journal of the National Society: this was partly because they lacked local authors who could generate material for publication, but also because they wanted to keep up with what was going on in the capital and at a national level. Certainly, the readership of the *Gazdasági Lapok* was much more extensive than the membership of the society itself, as it was posted to county societies as well. County societies either subscribed as institutions or, in many cases, individual members signed up for the journal; *Gazdasági Lapok* thus reached a sizeable audience in many rural locations, creating a strong link between the capital and the counties that was fundamental both in terms of the communication of organizational issues and for the transmission of knowledge. Finally, local society journals published news, letters and requests from more distant fellow societies. This was one of the fastest ways to send messages from one society to another.

For a better evaluation of the scope of professional journals as a means of communication it is necessary to estimate the size of the audience they reached. According to the limited data available on the publication's circulation, 1,300 copies of *Magyar Gazda* (Hungarian Farmer, which was the predecessor to the *Gazdasági Lapok*) were printed twice a week before 1848, at a time when the membership of the National Society was about 1,000.[27] Thus, almost a quarter of all copies were being sold outside of the society (meaning that most issues were read by county dwellers, since the National Society's membership was mainly located outside the capital). In the 1850s, *Gazdasági Lapok* had about 1,000 regular subscribers (and presumably sold more copies than this). This has been viewed as a success by later scholars.[28]

As a point of reference, however, it is also important to note that, apart from *Gazdasági Lapok*, the National Society was also the publisher of a cheaper periodical from 1839 onwards – the *Mezei Naptár* (Agricultural Calendar). This popular calendar had a diverse content, including some professional information and popular scientific articles, but also riddles, horoscopes and other similar items. It was aimed at the lower strata of the rural population (who were presumably not members of any society) across the country. Its popularity is clear from the enormous growth in the number of copies that were sold: from 5,000 to 80,000 copies per year by 1845, and it also remained widely popular afterwards. This seems to suggest that the demand for news (in part agricultural knowledge and know-how) and other reading material was much greater than society journals could satisfy.[29] The importance of such publications as sources of popular knowledge should be appreciated, but not overestimated. It should be kept in mind that the level of literacy was low. The figures for Zala County for 1870 (when a systematic population census that met international standards was carried out) show that 64 per cent of the total adult population was illiterate (a figure that was somewhat lower than the national average).[30] There is no detailed information available about the degree of literacy among the population engaged in agricultural occupations, but the rates within this group were presumably even lower.

In Zala County, *Dunántúli Társadalmi Közlöny* (Transdanubian Journal), a journal owned and edited by an estate administrator and an expert on sericulture, József Péterffy, served as the official channel of communication

---

27 K. Galgóczy, *Az OMGE évkönyve* (3 vols, Budapest, 1883), III, p. 105.
28 Vári, *Urak és gazdászok*, p. 154.
29 On the other hand, 80,000 copies is a tiny number if we consider that, out of a total population of about ten and a half million people living in Hungary in 1870, approximately five million were occupied in agriculture (the greater part of whom – 60 per cent – were agricultural labourers (annual or dayworkers predominantly), with the smaller part consisting of landowners or tenants).
30 *A Magyar Korona országaiban az 1870. év elején végrehajtott népszámlálás eredményei a hasznos háziállatok kimutatásával együtt*. Országos Magyar Királyi Statisztikai Hivatal (1871), p. 239.

for the Agricultural Association between 1861 and 1864. When launching the journal, Péterffy published a manifesto:

> in a country where agriculture is the main sector of production, we experience that the number of regular subscribers to agricultural literature is barely 8000 [...] but I have decided to take up the gauntlet.[31]

His intention was to provide a space where 'we can exchange our views without previously notifying the capital' (i.e. Budapest).[32] This was a clear indication that the journal was designed to serve as an independent forum for discussing regional matters without the oversight of the National Society, thereby serving as a means for the further integration and facilitation of communication among the population of the region. Also, the association used the journal for communicating with its members: it regularly published invitations to its meetings, extracts from its minutes, and so on.

Regular authors participating in the journal included local agricultural experts (such as Pál Sommsich, who published widely on viticulture) and well-known public figures living in the region (for example, Sándor Kozma, MP and judge); veterinary articles from local doctors frequently appeared. However, articles related to agronomic theory and agricultural practice were partly copied from *Gazdasági Lapok* or translated from foreign journals (articles presenting the theory of Friedrich List or Justus von Liebig's chemistry, for example), but in many instances local issues were discussed with a sensitivity to their implications (for example, a series of articles about the reasons for and the results of draining Lake Balaton). Notices about grain prices in the region and on the Vienna stock exchange were also published.

Unfortunately, there is no precise data about the number of copies that were sold; the only evidence is the remarks made by Péterffy in 1863. He reported that his newspaper had only 160 regular subscribers from the membership of the county associations of Zala and the neighbouring county, Somogy, which used the journal as their gazette. On his calculations, only 20 per cent of members had subscribed to the journal.[33] These figures may underestimate the real number of subscribers,[34] but they are illuminating in that they reflect the disenchantment of a committed agrarian. It is also relevant to note that the readership of the journal was certainly broader than the membership of the association, as its

31 *Dunántúli Társadalmi Közlöny*, 14 Oct. 1861, p. 1.
32 *Ibid.*
33 *Dunántúli Társadalmi Közlöny*, 12 July 1863, p. 1.
34 In 1862, the Agricultural Association of Zala County had 187 members. It is more than likely that none of the other associations had many more than that. One hundred and sixty regular subscribers in this case would have meant 35–40 per cent of the total membership of the two associations.

content included not only news and articles on farming, but other items of interest. Those who bought the journal for its news and other content were, perhaps unintentionally, confronted with agricultural matters pertaining to the region as well.

In 1864, Péterffy left the county, moving first to Pest and then to Vienna. Although the journal he edited ceased publication, its role as a channel of communication for the Association was taken over by the most popular regional journal of the time, the *Zala-Somogyi Közlöny* (Gazette of Zala and Somogy Counties).

The 1860s witnessed the establishment of a regional press in Hungary. The new journals may well be perceived as links between the capital and the rural localities that facilitated the flow of information and knowledge from the centre to the regions. However, Péterffy's remarks reveal that this one-directional flow (from capital to country) had become unwelcome. Local members sought an independent forum in which to discuss their own issues without any external control. After decades of the centralized supervision of all political and public terrains, even an independent journal was regarded as a small step towards independence. However, it is also apparent that the local agrarian circles of the time were too small to sustain such an independent forum without difficulties: on the one hand, the content of regional journals was in many cases copied from the journal of the National Society; on the other hand, the low number of subscribers made newspapers financially unviable. In any case, the Zala County periodical fulfilled practical needs (communication within the regional association) while creating the ground for the emergence of a group of professionally-aware readers by publishing theoretical and practical articles on agrarian issues.

The Association of Zala County circulated knowledge in forms other than the printed. This activity was all the more important, since the journal – as shown above – presumably reached only a minor proportion of the total population of the county, even of those who were involved in agriculture.[35] Another way of reaching a wider audience was by organizing public events: exhibitions (of farm animals, products and machinery), races, contests of all kinds and lectures. As early as in the first year of its existence, the association put on an 'economic exhibition and competition' where wines and farm animals were displayed and a horse race was held. Regarding the exhibition, special emphasis was put on the rule that only 'sheep, horses, cattle, pigs and poultry that were bred in the county' could be shown, and that it was those breeders 'who bred eminent farm animals due to their diligence, not their privileged position' who should receive awards.[36] This tactic was definitely aimed at including lower-strata county dwellers. Such public programmes were

35   See n. 17.
36   *Gazdasági Lapok*, 23 June 1861.

established ways of publicizing local successes in farming and popularizing both new practices and methods of breeding and cultivation. These
events were also described in the press. The effectiveness of such shows
in transmitting knowledge and new ideas was multiplied by the detailed
information that was published about the winners and their prominent
products, breeds and methods.[37]

The association was the initiator and supporter of agricultural education
in various forms. Public agricultural education in Hungary was rather
underdeveloped during this period. Despite the significant share of the
population involved in agricultural occupations, the first government
regulation on elementary level agricultural education was only issued in
1896.[38] At a higher level, five public agricultural colleges in the Hungarian
part of the country were organized (or reorganized from pre-existing
private institutions) in the 1860s and 1870s.[39] One of these colleges was
situated in Zala County at Georgikon in Keszthely. The institution had
a long and successful history as the first professional agricultural school
before 1848: it was started as a private initiative.[40] It was shut down
during the revolution of 1848 but reopened as a public college in 1865
with the assistance of the association. The new institution provided
education at different levels: it contained an elementary school and a
secondary level college, which trained professional farmers; additionally,
it also incorporated a secondary level school for training viticulturists.
The association supported Georgikon through an annual contribution
and also provided educational grants for indigent pupils and students at
both levels of education.[41]

---

37 The exhibition in 1861 had 900 visitors. Two years later, a similar exhibition
was organized by the 'housewives of the county', again combined with a
horse race, which was attended by 10,000 (!) visitors: *Zala-Somogyi Közlöny*, 20
May 1863.

38 The regulation issued by the Minister of Religion and Public Education, no.
60.764/1896 ordered the establishment of elementary level agricultural schools
in all municipalities where the number of children of parents occupied in
agriculture reached 40.

39 The eagerness for a professional agricultural education in Hungarian in
1860s and 1870s was part of the European enthusiasm for science-based,
experimental agriculture at the time; Justus von Liebig's criticism of purely
practice-based agricultural research was willingly integrated into plans for the
professional college system by policymakers of the period: see J. von Liebig,
Die moderne Landwirtschaft als Beispiel der Gemeinnützigkeit der Wissenschaften
(Braunschweig, 1862).

40 See G. Kurucz, 'Advanced Farming and Professional Training: the First
Hungarian College of Farming', in N. Vivier (ed.), *The State and Rural Societies:
Policy and Education in Europe, 1750–2000* (Turnhout, 2008), pp. 195–214.

41 National Archives of Hungary, Zala County Archive (hereafter, 'ZCA') X. 107,
Archives of the Agricultural Association of Zala County (hereafter 'AZC'),
General Assembly Minutes, 23 Feb. 1863, 13 Apr. 1863.

Apart from its commitment to the college at Georgikon, the association was keen to organize popular theoretical and practical courses for farmers of all ages and of any educational experience. Fundamentally, the aim of the organizers was to introduce farmers to the daily routines of professional farming. Thus they provided a theoretical grounding on long-term planning in farming, but the emphasis was on conveying practical knowledge. Traditional and modern tools, machines and chemicals were brought to classrooms or to nearby fields where all participants could try them. Experimental fields, orchards and vineyards were established where various species of crops, vegetables, grapes and other fruits were grown and where students were taught how to cultivate them.[42] Contests were announced each year for professional agronomists and non-professional practitioners to write informative booklets on various topics in terms that would be comprehensible to less-educated farmers.[43]

The association was extensively engaged in the dissemination of knowledge. It should be pointed out, however, that the forms of knowledge dissemination described here were in many instances also the means of creating new knowledge. Competitions and exhibitions were events at which new and better species, whether plants or animals, could be introduced. Experimental fields and popular courses were also a way in which new breeds, techniques and methods could be introduced. Encouraging authors to publish on given topics was likewise a way to spread existing knowledge, but also to launch and popularize new ideas and techniques.

However, it is doubtful as to whether these initiatives achieved their aims. We do not know how many people attended the association's events. Exhibitions and competitions seem to have been popular,[44] but neither the association's own records, nor reports in journals, describe the effectiveness of either the courses or the open experimental fields and orchards maintained by the association, nor do we have data on the numbers of pupils or visitors. Statistics are only available for Georgikon, where the number of pupils studying at the elementary level was reported as being 110 in total for the whole decade from 1865 to 1874, and 445 for the secondary level two-year course during the same period.[45] These numbers are not high, especially in relation to the sizeable proportion of

---

42 *Gazdasági Lapok* acknowledged the activity undertaken at the so-called 'central orchard' in 1868, highlighting that the orchard was open to all who were interested in plant breeding or any other practical work with plants. The same article reported on two grants established by the association: one to support schoolmasters who participated in maintaining tree nurseries; and the other to recognize those pupils who had made advances with fruit tree breeding: *Gazdasági Lapok*, 3 June 1868.

43 See, for example, ZCA, AZC, Assembly of the Directorial Committee, 8 May 1865.

44 See n. 29.

45 Á. Balás (ed.), *Magyarország mezőgazdasági szakoktatási intézményei 1896*

the population engaged in agriculture in the county, and considering the fact that a few pupils and students came to these institutions from outside the county each year. The repetitive calls for informative booklets and the large number of grants available for educational purposes might signal a considerable need for such initiatives, but it may also show that constant incentives were needed to mobilize the rural population.

Recipients: the membership of the association

Who were the recipients: that is to say, which individuals did the message reach and who benefited from the knowledge that became available through the activities of the association? The association had 50 founding members and 350 regular members when established in 1861. Regulations about the rights of different membership types reveal internal differences among members.[46] Analysis of the everyday activities and practices of other Hungarian agricultural societies has shown convincingly that the stress placed on the democratic organization and equality of members was an ideal rather than the reality.[47] Consequently, the Zala Association, which on a discursive level at least (in its statutes) emphasized the equality of its members, actually functioned as an institution that maintained social differences. It did this in two ways. First, positions of leadership were generally occupied by the socially most prominent and wealthy members. The majority (more than 60 per cent) of the founding members occupied high public administrative positions before 1849 or after 1865 and/or were members of traditional local noble families who owned properties of a significant size.[48]

Second, the elite position of these groups was not only reproduced but also reinforced by the association. The vast majority of regular members were wage earners in various agricultural occupations: land agents mainly, but also labourers on estates. Tenants, as in the case of the National Society, were present at only to a marginal degree in the Zala

---

(Magyaróvár, 1897), p. 78. It is important to note that Gregorikon was soon overtaken by the other agricultural schools in terms of the number of students.

46 The two types of membership differed regarding membership fees (founders paid higher fees than regular members), and also regarding entitlements: governing positions could be occupied only by founders, whose votes also counted double regarding all issues that concerned the possessions and revenues of the association.

47 This was generally the case, and is not characteristic of the County of Zala alone. For details, see Vári, *Urak és gazdászok*, p. 176.

48 The noble (or even aristocratic) character of the governing boards was apparent both in the National Society and other county associations as well at least until the 1870s. See Vári, *Urak és gazdászok*, pp. 406–16 and Z. Kiss, 'A Zala Megyei Gazdasági Egyesület megszervezése a neoabszolutizmus korában', *Korall* 3 (no. 13) (2003), pp. 107–24.

Association. Many regular members were in fact employees of the leaders of the association, and although it was certainly not mandatory for such employees to join the association, it was highly unlikely that they could refuse the suggestion when made by their employers. Indeed, they either joined voluntarily, or complied with their employers' desires, reinforcing their own dependent position in this way and strengthening the leading role of the local elite.[49] However, being a member of the association was certainly advantageous. Members reinforced their own position as 'faithful' employees but also, and more importantly, they obtained fast and easy access to resources (both material and intellectual) and personal connections that they could take advantage of for their own advancement.

This is especially true for the smallest group within the association, though their number belies their importance as members: the better-off farmers or smallholders who generally joined the association as regular members or annual subscribers. Taking part in the association was, for many of them, their only way of receiving any kind of education in what was actually their occupation (that is, farming), and to obtain access to devices, technologies and knowledge.

Finally, it should be mentioned that the great majority of the agrarian population of the county – peasant smallholders or day labourers – were excluded from membership by the membership fee. Other factors too had an important role in delineating the borders of the association.[50] Participation in the everyday activities of the association required a relatively high level of independence: those who wanted to be involved had to be able to spend time and money on attending events (be they meetings, competitions, or farming courses), which were thus the privilege of only a few. These 'outsiders' may still have received the messages transmitted by the association (for example, through informal conversations or by observing the farming practices of their fellow farmers), but the means by which this was achieved goes beyond the scope of this chapter.

Conclusion

In the years after the revolution of 1848, and similar to what was happening all over Europe, an extensive network of agricultural associations was established in Hungary. Knowledge dissemination was a central feature of their purpose, and they soon became an instrument for implementing 'proper' (that is, fair, rational and modern) values

---

49 Vári, *Urak és gazdászok*, pp. 198–205; Z. Kiss, 'Urak és szolgáik – a Zala Megyei Gazdasági Egyesület tagsága az alakuláskor (1861)', in É. Gyulai (ed.), *Úr és szolga a történettudomány egységében. In memoriam Vári András* (Miskolc, 2014), pp. 134–9.
50 For data on the social distribution of the population, see n. 25.

into agriculture. Analysis of the activity of one association based in Zala County has shown the diversity of channels that an association could establish and maintain in order to translate theoretical ideas about 'proper values' into practice. In investigating the association as part of a broader communication system, the chapter has treated its publications, educational practices (formal and informal schools maintained or supported by the association) and other public events (races, contests, shows) as means of knowledge dissemination.

However, the analysis has also revealed that the 'translation' of the values formulated at a national level was not without its problems, since local actors had specific and particular aims and goals and were not inclined to unreservedly follow a model tailored to meet – from their perspective – somewhat abstract needs. This fact was demonstrated prominently by the desire for an independent agricultural press in the county that was beyond the reach and influence of the National Association. Another characteristic feature that highlights the limitations placed on both the National Association and the Zala Association was the composition of their membership. Here, as elsewhere, this not only reflected the social inequality that existed at the time, but, due to the various types of membership available, actually reinforced it. This presumably resulted in the knowledge transmitted by the association reaching only a socially-selected proportion of the rural population.

The focus of this chapter has been the various roles that an agricultural association played as a disseminator of knowledge. Further analysis is needed to reveal how effective this knowledge transmission was: that is to say, how many of the 'proper values' were in fact integrated into the daily routine of farming.

7

'The Eye of the Master': Livestock Improvement and Knowledge Networks in Belgium, 1900–1940

Dries Claeys and Yves Segers

In his essay *The Theory of Social and Economic Organization* (1947), the German sociologist Max Weber unravelled how modern societies became increasingly organized. Interactions and transactions between individuals and organizations were structured according to well-defined social principles, while bureaucracy grew in order to support and defend public interests.[1] The economy did not escape this need for ordering. Scott Lash and John Urry have explained how, at the end of the nineteenth century, an organized capitalism was constructed. At a time when the invisible hand created social inequality and environmental problems, government departments and civil society organizations such as trade unions and farmers' associations were established to deal with socio-economic tensions and challenges and to structure the (inter)national markets.[2] Agriculture was no exception in this regard. After all, the increased globalization of the agricultural and food economy, which was partly the result of a transport and communication revolution, resulted in a deep agricultural depression in Europe that lasted from about 1880 to the mid-1890s.

That crisis led to structural changes in the agricultural sector. Farmers' organizations looked to government for measures to support national agriculture and to arm it against growing international competition. Among other things, this led to discussions about the degree of free trade and protectionism, to a search for future-oriented activities, and to the widely-supported ambition to modernize agriculture. One way out of the

---

[1]   M. Weber, *The Theory of Social and Economic Organization* (London, 1947).
[2]   S. Lash and J. Urry, *The End of Organized Capitalism* (Cambridge, 1988).

crisis was an increase in productivity, which could be achieved by means of a more scientific approach, through innovation and the development of more profitable sectors and crops, such as horticulture and livestock farming. To make this modernization offensive a success, the state and agricultural organizations in European countries increasingly worked together. They did this in different ways, with varying intensity and sometimes with different objectives. Anton Schuurman has written about the emergence of an 'institutional matrix', in which cooperation between state and civil society is the central motor.[3]

In this chapter, we examine how state and civil society worked together in Belgium to organize scientifically-based livestock improvement in the period 1900–1940. Our approach can be explained in terms of four well-defined questions. Firstly, this chapter examines the role of the First World War in the development of scientific cattle breeding. Did wartime devastation indeed accelerate the search for better livestock? Secondly, we concentrate on the appearance of a 'modern' cattle breeding network. Who was involved in the process of livestock improvement? Thirdly, we analyse the involvement of farmers within the rationalization of stock-breeding. To what extent did they actively participate in the diffusion of scientific knowledge on cattle breeding? Fourthly, and lastly, how successful were the attempts to change the farmers' traditional practices? How successful was the initial programme?

Recent research by Bert Theunissen and Steven van der Laan, among others, has indicated that livestock improvement was not an uncomplicated, linear process. The rationalization of cattle breeding was, on the contrary, the result of complex interactions between government institutions and their initiatives, scientists and laboratories, civil society organizations, the farmers and their cattle.[4]

Was that also the case in Belgium? The institutional and economic aspects of cattle breeding in Belgium have been investigated in the past, but the dissemination of the new knowledge of cattle breeding and

---

3   A. Schuurman, 'Agricultural Policy and the Dutch Agricultural Institutional Matrix during the Transition from Organised to Disorganised Capitalism', in P. Moser and T. Varley (eds), *Integration Through Subordination. The Politics of Agricultural Modernisation in Industrial Europe* (Turnhout, 2013), pp. 65–85; also J. Planas, 'Cooperation, Technical Education and Politics in Early Agricultural Policy in Catalonia (1914–1924)', *Rural Hist.* 32 (2020), pp. 211–12; G. Federico, *Feeding the World. An Economic History of Agriculture, 1800–2000* (Princeton, 2005), pp. 189–96.

4   B. Theunissen, 'Breeding without Mendelism: Theory and Practice of Dairy Cattle Breeding in the Netherlands, 1900–1950', *Journal of the History of Biology* 41 (2008), pp. 637–76; B. Theunissen and S. van der Laan, *Een Varken voor iedereen: De modernisering van de Nederlandse varkensfokkerij in de twintigste eeuw* (Utrecht, 2017).

acceptance of the new insights it provided has remained unexamined.[5] Academic research into the functioning of knowledge networks in other sectors has been limited to specific actors and on aspects and largely institutional questions such as the establishment of higher agricultural education in Gembloux and Leuven, the relationship between agronomy and agricultural policy and the development of (agricultural) laboratories before the First World War.[6] The dissertation by Hanne De Winter forms an exception to this. She studied the circulation of knowledge and advice about fertilization in the years 1840–1991 and looked at the development of the Soil Science Service of Belgium from the perspective of knowledge networks. De Winter particularly emphasizes the role of consultants employed by the government, private institutions and companies as mediators between experts and farmers. As 'cultural amphibians' they brought together the worlds of theory and practice from the end of the nineteenth century, with the aim of shaping a more modern and rational agriculture.[7]

Another point which received much attention in the knowledge offensive that began at the end of the nineteenth century was the modernization of livestock farming. The functioning of knowledge networks therefore forms an interesting and relevant case for study. The production of animal products was the most important sector of the Belgian agricultural economy around 1910. Both the government and civil society organizations devoted a great deal of attention and resources to it. Moreover, the First World War led to a severe reduction in the Belgian livestock population. A speedy recovery of livestock numbers was necessary after the war, and this provided a unique opportunity for scientists and policymakers to both disseminate and implement modern principles of livestock improvement in a coordinated manner. But how was this tackled and what role did the various actors play within the knowledge network?

---

[5]   Y. Segers, E. Niesten and J. Raymaekers, 'Over de maakbaarheid van dieren. Veeteelt, wetenschap en vleesconsumptie in België gedurende de negentiende en twintigste eeuw', *Jaarboek voor Ecologische Geschiedenis* (2004), pp. 19–50; J. Blomme, *The Economic Development of Belgian Agriculture, 1880–1980: A Quantitative and Qualitative Analysis* (Brussels, 1992), pp. 119–22; B. Demasure, 'De aanslag op de veestapel in het Kortrijkse tijdens de Eerste Wereldoorlog', *De Leiegouw* 56 (2014), pp. 129–56.

[6]   L. Diser, 'Laboratory versus Farm. The Triumph of Laboratory Science in Belgian Agriculture at the End of the Nineteenth Century', *Agricultural Hist.* 86 (2012), pp. 31–54; Y. Segers and R. Hermans, 'Between Ideology and Science. Higher Agricultural Education in Belgium and the Development of a Catholic Agricultural Network', *Agricultural History Rev.* 57 (2009), pp. 236–56.

[7]   H. De Winter, 'Kennisnetwerken in de landbouw. Circulatie van bemestingskennis en -advies in België, 1840–1991' (unpublished Ph.D. thesis, University of Leuven, 2015).

Conceptually, this chapter makes use of Michel Callon's four-phase theory of translation. In order to validate their knowledge, agricultural scientists had to implement their theories in practice through processes of problematization, 'interessement', enrolment and mobilization. Problematization refers to the moment when actors offer problem statements and seek to convince others that they have the correct solutions. 'Interessement' corresponds to the strengthening of the links between the interests of various actors. Enrolment then refers to the participation of actors and their acceptance of their role in prioritizing a particular problematization. Last, but not least, mobilization concerns the maintenance of the network by ensuring that spokespersons act according to its interests. Translation, then, is a process of 'creating convergences and homologies by relating things that were previously different'.[8]

The structure of this chapter is inspired by this four-phased model of translation. The first section focuses on the problems that Belgian farmers faced before and during the First World War. The second analyses the creation of a stockbreeding network after 1918 and the following decade. The third studies the modern practices of cattle breeding, while the fourth and final section describes the (productive) qualities of the post-war national herd. Legislation, official documents, contemporary publications and articles on livestock improvement as well as annual reports were consulted in order to reconstruct the characteristics and functioning of this knowledge network. Due to the nature of the available sources, our emphasis is upon the institutional aspects of innovation and change. A bottom-up analysis, in which the voice and vision of the breeders and livestock keepers are central, will be undertaken in future research.

Belgian cattle farming and the First World War

Belgium was the only country to be almost completely occupied during the First World War. Four years of German occupation left its marks on the agricultural economy. A great deal of its livestock was confiscated for military purposes or transported to Germany, while other animals died during combat or were slaughtered in order to provide food. The number of cattle in 1919 was only two-thirds of that of 1914. Jan Blomme has estimated that the First World War decimated the Belgian breed of horses by 40 per cent and the number of pigs by not less than 76 per cent. The lack of concentrated feeds also had an impact on average milk yields. According to Blomme, Belgian agriculture suffered from reduced milk yields until the early 1920s.[9]

---

8   M. Callon, 'Some Elements of a Sociology of Translation: Domestication of the Scallops and the Fishermen of St Brieuc Bay', in J. Law (ed.), *Power, Action and Belief: A New Sociology of Knowledge?* (London, 1986), p. 211.
9   B. Demasure, *Boter bij de vis. Landbouw en voeding tijdens de Eerste Wereldoorlog*

As tragic as the loss of cattle was for producers (and consumers), zoologists pointed to the First World War as an opportunity to completely redesign the selection methods used for livestock improvement. Leopold Frateur (1877–1946), a young professor in zoology at the University of Leuven, had already suggested in his *Overview of the Situation of Cattle Breeding* (published in 1915) that the

> selection based on the latest scientific findings, the systematic quest for greater profitability of the agricultural enterprise [stockbreeding] and rigorous bookkeeping are the positive ways to follow in order to really engage in livestock improvement in Belgium.[10]

Simultaneously, he emphasized the importance of indigenous breeds for the reconstruction of the Belgian livestock once the war was over. Uncontrolled cross-breeding with foreign animals would hinder the creation of breeds adapted to Belgium's agricultural, geological and climatological circumstances. In other words, post-war recovery was not only to entail a reconstruction, but also an improvement, of the national herd.[11]

Frateur suggested that a better, more productive (cattle) stock was more than necessary for Belgian agriculture to survive. The agricultural depression of the late nineteenth century had resulted in a shift from arable farming to horticulture and mostly cattle breeding. Belgian arable farmers were unable to compete with the large farms of the United States and other overseas countries. Because of their economies of scale, their enterprises could produce more cheaply. The increasing importation of bread grains from the 1870s onwards was a direct consequence of this, facilitated by the liberal economic policies of most Western European governments. Under pressure from imports of foreign grain, Belgian farmers identified cattle farming as an opportunity to increase their income and progressively shifted their production into dairy products and meat for the (international) market. While animal husbandry represented 45 per cent of the nominal output of Belgian agriculture in 1880, that figure had grown to 65 per cent of total value in 1910. With arable farming plummeting from 47 to 28 per cent of output by value, cattle farming became the undisputed flagship of Belgium's primary sector.[12]

The growing importance of cattle farming resulted in and was stimulated by an increasing (scientific) interest in stockbreeding. The value

---

(Leuven, 2014), pp. 189–93; Blomme, *Economic Development of Belgian Agriculture*, pp. 119–22.

10 J.-L. Frateur, *Aperçu sur la situation de l'élevage bovin en Belgique avant la guerre* (Leuven, 1915), p. 35.

11 A. Gobin, *Professor J.-Leopold Frateur en de omwenteling in de veehouderij* (Utrecht, 1999), pp. 2–8; J.-L. Frateur, 'Herstelling, ontwikkeling en verbetering van de Belgische veeteelt', *De Boer*, 5 Apr. 1919, pp. 2–3.

12 Blomme, *Economic Development of Belgian Agriculture*, pp. 197–9.

of an animal was no longer determined by its utility for the farmer's household and the value of its manure for an arable regime. Meat production and dairy farming turned into a market-oriented sector, which altered the requirements of every breed and animal. Milk yields and the fat percentage became increasingly important. Given these developments, it should come as no surprise that academic and government institutions started to investigate the possibilities of improving the productivity of livestock. If Belgian agriculture wanted to survive in a growing competitive international market, a significant improvement in the national livestock was necessary.

Before the 1880s, the 1.2 million head of cattle were a colourful collection of animals. The national herd consisted of various breeds without pure bloodlines, which were often crossed in response to local and individual needs. The first attempts to improve livestock dated back to the 1840s. That is when the Belgian government encouraged cross-breeding experiments with the Durham Shorthorn. This British breed – the first to have its own herd book (1822) – was selected for its exceptionally high milk fat and slaughter value. This was important in order to provide the expanding working population with sufficient food and calories. Unfortunately, those efforts were largely in vain. While the quality of the first offspring was good, the productive characteristics tended to become diluted in subsequent generations. Furthermore, the milk yield of the Durham cows was inadequate, which meant that the breed was not suited for Belgian farmers who preferred dual-purpose cows.[13]

The cross-breeding experiments with the Durham Shorthorn laid bare one of the main shortcomings of 'traditional' nineteenth-century breeding methods. These methods were based on the assumption that desirable hereditary elements could simply be detected in the 'extérieur' of the cattle, namely in their physical appearance. This resulted in the method of 'mass selection', whereby animals with the right stature were chosen for breeding. Gregor Mendel's genetic theory would later expose two weaknesses that were inherently interrelated to the 'mass selection' technique. First, the existence of heterozygotes made it possible that animals without pure bloodlines were nevertheless selected because unwanted traits were inherited recessively. A second, but interconnected, disadvantage was that it would take a long time to create a pool of purebreds. As a consequence, from the 1870s onwards, questions were raised about the breeding methods being employed. New scientific breeding techniques informed by genetic theory were devised. The shift from *phenotypic* to *genotypic* breeding methods was encouraged from the end of the nineteenth century.[14]

13 Segers, Niesten and Raymaekers, 'Over De Maakbaarheid Van Dieren', pp. 21–4.
14 D. Brullot, '"Het Oog Van De Meester Maakt Het Vee Vet"? Rundveeverbetering

In 1884, the Belgian government established a Ministry of Agriculture in order to find solutions to the difficulties in which the national primary sector found itself. The National Society for the Improvement of Cattle Breeds in Belgium (Nationale Maatschappij voor de Verbetering van de Rundveerassen in België) established in 1890 was intended to be one of the principal instruments to revitalize the sector. The creation of this government service signalled the beginning of cattle breeding along modern, scientific lines, and can be regarded as the moment when the problematization phase passed into the interest phase. The main goals of the National Society were the selection of well-defined regional cattle breeds and the establishment of herd books.[15]

Research on the application of genetic theory to livestock improvement resulted in the establishment of an Institute for Zootechnics (Instituut voor Huisdierkunde) at the University of Leuven in 1908. The institute (which received funding from both the government and private donors) was headed by Leopold Frateur and had a special status, being independent of the agricultural college of the university. It is probably this status that led to the situation in which the institute was the only functioning research unit of the university during wartime. For Frateur, the institute served as a vehicle with which to apply Mendel's genetics to the field of animal husbandry.[16] A number of farms on the outskirts of Leuven served as research stations. In this way, a limited network, with links to active breeders and livestock keepers, was in existence before the war. Frateur had already published more than 60 articles on animal husbandry based on the experiments carried out in the stations before 1914. His scientific insights were inspired and influenced by the publications of Wilhelm Johanssen (Copenhagen) and William Bateson (Birmingham) and through his many working visits to universities and research centres throughout Europe. Frateur had a special interest in Danish cattle improvement. As early as 1906, he gave lectures to farmers on cattle breeding in Denmark.[17]

In the conclusion of his overview of livestock improvement in Belgium at the outbreak of the First World War, Frateur showed some ambivalence about developments in the field. Frateur stated that 'the efforts made in recent years with regard to livestock improvement have certainly been big. Nevertheless, the results have never completely met expectations'.[18]

---

in België (1880–1919)' (unpublished M.A. thesis, Leuven, 2010); Gobin, *Frateur*.

15 A. Pfeiffer, *L'Amélioration du bétail en Belgique et les syndicats d'élevage* (Kortrijk, 1894), pp. 6–13.

16 R. Hermans, Y. Segers and B. Woestenborghs, *In Het Spoor Van Demeter: Faculteit Bio- Ingenieurswetenschappen K.U.Leuven, 1878–2003* (Leuven, 2005), pp. 65, 77, 84; L. Frateur, 'Note sur l'Institut de Zootechnie de Louvain', *Institut de zootechnie de Louvain* 14 (1913). pp. 5–6.

17 Gobin, *Frateur*, pp. 13–16; Hermans, Segers and Woestenborghs, *In het spoor van Demeter*.

18 Frateur, *Aperçu sur la situation*, pp. 34–6.

Knowledge about livestock improvement was certainly being circulated in academic and in government circles, but there was still a massive gap between theory and practice, between the laboratory and the livestock shed. For instance, the first handbook on genetic theory in stockbreeding written in Dutch – a large majority of Flemish farmers were unable to read French to a high level – was only published in the 1920s. The first organizations to implement Mendelism in agriculture, such as the 'Veekweeksyndicaten' en 'Veebonden' (further information about which can be found later on in this contribution) had only been recently established on the outbreak of the First World War and their impact remained limited. Furthermore, it seemed difficult to implement a satisfactory application of the Mendelian principles. Breeders and pastoralists did not want to simply replace their traditional practices with new methods that had still had to prove their worth. Moreover, the support provided by experts and consultants was very limited, as was the financial support. The destruction of Belgian livestock in wartime therefore provided a unique opportunity to create a new body of livestock on a rational basis.[19]

The post-war construction of a stockbreeding knowledge network

The exceptional situation of the Institute for Zootechnics and the financial support it received enabled Leopold Frateur to continue his research during the war and to design a programme for reconstruction of the national herd. He also managed to expand his political and social network during the war and enhance his reputation. For example, he was vice president of the Agricultural Committee of the National Aid and Food Committee (1914–1918) and became vice chairman of the Belgian Farmers' League (Belgische Boerenbond). Naturally, these contacts helped policymakers to pick up his ideas more quickly. Frateur presented his insights in *New Methods For Livestock Improvement* (1922).[20] In order to create more productive animals, breeders had to work through three consecutive phases. A first step was to create new bloodlines for every breed that contained all the desirable elements. The second step of the process was to multiply these new bloodlines and allow them to replace the old, less productive breeds. In a final phase, it was necessary to 'place them in the environmental conditions most suitable for their exploitation, in order to obtain maximum output'. Frateur, in other words, advocated the creation of regional breeds. This

---

19 Y. Segers, L. Van Molle and G. Vanpaemel, 'In de greep van de vooruitgang 1880–1950', in Y. Segers and L. Van Molle (eds), *Leven van het land. Boeren in België, 1750–2000* (Leuven, 2004), pp. 49–109.

20 J.-L. Frateur, *Les nouvelles méthodes d'amélioration du bétail* (Aarschot, 1922), pp. 9–14.

three-phase stockbreeding plan would serve as the basis for the transformation of Belgian livestock after the war.[21]

Frateur's ideas about cattle breeding were known to policymakers and influenced the Royal Decree on Livestock Improvement issued on 16 August 1919. This sought to 'ameliorate cattle breeds' by constructing a network of public and private actors (research units and civil society organizations) and the farmers themselves. It recognized that only such a broad knowledge network, supported by all relevant actors, would be able to bridge theory and practice and improve the quality of the Belgian livestock according to modern, scientific methods. Figure 7.1 presents the elements of the knowledge network it envisaged. This initiative illustrates the growing collaboration between the state, experts and civil society organizations at the beginning of the twentieth century, in which the latter received financial support in order to deal with questions of public interest. The government itself provided a legal framework, but remained largely in the background, supporting and controlling the actions of civil society. In his small publication entitled *Le rôle des Elevages d'Elite dans l'amélioration du bétail et des Syndicats d'Elevages et d'Exploitation dans l'amélioration du bétail* (*The Role of Breeding Stations, Breeding Syndicates and Exploitation Syndicates*, 1922), Frateur explained how these three civil society organizations could be called on to manage the three steps of his breeding programme.[22]

Let us begin by taking a closer look at the role of the breeding stations. They formed part of the Institute for Zootechnics at the University of Leuven. They served as laboratories for the implementation of genetic theory in animal husbandry. This role remained unchanged in the context of the post-war recovery programme. Due to his established reputation and his institute's contacts with policymakers, Frateur, his Institute for Zootechnics and its breeding stations were designated to carry out the first phase of the livestock improvement process. This means that the research unit was responsible for the selection of the breeds and varieties that would serve as the basis for Belgium's new body of livestock. While the theoretical work was to be done in the institute, the practical work was to be undertaken at the breeding stations. These were, in fact, active farms that signed agreements with the government, undertaking that the animals bred by the stations according to the institute's requirements would be sold to the state. Because the stations were spread across Belgium and its agricultural regions, the adaptation of breeds to regional

---

21 *Ibid.*, p. 10.
22 J.-L. Frateur, *De rol der keurkweekerijen, der veekweeksyndicaten en der veebonden in de veeverbetering* (Leuven, 1922); id., 'Omwenteling in den veekweek', *De Boer*, 18 Oct. 1919, p. 2.

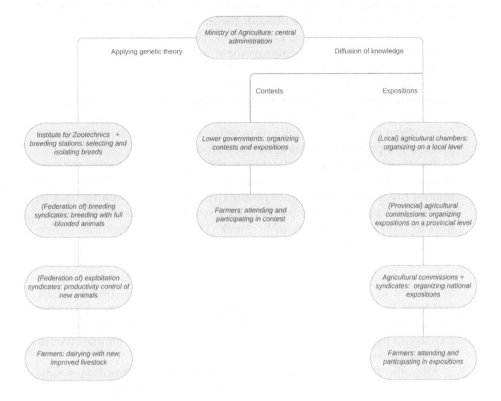

FIGURE 7.1 The network of actors participating in livestock improvement in inter-war Belgium. Source: J. De Tilloux, 'Premiers résultats de la méthode actuelle d'amélioration du bétail', *Journal de la Société Centrale d'Agriculture* 72 (1924), p. 23 and authors' insights.

conditions could easily be assessed. This collaboration with active farmers formed a crucial element in the enrolment phase.[23]

In addition to this expanded breeding network and the Institute for Zootechnics, the Belgian government established a pair of public agencies whose role was to manage the livestock improvement programme. The first one, the Technical Committee, formed part of the Ministry of Agriculture's central administration. It served as an advisory board and

---

23 '16 août 1919 – Arrêté royal: élevage des races bovines, subsides', *Pasinomie* (1919), p. 342; L. Martens, *De veestapel onder schot. De invloed van de Eerste Wereldoorlog op de Belgische veeteelt* (unpublished M.A. thesis, University of Leuven, 2011).

included among its members a number of specialists appointed by the Minister of Agriculture, the head of the administration at the ministry, the head of the Institute for Zootechnics (i.e. Leopold Frateur) and the directors of the Livestock Improvement and Veterinary Services. The Minister of Agriculture could also call on the expertise of consultants from the Livestock Improvement Service. In contrast to the Technical Committee, which mainly focused on theoretical issues, the Livestock Improvement Service primarily focused on the implementation of government policy. Its consultants monitored the livestock improvement process and provided technical advice in the field.[24]

The breeding syndicates (*Syndicats d'Elevages* or *Veekweeksyndicaten*) played an important role assisting the breeding stations in replacing inferior breeds with new, more productive animals. They dated back to the pre-war period, when the Belgian government took its first initiatives to improve the quality of livestock. The breeding syndicates were actually private organizations but were financially supported by the Ministry of Agriculture.[25] In return for this financial support, the syndicates were commissioned to improve six types of cattle: the Belgian blue breed in central Belgium, the red and red and white breed in East and West Flanders, the Herve and Campine cattle breeds, as well as the Frisian breed in the Flemish Polders. Pre-war livestock improvement had focused on hybrid varieties. The creation of pure-blooded animals would only start after 1918.[26]

After the First World War, Frateur considered the breeding syndicates as 'reproduction centres for those breeds selected by the breeding stations'. Because this was a work of national interest, Leopold Frateur argued that the syndicates were only to consist of 'the best breeders who understand the importance of their work'. For him, the breeding syndicates formed an extension of the breeding stations beyond the university walls.[27] They were mandated to breed using the animals placed at their disposal by the Institute for Zootechnics. All animals were to be registered in a herd book, so that their pedigree could easily be verified. This was necessary in order to maintain pure bloodlines and thus produce high-quality breeds (Figure 7.2). In order to fulfil their assigned tasks, local breeding syndicates were also encouraged to have their own bull as an ancestor for one or more generations. The investment would be shared by all the members of the syndicate, spreading the cost and ensuring the

24 Gobin, *Frateur*; Martens, *De veestapel onder schot*.
25 L. Van Molle, *Katholieken en landbouw. Landbouwpolitiek in België, 1884–1914* (Leuven, 1989), pp. 137–9, 204–6 and 280–1.
26 Segers, Van Molle and Vanpaemel, 'In de greep van de vooruitgang, 1880–1950', p. 100.
27 Frateur, *De rol der keurkweekerijen*.

improvement of the local livestock. According to Frateur's own estimates, the work of livestock improvement – the creation of six regional cattle breeds – was to be completed within an 18-year timeframe (i.e. six generations of three years a piece). An improved body of livestock for Belgian farmers was to be achieved by 1940.[28]

The final phase of Frateur's improvement programme, the integration of the new breeds into agricultural practice, was in the hands of so-called exploitation syndicates (*Syndicats d'Exploitation* or *Veebonden*). While the breeding syndicates quite logically concentrated on breeding, exploitation syndicates aimed to exploit the cattle delivered by the breeding stations and breeding syndicates.[29] The first exploitation syndicates, founded in the decade before the First World War, concentrated on improving living conditions and checking hygiene standards, feed and milk yields. Of particular importance here was the shift from the aesthetic qualities of the animals to the input and output of cattle farming.[33] This shift persisted after the war, when Frateur claimed that the improvement of the productivity of cattle farming was precisely the task to be undertaken by the exploitation syndicates.[30]

In Frateur's plan, these syndicates were to play a crucial role in ensuring the optimal functioning of the knowledge networks. They were complementary but also dependent on each other. The success of one actor partly determined the success of the other. They took the form of a collaboration between experts, breeders and livestock farmers, between government and civil society, in which they all brought their networks together and pursued a common goal. In all this, the Belgian Farmers' Union occupied a special position.

Belgium's largest agricultural organization, the Belgische Boerenbond, actively promoted the work of the exploitation syndicates. As a Leuven-based civil society organization established in 1890, the Farmers' League had close connections with the Institute for Zootechnics (in fact, both organizations were situated in the same street). Leopold Frateur understood the workings of the Farmers' League better than anybody else. He held several board positions and published many articles in the league's magazines. In 1906, Frateur convinced the league to encourage the establishment of new exploitation syndicates. Indeed, in the decade before the First World War, some 67 local branches of the league created their own syndicates. This can be considered as the starting point of modern livestock improvement in Belgium. In addition to the local syndicates, the Farmers' League established a Federation of Exploitation Syndicates (Federatie

28 Gobin, *Frateur*.
29 Frateur, *De rol der keurkweekerijen*; J.-L. Frateur, *Reconstitution, développement et amélioration de l'élevage belge* (Brussels, 1918), pp. iii–viii and 2–3.
30 Van Molle, *Katholieken en landbouw*, pp. 204–6.

van Veebonden). This umbrella organization monitored the work of all syndicates. Alongside that federation, other syndicates organized the improvement of other farm animals, such as pigs and small livestock.[31]

The monitoring of progress in breeding was the task of the provincial administrations and of two well-established organizations: the local agricultural chambers (*comices agricoles*) and the provincial agricultural commissions. They were responsible for the diffusion of knowledge via contests and exhibitions, a task that they had performed during the nineteenth century.[32] The royal decree of 16 August 1919 declared that livestock shows could only be organized by the Ministry of Agriculture or the provincial administrations. They were designed 'to select the cattle allowed for breeding'. Every jury was to consist of three members, selected from candidates put forward by the provincial agricultural commissions, the breeding syndicate of the province in question and the Technical Committee for Cattle Farming. They were to evaluate and reward the breeding animals on scientific grounds. The aim of the exhibitions and contests was to 'draw the attention of farmers to the importance of livestock improvement and professional education in the subject'. The royal decree stated that exhibitions arranged by the local *comices agricoles* would take place every three years, while provincial exhibitions were to be organized every nine years by the joint effort of the agricultural commission and the breeding and exploitation syndicates. National exhibitions of livestock improvement were to be organized every four years by the federations of both syndicates.[33]

Livestock keepers are not breeders

The growing popularity of the livestock improvement programmes gradually drove a wedge between farmers and breeders. Farmers concentrated on the commercial exploitation of their cattle. Breeders considered livestock breeding as a source of income. While all cattle breeders were farmers, not all farmers were cattle breeders.[34] Engineering new livestock was no longer the privilege of scientists working in university laboratories or within bureaucratic institutions. From the beginning of the twentieth

---

31 Frateur, *Les nouvelles méthodes d'amélioration du bétail*, p. 21; L. Van Molle, *Ieder voor allen. De Belgische Boerenbond 1890–1990* (Leuven, 1990), pp. 136, 139–40.

32 *Verbetering der rundveerassen in België* (Brussel, 1920), pp. 10–16; M. Van Dijck, *De wetenschap van de wetgever. De klassieke politieke economie en het Belgische landbouwbeleid, 1830–1884* (Leuven, 2008), pp. 177–85.

33 J.-L. Frateur, *Systematische stamvorming als voorbereiding tot wetenschappelijke rundveeverbetering* (Brasschaat s.d.), p. 30; '16 août 1919 – Arrêté royal', pp. 344–5.

34 This was the case in Belgium, but also in the Netherlands: see Theunissen, 'Breeding without Mendelism', p. 654.

century onwards, and even more so after 1918, a network of breeding syndicates and exploitation syndicates supported the dissemination of new, scientific methods. Although the syndicates were supported by the government, it was the first time that farmers were directly and in a structural way involved in matters of livestock improvement. Representatives of the state and of the Federation of Exploitation Syndicates controlled and monitored the progress made in the field.[35]

In the decades before the First World War, as mentioned before, livestock farming pioneers established the first Belgian breeding and exploitation syndicates. In 1900, there were already 300 local organizations for livestock improvement with a total 12,300 members. Ten years later this number had grown to 500 syndicates with 20,000 members.[36] The number of syndicates seemed to drop significantly during the years immediately after the First World War. This was probably due to the complete disorganization of civil society between 1914 and 1918, from which the Belgian countryside only recovered slowly. According to the consultant, Joseph De Tilloux, the number of breeding syndicates in Belgium numbered 180 in 1923. These syndicates were responsible for the breeding of 24,300 cows, more than half of them being situated in the provinces of Hainaut, Namur and East Flanders (approx. 7,000, 3,500 and 4,200 respectively).[37] On the other hand, most exploitation syndicates in 1923 were situated in the provinces of Antwerp, Limburg and West Flanders. Respectively 24, 43 and 25 exploitation syndicates out of a total of 109 (with 2,400, 3,600 and 1,700 of 9,200 head of cattle) were established in these provinces. The reason why is unclear. It is possible that in those provinces, the most appropriate breeds were already selected, giving the exploitation syndicates the possibility of working with these animals.[38] The number of syndicates for livestock improvement doubled during the next years. According to the *Reports of the Ministry of Agriculture* – a government periodical only published in 1938 and 1939 – the number of exploitation syndicates at the end of the inter-war period had reached a total of 221, with 26,200 registered milking cows and 397 bull-breeding syndicates with 400 stud bulls.[39] Contemporary estimates show that the total number of breeding syndicates had slightly increased by the end of the 1940s (187 in 1949), while the number of pedigree cows had grown more spectacularly (to 86,800).[40]

35 Segers, Van Molle and Vanpaemel, 'In de greep van de vooruitgang, 1880–1950', p. 103.
36 Van Molle, *Katholieken en landbouw*, p. 399.
37 De Tilloux, 'Premiers résultats', pp. 29–30.
38 *Ibid.*, pp. 29–30.
39 Gobin, *Frateur*.
40 Gobin, *Frateur*.

The Belgian Farmers' League actively promoted livestock improvement policies by establishing its own network of exploitation syndicates. In 1920, its annual report recorded 36 active syndicates. This number had grown to 101 by 1922 and 114 in 1926. The management of the Farmers' League strictly controlled the functioning of these syndicates and dissolved those that did not fully operate in accordance with the rules of scientific cattle breeding. This explains why the total number of exploitation syndicates decreased during the late 1920s (see Figure 7.2). The graph also shows how the number of stud bulls, which were held by the syndicates to breed with, constantly rose during the 1920s. In 1930, 97 bulls were held by 89 special syndicates. The breeding of high-quality bulls had progressed in such a manner that, after a decade of scientific breeding, around a hundred bulls were available for exploitation in a commercial context.[41]

How and through which media and initiatives did the new knowledge about modern livestock improvement and livestock farming reach Belgian farmers? Few of the farmers involved in livestock improvement had received higher education. Knowledge was usually handed down from one generation to another (tacit knowledge), although the Belgian government had started to organize agricultural education from the late 1840s onwards. A second 'educational offensive' followed during the agricultural crisis of the 1880s. In the mid-1930s, Belgium had 16 secondary agricultural schools, 17 secondary agricultural departments, 17 secondary horticultural schools and two schools for agricultural mechanics. Meanwhile, and more importantly, adult education, evening and winter schools were organized all over the country in order to inform farmers and their wives about new insights and practices. Lectures were organized by the Ministry of Agriculture or by civil society organizations such as the Belgian Farmers' League. During the early 1920s, the Farmers' League organized more than 3,000 lectures a year.[42]

The existence of this agricultural knowledge network, with its lectures, adult schools and agricultural exhibitions, convinced the Belgian government that livestock improvement was possible 'without thorough scientific knowledge' and could be achieved by 'farmers who are aware of the importance of their duty'.[43] The government held that the basic

---

[41] E. Luytgaerens, *Belgische Boerenbond. Verslag over de dienstjaren 1919–1938* (Leuven, 1939), p. 52.

[42] L. Van Molle, '*Kulturkampf* in the Countryside: Agricultural Education, 1800–1940: A Multifaceted Offensive', in C. Sarasua, P. Scholliers and L. Van Molle (eds), *Land, Shops and Kitchens. Technology and the Food Chain in Twentieth-Century Europe* (Turnhout, 2005), pp. 139–69; Segers and Hermans, 'Between Ideology and Science', pp. 236–56.

[43] *Verbetering Der Rundveerassen in België.*

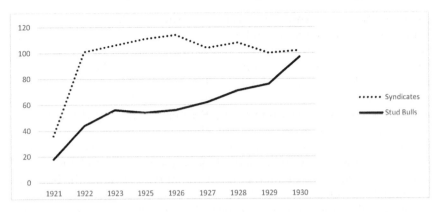

FIGURE 7.2 The number of exploitation syndicates (and their stud bulls) established by local branches of the Belgian Farmers' League (1920–1930). Source: E. Luytgaerens, *Belgische Boerenbond. Verslag over de dienstjaren, 1919–1938* (Leuven, 1920–1939), p. 52.

principles of genetic theory were relatively easy for farmers to understand. Their involvement in syndicates would serve to educate them further. Between 1920 and 1930, it organized more than 2,700 lectures on livestock improvement (not only relating to cattle, but also other farm animals). The local exploitation syndicates were frequently visited by breeding consultants and the Belgian Farmers' League meticulously recorded the number of visits made by their experts to both syndicates and cattle breeders. The frequency with which the Farmers' League verified its syndicates increased profoundly during the 1920s. While only 76 visits were organized in 1922, inspections were carried out more frequently in the remainder of the decade. In 1930, consultants from the Farmers' League carried out 462 visits. During these 'propaganda visits', the consultants, as true cultural amphibians, actively promoted livestock improvement and explained the basic insights of modern stock breeding. Furthermore, livestock improvement was the subject of numerous lectures, popular articles in its members' journals such as *De Boer* and discussions at agricultural shows.[44]

The organization of agricultural shows and prize competitions was nothing new. It formed part of a government strategy that aimed to educate farmers by offering them a visual presentation of new methods and good practices.[45] The law on livestock improvement therefore built on a well-established tradition to disseminate Mendelian ideas across

44 Luytgaerens, *Belgische Boerenbond*, pp. 53–5.
45 Van Molle, *Katholieken en landbouw. Landbouwpolitiek in België, 1884–1914,*

the network of stockbreeders. The post-war exhibitions on livestock improvement differed in a number of ways from those organized before the war. While the pre-war exhibitions made a virtue of the aesthetic qualities of the participating animals, events after the First World War assessed cattle on their productivity. In 1925, *De Boer* emphasized the need for contests 'based on in-depth inquiries instead of first impressions'. The contests, according to the Farmers' League, had the aim of persuading farmers 'not to arbitrarily choose the animals that appeared best for breeding purposes, but to train the public to become good breeders'.[46] This is why the deliberations of the jury had to be made on objective criteria: the affiliation to the regional type of cattle, the build of the animals as well as their yield and the fat ratio of the milk (Figure 7.3).[47]

We can therefore see how, especially after the First World War, increasing efforts were being made to bring modern insights to breeders and pastoralists. Government and civil society organizations worked closely together within an expanding knowledge network. But how should we assess its impact? Despite all efforts and the increasing deployment of people and resources, the livestock improvement programme did not reach the mass of Belgian farmers before 1940. Taking the number of organizations as the basis for further calculations allows us to estimate the relative importance of exploitation syndicates. In 1930, the Belgian Farmers' League coordinated 102 exploitation syndicates. Given the fact that the Farmers' League had 1,228 local branches across the country that year, it becomes clear how limited the scale of livestock improvement was at that date. Only 8 per cent of the local Farmers' League guilds (*boerengilden*, the name stresses the corporative spirit in which they were established) had their own exploitation syndicates. In 1930, the exploitation syndicates of the Belgian Farmers' League consisted of approximately 10,400 cows. This was only 1 per cent of the Belgian cattle stock. If the exploitation syndicates outside the Farmers' League are also taken into account, 26,218 dairy cows were registered in the herdbooks in 1938. With a total of 1.09 million cows in Belgium, 'adapted' animals still represented a marginal share (2 per cent) of total livestock.[48]

Just after the Second World War, E. Warnants, a former director-general of the Ministry of Agriculture, published an analysis of livestock improvement in Belgium, *L'amélioration des animaux domestiques en*

---

pp. 204–6, 223; E. Warnants, *L'amélioration des animaux domestiques en Belgique, 1880 à 1940* (Leuven, 1947), p. 42.

46 'Over de puntenschaal', *De Boer* 31 (7 Feb. 1925), p. 3.

47 *Prijskamp voor melkkoeien van het Kempisch ras* (Namen, 1924).

48 Gobin, *Frateur*; Blomme, *Economic Development of Belgian Agriculture*, pp. 231–3, 262–6; Luytgaerens, *Belgische Boerenbond*, pp. 52–3.

BELLA. — N° 244 Lim.
1ʳᵉ pour la production laitière avec **7980** litres à **3,6** °/₀ de graisse.
Appartenant à M. GERMEYS, V., à Linckhout (Limbourg).

FIGURE 7.3 Productivity (milk yields and fat percentage) of new livestock during local and regional contests (Campine area in northern Belgium: province of Limburg). *Concours de vaches laitières de race Campinoise* (Namur, 1924), p. 41.

Belgique 1880–1940 (1947).[49] Warnants investigated the extent to which regionally-adapted types of cattle had been formed during the inter-war years. According to his calculations, the creation of regional breeds was far from completed in 1940. Table 7.1 compares the actual number of animals per region with the planned number of 'new' heads of cattle. For the whole of Belgium, only 4 per cent of the livestock improvement programme had been completed. Especially in the Flemish agricultural regions – West and East Flanders and the Campine area – a lot of work remained to be done. Warnants nevertheless remained quite optimistic about the chances for the project to succeed. He argued that for the entire body of livestock to experience the positive effects of rationalization, only 6–12 per cent of the pure-blooded animals were needed.[50]

49 Warnants, *L'amélioration des animaux domestiques*, pp. 62–74.
50 Gobin, *Frateur*.

TABLE 7.1 Planned number of regional breeds in Belgium compared to results in 1940, both in absolute and relative terms.

Breed	Region	Planned number	Number achieved by 1940	%
Red	West Flanders	278,000	5,500	1.98
Blue	Central Belgium	928,000	56,000	6.03
Red and white	East Flanders	250,000	7,000	2.80
Black spotted	Herve	125,000	15,000	12.00
Red spotted	Campine	216,000	2,800	1.30
Frisian	Flemish Polders	76,000	450	0.59
Total	Belgium	1,873,000	86,750	4.63

Source: E. Warnants, *L'amélioration des animaux domestiques en Belgique 1880–1940* (1947), pp. 21–2.

Why did the improvement of the Belgian livestock take off so slowly? How can we explain the fact that ordinary farmers seemed so hesitant in accepting the results of scientific stockbreeding? Further research is needed to provide a comprehensive answers to this. For now, we can refer to a few factors that certainly had an influence. One explanation has already been given by Warnants. He referred in the 1940s to the (alleged) conservative mentality of the farmers as a hindrance to the dissemination of knowledge and new insights into livestock improvement. Laboratory science and practical expertise seemed to be incompatible, and he thought that this was a further impediment to the achievement of a 'modern' Belgian agriculture.[51]

Second, Warnants pointed to the small size of Belgian farms and their limited financial reserves. The purchase of pure-blooded animals (high-quality bulls in particular) was certainly not cheap, despite government subsidies. Moreover, the introduction of scientifically-improved breeds and the application of new insights created risks and uncertainty. Genetic theory was put forward as a solution to overcome the weaknesses of traditional stockbreeding and ensure the future of the meat and dairy sector. According to the German sociologist Ulrich Beck, the application of science to contain (economic) crises was a key feature of future-oriented modern societies. However, new methods and techniques 'involve the

[51]   *Ibid.* Gobin, *Frateur*, pp. 21, 42–3.

production, distribution and consumption of [...] benefits and hazards'.[52] Certainly for businesses without or with only a limited financial buffer, the prospect of unforeseeable returns was problematic. In this respect, the waiting game played by Belgian farmers was not a consequence of their irrational conservative mentality, but a rational decision based on a pragmatic consideration of all the costs and likely profits. That the number of lectures on livestock improvement reached a yearly average of approximately 200 in the 1920s indicates that farmers were not the conservative individuals they were sometimes portrayed to be by agronomists and other experts. A growing number of farmers were interested in taking (evening) courses with the prospect of improving their own businesses and income. They increasingly seemed to trust science, modern insights and inputs as a means of overcoming crisis, a tendency that can also be noticed in the increasing consumption of artificial fertilizers.[53]

Third, there were also various technical (breeding) problems. A major challenge was the dependence on foreign cattle as the means of quickly rebuilding livestock numbers after the war. In the eyes of Frateur and many of his colleagues, the destruction of the First World War offered an opportunity to rationalize breeding methods in Belgium.[54] The quick recovery of the animal husbandry sector was necessary to revitalize the agricultural economy and to provide the Belgian population with enough food at a time of international protectionism and rapidly rising prices. The Belgian Ministry of Agriculture therefore acquired cattle from the Netherlands, Scotland and Switzerland. Belgium also received livestock from Germany as part of the war reparations agreed in the Treaty of Versailles in June 1919.[55] However, importing from abroad seemed to run counter to the creation of pure-blooded breeds through the cross-breeding of indigenous animals. According to Frateur, the importation of foreign animals and the engineering of domestic breeds were not necessarily incompatible. The main condition was that only those animals with the highest yields and the greatest likelihood of adapting to the Belgian

---

[52] U. Beck, *Risk Society. Towards a New Modernity* (London, 2009); E. Bullen, J. Fahey and J. Kenway, 'The Knowledge Economy and Innovation: Certain Uncertainty and the Risk Economy', *Discourse: Studies in the Cultural Politics of Education* 27 (2006), pp. 53–68.

[53] Luytgaerens, *Belgische Boerenbond*, p. 32; De Winter, 'Kennisnetwerken in de Landbouw'; Blomme, *Economic Development of Belgian Agriculture*, p. 264.

[54] *Parliamentary Reports, House of Representatives*, 10 Oct. 1919, p. 1998; *Parliamentary Documents, House of Representatives*, 1922, nr. 266; 'Begrooting van de ter uitvoering der vredesverdragen invorderbare uitgaven voor het dienstjaar 1922', p. 42; 'Bond der Geteisterden van Yper', *Het Ypersche*, 30 Oct. 1920.

[55] De Tilloux, 'Premiers résultats', 28; D. Claeys, 'Land, staat en bevolking. De wederopbouw van het Belgische platteland na de Eerste Wereldoorlog' (unpublished Ph.D. thesis, Leuven, 2019), p. 110.

environment (for example, by importing cattle from German border regions) should be selected. Despite all efforts however, the quality of the livestock received left much to be desired. Moreover, the outbreak of rinderpest in 1920 wiped out part of the efforts made to improve the Belgian livestock through managed importation. An additional problem was inbreeding; it hindered the translation of Mendelian ideas in the field. The close kinship between some breeding animals sometimes caused infertility, lower yields or decreased resistance to disease. The solution to this was found in the creation of herd books by the breeding syndicates, but the consequence was that the establishment of pure blood lines took longer than expected because the total pool of animals for cross-breeding shrank.[56]

Finally, we must also point to the evolving and even conflicting views of experts and scientists. During the 1930s, agronomists and consultants started to question the need for different breeds. The genetic pool was too small and progress too slow to justify the continuation of Frateur's original plan. The productivity, and not the regional variety, of the new livestock was of foremost importance. Furthermore, the organization of the syndicates by province and canton did not correspond with Belgium's agricultural regions. It is clear that syndicates that were situated in more than one agricultural region would have difficulties with the regional adjustment of their animals. The discussions about the usefulness of regional breeds increasingly paralysed the activities of the breeding syndicates during the inter-war period. This may help to explain why only a few syndicates were established during the 1930s. Moreover, the experts from the Technical Committee that monitored the livestock improvement programme changed their policies in the mid-1930s. Instead of regional variation, livestock improvement in future was to concentrate on the creation of a single high-quality white (formerly 'blue') breed. Their recommendation confirmed a tendency which was already under way. The Second World War further delayed the emergence of a single national breed.[57]

Conclusion

Niek Koning has argued that Western countries failed to modernize the peasant economy and create 'agricultural capitalism' in the nineteenth century.[58] After the First World War, further attempts were made to

---

[56] Martens, *De veestapel onder schot*, 57. Demasure, *Boter bij de vis*, 201–2; Gobin, *Professor J.-Leopold Frateur*, pp. 171–2.

[57] *Beoordeling der koe met tweeledig doel* (Brussels, 1927); Gobin, *Frateur*, pp. 391–4; A. Sevenster, *De rundveefokkerij in België* (Leuven, 1924), pp. 56–68.

[58] N. Koning, *The Failure of Agricultural Capitalism: Agrarian Politics in the UK, Germany, the Netherlands and the USA, 1846–1919* (London, 1994), pp. 243–5.

incorporate agriculture into the capitalist system. To effect that process, European states and civil society organizations cooperated in a range of areas. Their shared underpinning belief was that agriculture would only have a future within the national economy if peasants were assisted in making the transformation into farmers producing for the market and utilizing modern techniques based on scientific insights. This chapter has analysed how initiatives for livestock improvement after the First World War in Belgium, and in particular the setting up of new and efficient knowledge networks, were a part of that process of modernization. Four conclusions can be offered.

First of all, this case study shows how crises can stimulate innovation and the setting up or adaptation of knowledge networks to bring about innovation. Proposals for livestock improvement were formulated in response to the agricultural depression of the 1880s and 1890s, but a large-scale and coordinated programme was not established until after the First World War. Several actors became involved in different ways and entered into a partnership. The commitment of the national (and to a lesser extent provincial) government was important: it increasingly acted as the organizer and sponsor of breeding programmes. In addition, the participation of the largest agricultural organization, the Belgische Boerenbond, was of crucial importance. This organization mobilized its network in support of the government's livestock improvement programme. But this was not simply to modernize the livestock sector and increase livestock farmers' incomes. Naturally, the organization had its own reasons for collaborating with the government, including wishing to strengthen its prominence in the agricultural sector. Thanks to their central place in the knowledge network, the scientific world, and Leopold Frateur and his institute in particular, were able to realize their academic ambitions and strengthen their social and political influence. These observations lead us to a second conclusion: in the years 1900–1940, a complex knowledge network was established, which was based on cooperation between a variety of actors, government and civil society. Each of these actors had their own objectives, but shared a common goal: to ensure an adequate income for cattle farmers.

The role of Leopold Frateur is striking. Frateur was active in national and international academic circles, was an advisor to the Ministry of Agriculture and vice chairman of the Belgian Farmers' League. He was clearly the architect of the livestock improvement programme and the associated knowledge network. Under the 'eye of the master', a variety of actors and their networks were brought together. His prominence not only shows the importance of single individuals, people who have the ability to make a difference as a result of their ideas, dynamic attitude and personal contacts, but it also points to the interdependence (and dependence) of the actors within the knowledge network we have described above. We must therefore conclude that a strict division between the state on the one hand and civil society on the other is not possible or desirable. And within civil society too the connections between actors are stronger than we sometimes think at first sight.

Finally, we note that the knowledge network and the method used to transfer knowledge and insights were largely top-down in nature. The lines were drawn and facilitated by the government and relied heavily on the insights of scientists and experts. This involved a continuing search for the most effective system and required consensus to be reached between the actors. This, in turn, means that translation is a continuous process that runs through several different phases. Various ways were used and developed to circulate new knowledge, to convince breeders and livestock keepers to follow the desired practices (through the granting of subsidies, advice provided during on-site visits, the organization of exhibitions, competitions, and lectures). The role of breeders and livestock keepers was limited, but not entirely non-existent. Partly out of necessity, due to a lack of sufficient financial resources, Frateur used working farms as breeding stations. He increasingly appreciated the practical knowledge of livestock farmers and realized that their active participation and involvement was needed in order to make the livestock improvement programme a success. But despite all his efforts, only a small proportion of farmers became involved. A number of possible explanations for this have already been considered in this chapter, but additional research needs to explore this further. Why were some regions more involved in the livestock improvement programme than others? Could it be that some animal husbandry consultants in some regions were able to act as 'cultural amphibians', and were more effectively able to bridge the gap between theory and practice? And what characterized the breeders and livestock keepers who were involved before the Second World War? Who were those pioneers of livestock improvement in Belgium?

8

Bridging Rural Culture and Expert Culture: The Agrarian Press in Galicia, c.1900–c.1950[1]

Miguel Cabo and Lourenzo Fernández Prieto

The agrarian press is frequently used in historical research as a primary source for studying modern European rural society. Ernst Langthaler, for instance, used a number of periodicals to analyse the Nazi period in rural Austria, Johan Eellend to follow the development of the cooperative movement in Estonia, and Christine César and Nicolas Woss to reconstruct the genealogy of organic agriculture in France.[2] Although the agrarian press obviously reflected and stimulated processes of change, it has received surprisingly little attention from historians as an object of study in its own right. This chapter aims at describing the nature, function and position of the agrarian press in the tangle of knowledge, know-how and communication that surrounded farming in Galicia during the first half of the twentieth century.

---

1   This chapter draws on research undertaken by the Histagra Research Group (GI-1657) financed by the Xunta de Galicia (Galician Autonomus Government) as part of the Spanish Ministry of Economy Research Project 'Las dos vías de cambio y desarrollo agrario del siglo XX. Pluralismo de saberes en un marco orgánico y tecnocracia de la revolución verde. La agricultura atlántica, 1880–2000' (MINECO) (PID2020–112686GB-I00).
2   E. Langthaler, 'Massenmedien in der ländlichen Gesellschaft im Nationalsozialismus am Beispiel der Agrarpresse', *Zeitschrift für Agrargeschichte und Agrarsoziologie* 58 (2010), pp. 50–64; J. Eellend, 'Unity through Modernity: The Agrarian Media and the National Question in Estonia at the Turn of the Twentieth Century', *Nordost-Archiv. Zeitschrift für Regionalgeschichte* 18 (2009), pp. 25–43; C. César, 'Les metamorphoses des idéologues de l'agriculture biologique: la voix de *La Vie claire* (1946–1981)', in P. Cornu and J-L. Mayaud (eds), *Au nom de la terre. Agrarisme et agrariens en France et en Europe du 19e siècle à nos jours* (París, 2007), pp. 335–47; N. Woss, 'Un monde agricole insoumis: agriculture biologique et agrarisme à travers la revue *Nature et progrès* (1964–1974)', in Cornu and Mayaud, *Au nom de la terre*, pp. 349–60.

Galicia is situated in the north-west of the Iberian peninsula and is divided into four provinces (A Coruña, Lugo, Ourense and Pontevedra). It contained a little over 10 per cent of the total Spanish population in 1900. Its many peculiarities, including its language (kindred to Portuguese), was never acknowledged by the Spanish government or its legislation. Alienation from the Spanish state formed the basis for a political movement that sought autonomy (rather than separation) from the end of the nineteenth century onwards. It failed to attract much popular support until the 1930s.

The period under consideration – broadly the first half of the twentieth century – is important in many respects. It is marked by an explosion of local and, more specifically, agrarian periodicals in the context of a series of social transformations. In the first place, the rapidly declining illiteracy rates made the public receptive to published material: in 1887, barely 29 per cent of the Galician population knew how to read and write, compared to 35 per cent per cent in 1900, 43 per cent in 1910, 53 per cent in 1920 and 67 per cent in 1930.[3] This improvement came about as a result of efforts by the state and civil society, in particular remittances from emigrants living in the United States to help build schools and raise the educational level.[4] The rural population itself was eager to acquire reading and writing skills, as the mass transatlantic emigration required them to maintain family ties by letter, and because the written word had become a new tool in the advancement of social reproduction and rural development.

Second, the boom in periodicals went hand in hand with the gradual political socialization of the masses during the Bourbon Restoration (1874–1931), including the freedom of association (law of 1887) and the introduction of universal male suffrage (1890). Among the main issues of political and social debate during the first decades of the twentieth century were the abolition of the *foro* (a peculiar form of hereditary lease) and the deficiencies and corruption of government during the *Restauración*, the period between 1874 and 1923 when Spain was governed by a moderate liberal regime based on the alternation of liberal and conservative governments.[5]

3   The averages hide significant gender differences, namely much higher illiteracy figures among women: see C. E. Núñez, *La fuente de la riqueza. Educación y desarrollo económico en la España contemporánea* (Madrid, 1992).

4   X. M. Núñez Seixas, *Emigrantes, caciques e indianos* (Vigo, 1998); A. Costa Rico, *Historia da educación e da cultura en Galicia* (Sada, 2004). The link between migration and an improvement of the literacy rates is outlined in M. Lyons, *A History of Reading and Writing in the Western World* (Basingstoke, 2010), p. 180.

5   M. Cabo and A. Miguez Macho, 'Pisando la dudosa luz del día: el proceso de democratización en la Galicia rural de la Restauración', *Ayer* 89 (2013), pp. 43–65.

Third, the booming agrarian press reflected the expansion of the agrarian movement in Galicia, which was in line with the simultaneous associationist awakening in rural Spain in general. This movement relied on a variety of organizations that sought to improve the living conditions of rural people through education, cooperation, political consciousness-raising and protest (under different banners, ranging from Social Catholicism and Galician nationalism to Socialism and Anarchism). Interestingly, this rural-based associationism may have put the ruling elites of the Restoration in an awkward position, as some of their privileges (including the *foro*) were subject to fierce rural criticism. Earlier research revealed how the farmers' unions and their press played a mediating role between the local farming communities, the state and the markets (by buying inputs for agricultural production and selling their crop).[6]

The first part of the chapter presents the sources that have been used. The second part unravels the position and strategies of agrarian journalism in its efforts to connect with its target audience. The third section focuses on the bridging role of the press between farmers and experts. The last part of the chapter allows us to assess the major changes that took place in 1936, after the Second Republic was overthrown and replaced by the dictatorship of Franco, and to look at how regime change impacted on the agrarian journalism of the region.

Defining the agrarian press

In contrast to the main newspapers and scientific journals, the local press and the agrarian press in particular are often overlooked by historians, although they represent in themselves a valuable topic for research.[7] However, research into them is hampered by the institutional discontinuity of the publishers, who were often a political faction or an association, resulting in the loss of their memory and material legacy (correspondence, publications, etc.). Investigation is also not helped by the attitude of archival institutions and libraries, which have considered these publications to be ephemeral sources and unworthy of preservation. The result is that the researcher is destined to search for the surviving copies of periodicals scattered in many locations.

For the purpose of this chapter, a rather restrictive definition has been used that allows us to distinguish first of all the 'agrarian press' from local, political or working-class papers, despite the inevitable

6   M. Cabo, *O agrarismo* (Vigo, 1998); L. Fernández Prieto, *Labregos con ciencia. Estado e sociedade e innovación tecnolóxica na agricultura galega, 1850–1936* (Vigo, 1992).
7   Valuable, but not unproblematic, as discussed by M.-L. Legg, *Newspapers and Nationalism. The Irish Provincial Press, 1850–1892* (Dublin, 1999).

grey zone between them. Secondly, general newspapers have also been excluded, even those reporting frequently on questions regarding the rural economy or on the exploits of the agrarian movement, inevitably well-documented matters in many newspapers, given their importance at that time. Thirdly, agronomic and agro-technical bulletins are not included, nor the journals edited by the government and agronomist organizations or those published by commercial companies. Indeed, we have tried to distinguish between the more or less official 'agricultural press' and the 'agrarian press'. The former includes periodicals published in cities, all of them written in Spanish, issued directly or supported by public authorities (for instance, research centres), by semi-official bodies (such as the agricultural chambers) or professional organizations (of veterinarians or other agricultural experts), and often distributed for free. Although concealing a 'hidden agenda' aimed at driving agricultural interests towards a non-conflictive path based on the cooperative model, these periodicals mainly spread technical information, devoid of any social or political message.

Consequently, what has been taken into consideration for this chapter are the periodicals explicitly representing farmers' unions and federations of farmers' interests, those referring to agrarian issues and the agrarian movement, and those declaring the rural population to be their target audience, via their titles or subtitles. It is worth mentioning that the agrarian press often reprinted, summarized or paraphrased articles that were first published in agricultural journals, other periodicals or newspapers. Clear-cut dividing lines between the various types of journalism are, of course, in part artificial: the press constitutes a kind of loose and informal network on its own. The fact that a large part of the agrarian press was intimately linked to farmers' unions points at a second and much tighter form of connection.

With this definition of the 'agrarian press' in mind, our search for periodicals in Galicia managed to uncover 134 titles published between 1900 and the beginning of the Spanish Civil War (1936).[8] This chronological framework stretches from the launch in 1900 of the weekly magazine *El Campesino* in Lavadores, a village near the town of Vigo, up until the late 1930s when, in the wake of the military coup, the majority of the farmers' unions and agrarian federations were disbanded.

---

8   M. Cabo, *Prensa agraria en Galicia* (Ourense, 2002). Each periodical is described with its formal characteristics, chronological data, repositories of the periodical, contents, collaborators and ideological tendency.

Features and functions of Galician agrarian journalism before 1936

The 134 agrarian periodicals constitute a specific subspecies within the broader universe of the Galician press.[9] It is likely that many of the following statements are applicable to the agrarian press throughout Spain, despite the absence of studies that can confirm such with any certainty.[10] The position and influence of the Galician agrarian press in the web of knowledge transmission in the countryside cannot be measured by solely taking the number of relevant titles. Many questions then arise. We begin by considering the exterior features of the periodicals, ranging from their distribution through space and time, to their periodicity and readership, staff and (in)stability.

The geographical scope and distribution of the agrarian press give a first indication of its position in the region (Figure 8.1). The majority of the 134 papers in the selection were published in the two western provinces, namely Pontevedra (35.1 per cent) and A Coruña (29.1 per cent), which was in line with the demographic weight of these regions within Galicia, as well as with the early formation and high number of agrarian organizations there. The province of Lugo in the north-east contributed 14 per cent of agrarian periodicals with a predominantly social-Catholic stamp. The principal anomaly remains the low percentage of periodicals in the province of Ourense in the south-east (5.8 per cent). The remaining 16 per cent are papers that were published in Latin America or Madrid but aimed for distribution within Galicia. The under-representation of Ourense may be partially explained by the fact that the principal paper of the region was the daily *La Zarpa* (The Claw), established in its capital (the city of Ourense) in 1921, by the polemical priest and agrarian activist Basilio Álvarez (1877–1943) (Figure 8.2).[11] With a circulation of nearly 3,000 copies a day in a province with 412,000 inhabitants in 1920, and relying on a broad network of correspondents throughout the province, usually comprised of local union organizers and politicians from the opposition, this newspaper may have discouraged the emergence of other local agrarian periodicals.

In summary, the focus of the vast majority of papers was local or, at most, provincial. This fragmentation reflects both the organizational scattering of the agrarian movement, which never realized its dream of forming a federation to represent the whole of Galicia, and the electoral

9   Cf. the detailed presentation of each publication in Cabo, *Prensa agraria*.
10   With the partial exception of Y. Acosta Meneses, *La información agraria en España. Desde sus orígenes hasta la agenda 2000* (Madrid, 2007).
11   Álvarez became an MP of the Radical Republican Party in the Spanish Second Republic and died in exile in Tampa (Florida) among a strong Galician community of emigrants.

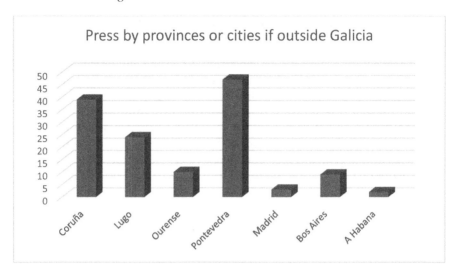

FIGURE 8.1 The agrarian press, number of titles by province or (if outside Galicia), city, 1900–1938. Source: Cabo, Prensa Agraria.

fragmentation of the region during the Restoration (until 1923), when Galicia was divided into 40 single-member districts for parliamentary elections (only A Coruña and Lugo were allowed to elect three deputies).

In terms of chronological evolution, the agrarian press quite reliably reflected both the progress and decline of the agrarian movement. The founding of agrarian periodicals progressed slowly, with ups and downs up until 1907. It took place against a backdrop of turbulence: the various projects aimed at the creation of Galician agrarian federations that all ultimately failed, the anger that accompanied the struggle to abolish the *foro* and the acquisition of full land ownership, and the success of the first Galician Agrarian Assembly in 1908 in Monforte, which served henceforth as a forum where the diverse elements within the agrarian movement, including those of the experts, could articulate their stand-points. Between 1908 and 1914, more farmers' unions and periodicals surfaced. During the First World War however, few new agrarian papers were launched, while many of those already in existence disappeared. This was a result of the repressive policies introduced by the authorities in their desire to suppress social and political unrest. The post-war years, from 1918 to 1923, by contrast, became the period of the greatest agrarian and journalistic activity, with a radicalization of the fight against the *foro* and the maximum expansion of the Catholic agrarian movement in response to the republicans and left-wing mobilization. The dictatorship

Figure 8.2 Advertisement of the agrarian daily *La Zarpa*, founded by Basilio Alvarez and published in Ourense between 1921 and 1936.

of Primo de Rivera (1923–1930) was a period of decline, both in terms of organizational and press activity, which was reversed during the Second Republic (1931–1936) when an acceleration in the political socialization of the population took place and an active political mass market arose. But the success of the military coup in Galician cities at the very beginning of the Spanish Civil War in 1936 put an abrupt end to both the agrarian movement and almost all its associated press.

What did the agrarian press, with all its ups and downs, offer to the inhabitants of rural Galicia? For 103 of the 134 papers we were able to determine the frequency of publication (Figure 8.3). Weekly publication was the most usual (44), followed closely by monthlies (30) and fortnightly editions (21). There were just two daily publications, both from Ourense and both connected to the charismatic priest Basilio Álvarez: *El Heraldo de Galicia* (1913), linked with the agrarian federation Acción Gallega (Galician Action), and *La Zarpa* (1921–1936).

However, the number of copies printed was generally modest. For the 30 papers prior to 1936 for which information is available, the average circulation came close to 2,000. However, this figure is skewed by a minority of papers, including *La Zarpa*, which printed 3,000 copies a day. The bulk of the agrarian press printed around 400 copies, as was the case for *El Agricultor* of Riotorto (1906–1916) in the province of Lugo. As a comparator, at the beginning of the 1920s the main Galician newspapers (*La Voz de Galicia* from A Coruña in the north and *Faro de Vigo* in the south) had a print run of some 15,000 copies a day. In short: the rather

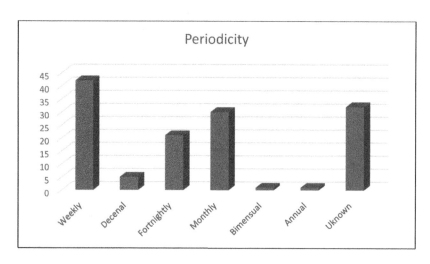

FIGURE 8.3 Periodicity of the agrarian periodicals, 1900–1936. Source: Cabo, Prensa Agraria.

modest frequency (half of the papers were fortnightly or monthly editions), the local scope, and the limited circulation of most papers demonstrate that the reach of the agrarian press as bearer of knowledge should not be overestimated.

There are also other features that put into perspective the relevance and durability of these publications. The staff who worked on them were seldom full-time journalists. The papers relied on part-time contributors, usually linked to agrarian organizations. They might be farmers, young lawyers or writers looking for prestige and to further their careers in politics or literature. The Galician agrarian press was miles behind the professionalism of agrarian journalism in the American Midwest, as observed by John J. Fry.[12]

The close connections between the Galician periodicals and the agrarian organizations that sponsored them contributed to their instability and precarious character. The papers were under constant threat, either by the vicissitudes (internal conflicts, political repression) of the organizations that funded them, by financial constraints, by reprisals by local power groups and pressure from different levels of the public administration or even from the Catholic Church. More often than not, rival papers launched by the monarchist party when it came to power locally were seen by the agrarian papers as a threat to their subscribership. These 'close enemies' would put all their energies into creating a polemic with 'the other', with the defeat of the agrarian paper being followed shortly after by the subsequent disappearance of its rival. The following comment in the newspaper *La Defensa* of Marín (Pontevedra) clearly summarizes some of the dangers threatening local and agrarian periodicals:

> One may constantly observe the disappearance of newspapers, victims of cacique oppression; or others founded to counteract their opponents, newspapers whose readers are bribed to 'change jackets', or others thrown out by caciques for failing to create a 'bombshell'; and if there ever were to exist a newspaper that sincerely defended the interests of the people, another would quickly emerge from the cacique world to steal subscribers in one clean swoop, forcing it to succumb.[13]

And this was not all: other forms of pressure on the agrarian press, because of its links with the agrarian social movement, included fines, the interception of postal applications for subscription, the harassment of the staff with complaints of slander, not to mention the cases of direct

---

12 John J. Fry, *The Farm Press, Reform and Rural Change, 1895–1920* (New York, 2005).
13 'La prensa y el cacique' (The press and the cacique), *La Defensa* 4 (1), Sept. 1914. By *'cacique'* we understand local political leaders who used their power for corrupt or partisan purposes such as electoral fraud, corruption, promoting friends to public positions and so on.

physical aggression and attacks on editorial premises. No wonder that over a third of the periodicals in this analysis did not survive their first year of publication, while more than two-thirds had failed within four years. Only a small number of papers lasted over a period of decades, thanks to the support of powerful Galician bodies or groupings of migrants, such as *El Emigrado* (A Estrada, 1920–1940), *El Noticiero del Avia* (Ribadavia, 1910–1936), *El Tea* (Ponteareas, 1908–1936), *La Comarca* (Ribadeo, 1919–to date), *La Voz de Ortigueira* (Ortigueira, 1916–to date) and *El Heraldo de Viveiro* (1912–to date). The newspapers that were able to survive were published in small Galician towns: centres of an electoral district with a significant market function and that provided their rural surroundings with information.[14]

It is important to consider the internal characteristics of the periodicals. Their *raison d'être* was to be found in their content, but their success was also indebted to the tactics they used to appeal to their readership. Content-wise, agricultural journalism in Galicia was far from an independent undertaking, but subordinated to the objectives of its driving forces. The contents of the papers were determined by the organizations and the ideologies they served, and their purpose was to popularize and defend the desired standpoints, converting each edition, in the words of Basilio Álvarez, into a 'daily meeting'. In other words: the press was not the centre of the organizational network, but its spokesperson. A large part of the four- or six-page issues covered the activities of the corresponding agrarian societies or federations: the renewal of their board of directors, reports on their meetings, cooperative activities and actions, the actions of their political enemies (mayors in particular were targets if they were not supportive), and so on. Often, they published news about the current situation in the region (interpreted in their own favourable way), as well as some news on international matters (the Moroccan Wars, Spanish and international current affairs, etc.). One or more sections in the paper was devoted to agriculture, offering practical advice on the cultivation of particular crops, cattle breeding or livestock health, and reproducing information on new technologies from specialized journals, etc. Sometimes, long texts and even entire books – about arable or livestock farming, leasehold legislation etc. – were published in serial form, which discouraged readers from buying single copies.[15]

---

14 These towns have been named *vilas* since the Middle Ages and can be found in all four provinces of Galicia and also in the north of Portugal (the Ancient Roman province of Gallaecia). G. Pereira Menaut and Ermelindo Portela Silva (eds), *El territorio en la historia de Galicia. Organización y control. Siglos I–XXI* (Santiago de Compostela, 2015).

15 The weekly *La Defensa* (Betanzos, 1906–1910) provides several examples of this formula and its potential applications.

The last one or two pages of the periodicals had a specific function: they offered diversion and publicity. Attracting advertising was fundamental for the economic survival of the periodical press, and the advertisements became simultaneously a crucial channel for the announcement and distribution of new farming tools and techniques.[16] The countless adverts on the back cover of the papers demonstrate the ongoing process of technological change, as well as the farmers' interest in modern practices.

Entertainment, for its part, may seem a restful diversion of little relevance: a rural novel, written in Galician and published serially, poetry, some jokes or cartoons. However, the importance of this component is not to be underestimated. The public had to be seduced into beginning to read, to read printed material in Galician and, if possible, in Spanish as well. This point needs some explanation. The intended readers of the agrarian press belonged to the peasantry and had been raised within an oral culture. Many farmers continued, during the first decades of the twentieth century, to rely on orally-transmitted knowledge and wisdom about their environment, farming and the outer world. As the nationalist journalist Antón Villar Ponte cleverly described, the true village newspaper was the one to which the inhabitants unconsciously related. There were

> publishers who thoroughly prepare an article. Then, there are others who specialize in the art of irony. There are those in charge of civil matters, reports of weddings, christenings and love stories [...]. Even world news has its journalists within these oral newspapers of the river banks and wells. News from America, above all, is daily exposed. Since, as you well know, there is practically no rural dwelling without family overseas. And now they even speak of the Moroccan War. For many, working arms were forced to abandon their hoes for rifles.[17]

Given this context, the agrarian press faced the challenge of bridging the gap between the oral culture and the written word. Other sorts of published material played the role of bridging two seemingly divergent traditions: almanacs and calendars for instance, and popular religious literature.[18] The blind journalist and writer, Valentín Lamas Carvajal (1849–1906), a defender of farmers' culture, became an important influencer in this aspect, opening doors to the written word and arousing

16   L. Fernández Prieto, *Labregos con ciencia*.
17   'Breviario de la aldea', *Galicia*, 11 June 1924.
18   This is also found in Austria: see E. Bruckmüller, *Landwirtschaftliche Organisationen und gesellschaftliche Modernisierung. Vereine, Genossenschaften und politische Mobilisierung der Landwirtschaft Österreichs vom Vormärz bis 1914* (Salzburg, 1977), p. 206; in the Netherlands, see J. C. Dekker, *Zuivelcoöperaties op de zandgronden in Noord-Brabant in Limburg, 1892–1950. Overleven door samenwerking en modernisiering. Een mentaliteitsstudie* (Middelburg, 1996), p. 508.

interest among the rural population. Lamas initiated the fortnightly *O Tío Marcos d'a Portela* (Ourense, 1876–1889) and published the booklet *Catecismo do Labrego* (1888), both in Galician. He criticized the Restoration because of the injustices caused by military service, taxes and *caciquismo*. And he paved the way in connecting with the rural population: *O Tío Marcos* had a circulation of 4,000 copies and *El Catecismo* ran to more than 20 editions. How did he achieve this? He wrote in the widely-spoken Galician language, used unorthodox channels of distribution (not only subscriptions, but also sales by vendors, at newspaper stands, in fairs and livestock markets), and adopted writing styles that referred to popular forms of expression and assisted collective reading. This practice is well documented, both orally as via the internal regulations of numerous agrarian societies: one literate member of a farmers' union would read the periodical aloud, to give the illiterate or hardly literate members access to the news and allow them to take part in the ensuing debate.[19]

Although Galician was the main language for over 90 per cent of the population, and for as good as 100 per cent of the rural population, the agrarian press was predominantly printed in Spanish.[20] This apparent contradiction is, firstly, due to the fact that Galician was not recognized as an official language before the 1980s and lacked a fixed vocabulary, spelling and grammar, which created a prejudice against its use for anything other than colloquial purposes. Socio-linguists call this a situation of *diglossia*, the coexistence of two languages with different social functions.[21] But, secondly, the use of Galician was more common in the agrarian press than in the general press and in the periodicals for the working class (as socialists and anarchists, with their internationalist objective and anti-agrarian prejudices, looked down on minority languages). Nevertheless, the use of Galician in the agrarian press was relegated to the last pages with their literary and humoristic contents, while the 'serious' matters (political news, technical articles, information about prices and markets, etc.) were always written in Castilian Spanish. This practice reinforced the gap between the official language, adapted to the needs of the modern world, and the regional language used in rural, informal contexts.

Taking this linguistic situation into account, the agrarian press employed a broad range of tactics to reach an audience that was still

---

19 Collective reading is a well-known practice, dating back to Ancient Roman times and enjoying a long tradition in many historical contexts, as analysed by A. Manguel, *A History of Reading* (London, 1996), p. 248.

20 There was only one agrarian periodical completely written in Galician, namely the fortnightly *O Tío Pepe* at A Fonsagrada (Lugo), published in 1913 to support the liberal PM and future president of the government (in 1935) Manuel Portela Valladares. He had strengthened his local following by creating a farmers' union and a rural bank.

21 H. Monteagudo, *Historia social da lingua galega* (Vigo, 1997).

generally unfamiliar with reading.[22] Or, in other words, the press adapted its outlook and style of writing to its intended readership. A first, visual tactic to attract readers consisted of the copious use of cartoons, images and, when they became economically viable, photographs. A second tactic consisted of the wrapping of current affairs into traditional Galician songs or poetry. A third one was to be found in the rhetorical style, often akin to the spoken language, with seemingly literal reproductions of common parlance, including exclamations and capital letters, direct appeals to the reader, and the like. Often, messages were phrased in the form of fictional dialogues, that is to say, conversations between two figures with opposed characteristics: an older and a younger man, an innovative farmer and a peasant reluctant to adopt new techniques, a villager tempted by left-wing ideas and a more conservative one, and so on. The desired posture was always advanced through confrontation: for instance, in breaching the widespread aversion to chemical fertilizers, for sustaining a political party, in criticizing the local authorities, warning against Protestant preachers, etc. Significantly, these dialogues were published in Galician to increase their credibility (it would be hard to imagine two peasants speaking Spanish to each other).[23]

A fourth tactic consisted of the use of *sueltos* (snippets), mottos or slogans, scattered over various pages, and aimed at bombarding readers with a simplified idea, one example being the slogan 'Farmers can't be socialists' that frequently appeared in the Catholic agrarian press. Fifth, the writers often tried to make their point via metaphors, religious metaphors for instance, as in the *Catecismo do labrego* by Lamas Carvajal. The agrarian press was saturated, and not solely in the Catholic periodicals, with a religious language that fitted perfectly with its moral-istic political ideas. Hence, speeches during meetings became 'prayers', campaigns were called 'crusades', splits in parties and political betrayals were compared to 'Judas', and agrarian leaders were labelled as 'apostles' or 'martyrs'.[24] The method had the advantage that even the illiterate were

---

22 These stylistic tactics coincided with the ones that were used in the British radical press in the first half of the nineteenth century: cf. for instance the Chartist weekly *The Northern Star* (1837–52); see D. Vincent, *Literacy and Popular Culture. England, 1750–1914* (Cambridge, 1993). Dekker (*Zuivelcoöperaties*, 508) mentions similar tactics used by the agrarian press in the two southern provinces of the Netherlands, in spite of the higher degree of literacy there in comparison to Galicia.

23 Mock dialogues to address the rural population were also common elsewhere, for instance in Austria: see Langthaler, 'Massenmedien', p. 62.

24 Italian socialist propaganda also reused religious language and symbols in the context of its proselytizing campaigns among the peasantry of northern and central Italy: see R. Zangheri, 'Contadini e politica nell'800. La storiografia italiana', in École française de Rome, *La politisation des campagnes au XIX siècle, France, Italie, Espagne et Portugal* (Rome, 2000), pp. 13–27.

familiar with this language, having heard it many times during Sunday sermons. Finally, the agrarian press (as well as speakers during meetings) sought to connect with the daily experiences of the rural population through the use of metaphors referring to farming: hostile politicians were branded as boars, foxes or other pests (and thus open to hunting), farmers' unions were compared to a flock of birds grouping together to protect itself against predators, vices among members of an association, such as selfishness or quarrelling, were compared to the tares in the cornfield, etc.

But such tactics were insufficient to remove the last obstacle to farmers buying periodicals: their price. Therefore, agrarian societies chose to support their papers. They offered their members reduced subscription prices, and collective subscriptions to their local branches. They recommended the collective reading of their contents. Many farmers' unions took up a subscription to more than one newspaper and journal, putting them at the disposal of their members within their premises. And it was far from unusual for provincial federations to force their local branches to purchase a fixed number of copies according to the size of their membership, as was the case of the Confederación Regional de Agricultores Gallegos (Regional Confederation of Galician Farmers), which in 1922 distributed copies among 122 local societies. In brief, the strategies that agrarian periodicals employed to survive and spread their message included a purposeful content, a well-considered format, low subscription rates, subsidies from agrarian unions and an income from advertisements. They were, thus, in many ways linked to and dependent on others.

The agrarian press and its contribution to technical change up to 1936

One of the important connections that echoed through the press were the links between the farmers' unions and the various kinds of experts (agronomists, veterinaries, technicians). Farmers and stock breeders mistrusted the experts, and vice versa.[25] The former considered the agricultural engineers to be too theoretical and condescending in their approach. Two other traits contributed to their lack of confidence: firstly, the experts were known as civil servants, and thus representatives of a state that imposed taxes and military duties without much in the way of compensation; and, second, most experts were born outside Galicia and unfamiliar with the peculiarities of Galicia, its language and its agriculture.[26] There was a single Central Agricultural Engineering College in Madrid, and Galician farmers rightly complained that its graduates did

[25] Fernández Prieto, *Labregos con ciencia.*
[26] The local networks of both monarchist parties (liberals and conservatives)

not understand their language, ignored the local names of plants and diseases, and had acquired a largely theoretical knowledge of farming in the drier regions and on large estates, none of it relevant to Galicia.[27] These prejudices applied to a lesser extent to the veterinaries, who were usually locals (Santiago had its own veterinary school between 1892 and 1924) and of a more socially modest origin than the agricultural (and forestry) engineers.[28] In 1900, an important change of direction took place when the new director of the A Coruña Regional Experimental Farm began to collaborate with the farmers in the region through a network of experiment stations.[29]

During the later nineteenth century, the efforts of the parochial clergy and the landed gentry to bridge the gap between modern science and actual farming practices had miserably failed: priests and nobility were not the best improvers. In the first decades of the twentieth century, experts began to accept that they were not the only ones with understanding of methods of cultivation, mechanization and cattle breeding, and that the farmers themselves could become key actors in the innovation process. However, in order to integrate the farmers into this process, they had to be organized. Farmers' unions therefore were welcomed as the prerequisite for a better understanding between *enlightened* and *practical* farming; that does not alter the fact that the experts never concealed their preference for unions that limited themselves to purely cooperative and technical collaboration, without political action and agitation around land-property issues. For the farmers, the agrarian unions offered an all-in path towards a more rewarding life: the fight against the *foro* to get full access to the land, technical improvements and better market conditions.[30]

How did the mutually beneficial collaboration between the experts and the unions take place? The latter were able to send samples of fertilizer to an official laboratory to detect imitations, they could ask experts to give lectures on issues that concerned their members, or they could deliver samples of insects or weeds to the Plant Disease Station (attached to the A Coruña Regional Experimental Farm from 1926) to identify pests and receive advice (at the same time helping the station to monitor the region with hundreds of samples every year). The collaboration also stimulated livestock shows, which allowed the demonstration of the most profitable

---

often offered access to technical advice as a means to attract voters through a system of clientelism.

[27] J. Pan-Montojo, *Apostolado, profesión y tecnología: una historia de los ingenieros agrónomos en España* (Torredolones, 2005); L. Fernández Prieto, *El apagón tecnológico del franquismo. Estado e innovación en la agricultura española del siglo XX* (Valencia, 2007).

[28] D. Conde, *Juan Rof Codina. Renovación na veterinaria e gandaría galega contemporánea* (Vigo, 2015).

[29] L. Fernández Prieto, *El apagón tecnológico del franquismo*.

[30] L. Fernández Prieto, *Labregos con ciencia*; Cabo, *O Agrarismo*.

breeds for the villagers. During the shows, discussions took place on the advantages and disadvantages of every breed, the importance of selecting the best bulls, which would then be kept by the farmers' union in order to improve their members' cattle. The shows, moreover, offered an opportunity for the unions to organize vaccinations and promote their cattle insurance service, efforts that were in line with the campaigns of the authorities to combat cattle diseases. There are many other examples of the close collaboration that took place.

The agrarian press, as part of the agrarian movement, had a clear role in the evolving mutual understanding between the experts and the farmers, namely as the disseminator and exponent of information. Research centres and agricultural stations published the results of their experiments with seeds, breeds, fertilizers and machinery, first in their bulletins or in specialized journals, and then their conclusions were republished by the agrarian unions in shorter, more accessible versions for their members. It was, incidentally, not unusual to include the table of contents of technical journals in the agrarian press. Articles in journals such as the *Boletín de la Granja Experimental* (1899–1904), brochures from the agronomic and veterinary services, the agricultural pages in the main newspapers and articles written by agronomists or vets were often reproduced in the agrarian press. The reprints were often accompanied by additional explanations in simple words; sometimes they were partly or fully translated into Galician. A remarkable example was the publication in 1913 in the fortnightly *O Tío Pepe* of a leaflet on meadows, written by the chief engineer of the provincial agricultural section and printed in Galician translation.[31]

After reading dozens of agrarian periodicals dating from the three first decades of the last century, it is easy to affirm a clear trend towards more articles concerning technical matters and innovations, although this trend is hard to quantify. During the 1910s, Basilio Álvarez personified the current suspicions against experts and technical improvements. They were seen to be diverting energy from the campaign over landownership and the demand by the farmers for full citizenship. This was an understandable fear, and not dissimilar to that of rural activists in Ireland who saw cooperatives as a stratagem of the so-called 'constructive Unionism' to tame Irish nationalism and rural unrest.[32] Typically, the press linked to Acción Gallega, the agrarian federation led by Álvarez between 1912 and 1916, published few technical articles. But just a few years later, the Confederación Regional de Agricultores Gallegos and its organ *La Zarpa*, both initiated and directed by Álvarez, started to pay assiduous attention to technical matters, and the staff of the provincial agricultural services

---

31 Juan de Eguileor, 'Los prados y el ganado', *O Tío Pepe*, 14, 20 Aug. 1913.
32 F. H. A. Aalen, 'Constructive Unionism and the Shaping of Rural Ireland, c.1880–1921', *Rural Hist.* 14 (1993), pp. 137–64.

became a regular contributor to *La Zarpa*. During the dictatorship of Primo de Rivera (1923–1930) this trend intensified because the regime did not allow political and electoral activities, whereas the favourable economic context encouraged the farmers' unions to strengthen their cooperative activities and technical support.

The experts for their part were aware of the opportunities offered by the press, and especially by the periodicals that were linked to the agrarian movement. Many developed a decades-long activity as specialized journalists. Juan Rof Codina (1874–1967), a Catalan veterinary, developed his career in Galicia and published over 3,000 articles.[33] The staff of the Plant Disease Station of A Coruña delivered around eight articles every year, while its director Pedro Urquijo (1901–1992) became a skilled photographer and enriched his science-popularizing activities with photos.[34] Javier Prado (1874–1942), the chief of the veterinarian services in the province of Ourense, was another prolific writer on rural matters.[35] He took advantage of his literary skills to communicate on vocational issues to a wider audience, for example by using the format of a poem in Galician to promote a cattle insurance association, or by using the dialogue formula to explain how to take care of farm animals (the characters being a well-fed cow versus a neglected one, or two hens, one raised outdoors and the other in a poultry house). Other well-known examples are Leopoldo Hernández Robredo (1864–1954), director of the A Coruña Regional Experimental Farm, and Cruz Gallástegui (1891–1960), founder of the Galician Biological Mission (Pontevedra), both the authors of dozens of articles in general newspapers.

The agrarian press after 1936

The military coup of 18 July 1936, and the repression that followed, caused the dismantlement of the agrarian movement. Not only were most of the leftist unions banned and their leaders fined, jailed or killed, local organizations, even when they had kept a low political profile, were suppressed. Simultaneously, countless agrarian periodicals ceased publication and many journalists were jailed, killed or forced into exile. Only the Catholic unions, most of the cattle insurance associations, a few organizations directly under the umbrella of right-wing local politicians and a handful of apolitical unions survived the move against the freedom of association. The Catholic unions had, in fact, decayed after having

33 L. Fernández Prieto, 'Estudio preliminar', in J. Rof Codina, *Reformas que se pueden implantar en Galicia para el progreso de la agricultura* (1913; annotated reprint, Sada, 1985).
34 M. Cabo Villaverde, *A Estación de Fitopatoloxía Agrícola da Coruña (1926–1951)* (Santiago de Compostela, 1999), p. 172.
35 M. Valcárcel (ed.), *Javier Prado 'Lameiro'. Obras completas* (Ourense, 1995).

reached their apex at the beginning of the 1920s, when they amounted to a third of the agrarian unions in Galicia. All of a sudden, rural Galicia lacked voluntary associations, and the expertise, know-how, material and cultural capital vanished into thin air in just a few fateful weeks in the summer of 1936. The new authorities rushed to destroy the associational network that had been patiently built up from the end of the nineteenth century. It took them almost a decade to implement their own Fascist alternative, the so-called Hermandades Sindicales de Labradores y Ganaderos (Brotherhoods of Farmers and Livestock Producers), launched in 1944. In between, the void was only partially filled by the Catholic unions, which managed to expand their role in Galician society during the Civil War and tried to monopolize the supply of meat to the national army.

The cessation of most agrarian periodicals was considered as 'collateral damage', resulting from the repression of the unions. Those that had their own printing press saw it confiscated and used henceforth by the Falangist party, which had tried to reverse its weak presence in Galicia prior to the war. This was part of the broader picture of dismantlement of the patrimony of the agrarian unions (premises, equipment, bank accounts, etc.) by the military and their civil supporters. Other press organs succumbed to the harsh conditions of the civil war (journalists drafted into the army, paper shortage, a climate of suspicion and of accusations). *Galicia Social Agraria*, a monthly edited in Mondoñedo (Lugo) and the main voice of the Catholic agrarian unions in the region, published its last edition in September 1936, after having enthusiastically welcomed the military coup and claimed some of the credit for Galicia remaining in the hands of the rebels. The real reason was simply that paper was in short supply and that the new authorities gave priority to other printed media. A few periodicals managed to survive by reinventing themselves as simple local papers, with a general content, just like any other.[36] During the three years of civil war, the only periodical on the scene worth carrying the label of the 'agrarian press' was the *Boletín de la Federación Católico-agraria de La Coruña*, a Catholic magazine that produced a single edition in 1938, arguing for a stronger role for the farmers in supplying the army and denouncing the commercial rivals of the Catholic unions as leftists and profiteers.

Even after having won the war in 1939, the Francoist dictatorship did not hasten to implement an alternative to the rural associations that had been dismantled. The first years of the regime were an interesting period from that point of view, because Catholics and Fascists (as well as other minor components of the coalition that sustained the regime) clashed

[36] That is how, for example, *La Voz de Ortigueira*, published weekly by a powerful agrarian federation in northern Coruña from 1916, managed to continue publication and still exists today, as does *La Comarca del Eo*, published in Ribadeo since 1919, linked as it is to an agrarian federation in north-east Lugo.

over the kind of associations that they would tolerate and, ultimately, over the nature of the regime itself. Catholics agreed with the repression of the leftist societies and of what they called, pejoratively, the *neutral* organizations, but they thought that they were entitled to retain their freedom of action due to their counter-revolutionary credentials and the complicity of the Catholic church with the *coup d'état* against the Second Republic. Hard-core Falangists, for their part, aimed at building a Fascist state, following the German and Italian models (Franco's allies during the Civil War), in which every single organization should be controlled by and placed at the service of the state. The outcome was that Catholic unions were tolerated under the guise of cooperatives, in accordance with the new law of 1942, which formally subordinated them to the only, in theory, kind of agrarian organization allowed to represent farmers thenceforth: the *Hermandades Sindicales de Labradores y Campesinos.*[37]

The trend in Galicia under the Franco regime was towards merging what we have previously called *agricultural* (or technical) journals and *agrarian* periodicals, now the voice of the *Hermandades* (Brotherhoods). In 1945, the first periodicals of the *Hermandades* in Galicia came out, entitled *Agro* (for the province of Pontevedra) and *Campiña* (for A Coruña), and later *Surco* (Ourense). Their characteristics differed substantially from the pre-war agrarian publications. To begin with, they were official publications and subject to the authoritarian regime, lacking the spontaneity and vitality of their pre-1936 ancestors. Their sphere of influence was the whole province, while before the Civil War most agrarian periodicals were local. Their print run amounted to thousands of copies (7,000 for *Agro* in 1945, 34,000 for *Campiña* in 1948), thanks to the financial support by the state and the free delivery via the network of the state-led unions. But, in accordance with the discrimination against all languages other than Spanish (identified with patriotism), Galician was absent in the *Hermandades* press, or at best confined to folk tales, poetry and humour, underscoring in this way the prejudice against Galician as a language unfit for science and modern communication.

Nevertheless, this press of the later 1940s and 1950s, published by the Francoist agrarian institutions, showed at first sight significant similarities to that of the pre-war period, mixing a romantic ruralist rhetoric with technical articles and information regarding the activities of the *Hermandades*, and explanations about governmental policy regarding rationing, agriculture, forestry and the like. However, in hindsight, the reality was quite different: the contents were produced by bureaucrats linked to the dictatorship and the voice of farmers and local activists was absent. Although now and then hints of criticism appeared, regarding

[37] D. Lanero, *Historia dun ermo asociativo. Labregos, sindicatos verticais e políticas agrarias en Galicia baixo o franquismo* (Santa Comba, 2011).

a specific political measure for instance, as well as traces of quarrels between factions within the heterogeneous alliance behind Francoism, the final objective of this press was to secure the passive support of the rural population for a regime in a quite precarious situation and isolated internationally (until the pact with the United States at the beginning of the 1950s). Finally, the organizational structure, the *Hermandades,* did not play at all the role that the pre-war farmers' unions had fulfilled. Recent studies demonstrate that they were distrusted by the rural population and seen as corrupt bodies, imposed on farmers from above, and accomplices of the forced levies on cereals and livestock.[38]

Consequently, the *Hermandades* press did not function as the link, as the meeting-point, between the needs of the farmers and the knowledge of experts, as the agrarian press had done before the war. The chain was broken because the *Hermandades,* although the only permitted form of farmers' association during Francoism (apart from some cooperatives with Catholic roots that were formally subordinated to them), did not engender the same cooperative attitude and willingness to implement technical improvements. The farmers did not consider them as tools to their own benefit, but as instruments of a state that was more alien and ruthless towards them than any of its predecessors. Inevitably, the regime made all the mistakes typical of policies imposed from above that Scott summarized under the name *high modernism.*[39] Farmers were unable to make their voices heard, nor have their local situation, knowledge, needs and complaints acknowledged and taken into account.

In the second half of the 1950s, the Spanish autarchic policy, inspired as it were by the former Axis powers, made way for a process of relative liberalization of agricultural production along the lines of the United States and its Agricultural Extension Service. Two new periodicals showed that something was changing in Galicia: *Galicia Avícola y Ganadera* (1954, for poultry and cattle breeders) and *Cooperativismo* (1966). Both used a far less ruralist rhetoric than the above-mentioned *Hermandades* press. They were supported by the more or less autonomous cooperatives (with Catholic roots) and displayed a business-like, profit-maximizing mentality, announcing a world in which farming and cattle breeding were a just profession, like any other, and not a way of life or the purest expression of the national virtues, as was the case in previous discourse.

---

[38] An updated overview in A. Cabana and A. Díaz-Geada, 'Exploring Modernization: Agrarian Fascism in Rural Spain, 1936–1951', in L. Fernández Prieto *et al.* (eds), *Agriculture in the Age of Fascism. Authoritarian Technocracy and Rural Modernization, 1922–1945* (Turnhout, 2014), pp. 189–218.

[39] J. C. Scott, *Seeing Like a State. How Certain Schemes to Improve the Human Condition Have Failed* (New Haven, CT, 1998).

Conclusions

All media occupy by nature an intermediate position between the senders and the receivers of information. Their descriptive, discursive and suggestive contents shape and confirm practices, opinions and emotions. This applies to the agrarian press in Galicia as well, as will be elaborated in a few concluding points.

The most obvious function of the agrarian press, before and also partly after 1936, is to be found in its bridging position between the local farmers, their unions, the state, and the agricultural and veterinary experts (with their more specialized agricultural press). The agrarian press served as a unique and most welcome channel to popularize new inputs (fertilizer, seeds, breeds, tools, etc.), farming methods and techniques. In short, the experts produced, within their state-funded institutions, science-based solutions to specific problems, the unions selected the published results that were considered to be useful to their members and the press reprinted and rephrased them, often complemented by explanations in simpler terms and advice for their application in a particular area. The farmers, for their part, made choices and redirected their requests and complaints to the unions. This circular system of knowledge transmission, through and around the press, helped to decrease the initial mistrust between the experts, the unions and the farmers and the system, based as it was on mutual dependencies that proved rewarding for all sides. But its strength was also its weakness: as soon as one link in the chain broke, being the dismantlement of the unions by the Civil War and the Franco regime, the fruitful avenues of the pre-war decades came to an end.

But there was more. The agrarian press contributed to the transformation and identity-building of Galicia. It played a role in the consolidation of the new political culture, characterized as it were by a greater mobilization of voters and a critical assessment of the behaviour of the politicians (accountability). The press summarized council meetings, analysed budgets and the distribution of local taxes, debated public works, etc. As was the case in Belgium, there was a marked correlation between the advance of the agrarian press and universal suffrage.[40] One could say that the press stole politics from the hands of a small ruling elite and launched it into the public eye. In this sense, the agrarian press helped to redefine the function of the journalist, not as the mere transmitter of facts and figures, but also as a whistle-blower, revealing the injustices of society, taking sides for a cause, participating in meetings and campaigns, etc.

---

[40] L. Van Molle, 'A State for the Peasants or the Peasants for the State? The Two Faces of Belgian Agricultural Policy, 1830–1914', in: N. Vivier (ed.), *The State and Rural Societies. Policy and Education in Europe 1750–2000* (Turnhout, 2007), pp. 159–76.

Hence, an alternative route into a political career was created for young people from the middle classes, or even from the peasantry.

The agrarian press contributed moreover to the construction of solidarities within the rural community and to the identity of the agrarian movement. During decades, if not centuries, the rural population had been undervalued and disregarded, but the establishment of unions and cooperatives, and the creation of the agrarian press, gave it a new self-image and a role in society. But this process involved ideological discord as well: the Catholic unions insisted on the farmers' role as the guardians of social stability and traditions, the Socialists on their shared interests with the industrial proletariat, the nationalists on their essence as the guardians of the authentic Galician culture.

In France, as Eugen Weber argued in his celebrated book *Peasants into Frenchmen*, the press tended to relegate local matters to the background, focusing on Paris, high politics and high society.[41] By doing so, the press, including the agrarian press, played a univocal role as a vehicle for the integration of all into the nation as an 'imagined community' and the basis of French nationalism, according to Benedict Anderson. This was not the case in Spain.[42] On the contrary, in Galicia the Madrid press seldom reached the countryside, and if the local and agrarian press made an effort to inform its readers on broader realities (reproducing articles from Spanish and the foreign press about the prices on international markets, legislation, etc.), it did so from a point of view that related the matter once more to the local situation. Moreover, the extra-local dimension in the Galician agrarian press did not come solely from Madrid, but from the Americas as well. A large part of the news, the collaborations, finances and subscriptions came from Hispano-American countries, thanks to the links with associations of emigrants. During the dictatorship of Primo, for example, the press published articles that unfavourably compared the political situation in Spain with that in Uruguay or Argentina, where thousands of people from Galicia experienced at first-hand the blessing of free elections, the right to strike and some social rights. In summary, in Galicia the local and agrarian press became more an expression of regional peculiarities than a force for homogenization.

---

[41] E. Weber, *Peasants into Frenchmen* (Stanford, CA, 1992); N. Fitch, 'Mass Culture, Mass Parliamentary Politics, and Modern Antisemitism: The Dreyfus Affair in Rural France', *American Historical Rev.* 97 (1992), pp. 55–95; M. Lyons, 'What did the Peasants Read? Written and Printed Culture in Rural France, 1815–1914', *European History Q.* 27 (1997), pp. 165–97.

[42] For a reflection on the relevance of this debate for the Galician case, see M. Cabo, 'Quelle nation dans les campagnes? État et nation-building en Espagne, un débat ouvert', in J.-L. Mayaud and R. Lutz (eds), *Histoire de l'Europe rurale contemporaine. Du village à l'État* (Paris, 2006), pp. 222–48.

9

Farmers Facing a Body of Expertise: the Activities and Methods of the Departmental Services for Agriculture in Oise (France), 1945–1955

Laurent Herment

During the latter half of the eighteenth and throughout the nineteenth century, agricultural knowledge made major advances in France. Many leading thinkers, such as Quesnay (1694–1774) and Turgot (1727–1781) in economics, or Lavoisier (1743–1794) and Boussingault (1802–1887) in chemistry, were involved in these advances and helped agriculture move forward. But scientific knowledge of this kind was not easily passed down to the French peasantry. The structure of French agriculture, with its millions of small or micro-farms, made it hard to transmit knowledge on a broad scale. So while the scientific knowledge networks of the 'enlightened' period around 1800 are quite well known,[1] the process by which scientific knowledge was transmitted to farmers, particularly to the innumerable small and micro-farmers, has been uncovered only in part.[2]

Few historians have given attention to the process of knowledge transmission. For them, and particularly with regards to France, there

---

[1]   P. M. Jones, *Agricultural Enlightenment. Knowledge, Technology, and Nature* (Oxford, 2016).

[2]   A. Bourde, *Agronomie et agronomes en France au XVIIIe siècle* (Paris, 1967); F. Reynaud, *L'élevage bovin. De l'agronomie au paysan (1700–1850)* (Rennes, 2010); N. Jas, *Au carrefour de la chimie et de l'agriculture. Les sciences agronomiques en France et en Allemagne, 1840–1914* (Paris, 2000). For a rare example of the level of knowledge of a small farmer in nineteenth-century France, see L. Herment, 'Julien Gabriel Sugy's agrarian knowledge', Rural History 2013, working paper, http://www.ruralhistory2013.org/papers/10.1.2._Herment. pdf.

were two preferential research topics. One was the careful study of the dominant scientific body, the Institut des Recherches Agronomiques (IRA), later called the Institut National des Recherches Agronomiques (INRA), as in the edited volume by Bonneuil, Denis and Mayaud.[3] The other topic appears in publications by Muller and other sociologists.[4] Muller gave a detailed account of the workings of the Departmental Agricultural Services (Services Départementaux de l'Agriculture) and the role of the agricultural engineers who headed these services (Directeurs des Services Agricoles). But his focus was mainly institutional and on the experts at the top. Conversely, Brunier presented an analysis of the activities of local advisers.[5] With this exception, no one has examined the spread of knowledge among French farmers in the course of the twentieth century. If the transmission of information has been dealt with at all, it was often from a limited viewpoint: the history of a particular scientific organization or of a state service, or of publicity to promote plants, seeds, fertilizers, pesticides, and the like. It is the farmers who are often absent from the historical accounts of the 'agricultural revolution' after the Second World War. Consequently, it is hard to see where they fitted into this revolution; they often seem outsiders to the process.[6]

This chapter aims to prove that the collective and individual agency of farmers in the transmission of scientific knowledge was important, not because they were at the centre of the knowledge system, but because they faced a mass of scientific, administrative, commercial, industrial, and other information with which it was difficult to come to grips. Moreover, this multi-expertise frame, surrounding the farmers, was not simply a top-down diffusion of popularized knowledge. Farmers were not passive subjects but managed to contribute to the process of defining the choice of products and practices that were characteristic of this revolution.[7]

At the end of the Second World War, French planners had great ambitions for French agriculture. They wanted France to become a major exporter of strategic staple foods, especially wheat, barley, beet sugar

3   C. Bonneuil, G. Denis and J.-L. Mayaud (eds), *Sciences, chercheurs et agriculture. Pour une histoire de la recherche agronomique* (Paris, 2008).

4   P. Muller, *Le technocrate et le paysan. Les lois d'orientation agricole de 1960–1962 et la modernisation de l'agriculture française, 1945–1984* (Paris, 1984).

5   S. Brunier, 'Conseillers et conseillères agricoles en France (1945–1983). L'amour du progrès aux temps de la 'révolution silencieuse' (Ph.D. thesis, Université de Grenoble, 2012); S. Brunier, *Le bonheur dans la modernité. Conseillers agricoles et agriculteurs (1945–1985)* (Lyon, 2018).

6   This last remark refers to historical studies. It does not apply to the work of numerous sociologists of the INRA, who integrated the perspective of farmers, but without using historical methods and focusing only on the most recent period. For the position of the peasantry, see P. Bourdieu, 'Une classe objet', *Actes de la recherche en sciences sociales* 17 (1977), pp. 2–5.

7   The question of the benefits to the farmer is beyond the scope of this chapter.

and, in the long run, maize (for animal feed). They also hoped to reduce the dependency on imported oil seeds and to improve the quality of other staples such as milk, meat, fruit, vegetables, and the like.[8]

To achieve these goals, they developed plans for a rapid modernization of French agriculture. This process had to follow various important paths: mechanization, the use of fertilizers and pesticides, selected seeds and farm animals, and the rearrangement of the rural landscape by reclamation (*défrichement*) and reallocation of land (*remembrement*). The outcome would be a raised standard of living for the French peasantry. But beyond these goals, there was another challenge: the modernization of agriculture through the modernization of men. Though France took pride in its very efficient agricultural research institution (the INRA), the country was extremely backward in popularizing agricultural knowledge. In the words of a 1953 report, the situation was dramatic in the English sense of the word, but also in the French meaning, that is to say, tragic: 'There is one extension agent for 240 farms in the Netherlands, 360 farms in Denmark, 2,700 farms in Italy, and 6,000 in France'.[9] Both for financial and political reasons – shortage of money, competition among firms and professional organizations – the channels for spreading agricultural knowledge were poorly developed in France.

The only available agent for popularization were the offices of the French Ministry of Agriculture at the level of the *département*. These services were presided over by an agricultural engineer, the Director of the Departmental Services for Agriculture (Directeurs des Services Agricoles, henceforth DDSA), supervising a small but diligent group of people. Until the late 1940s, and in some cases the later 1950s, the DDSAs were at the head of knowledge networks that allowed the gradual improvement of French agriculture.

The archives of the DDSA in the *department* of Oise, a Mr J. Guillemot, contain a very useful body of documentation that offers insights into the problems of modernizing French agriculture during the post-war period, in particular in the 1950s. Hübscher has already used these archives to examine the characteristics of Belgian farmers who settled in this *departement*, as I did too for research on the introduction of tractors in French agriculture.[10]

---

8   L. Herment, 'Tractorization. France, 1946–1955', in C. Martiin, J. Pan-Montojo and P. Brassley (eds), *Agriculture in Capitalist Europe, 1945–1960. From Food Shortages to Food Surplusses* (London, 2016), pp. 185–205.

9   Archives départementales de l'Oise (henceforth AD60), 515W/7019: note, 5 Oct. 1953. 'Présidence du conseil. Commissariat général du plan. Commissions de la Production Agricole et de l'Equipement Rural. Résumé du rapport général des commissions de la production agricole et de l'équipement rural'.

10 R. Hübscher, *L'immigration dans les campagnes françaises : XIXe–XXe siècle* (Paris, 2005) 190. Herment, 'Tractorization'.

The Oise was one of the more commercially-advanced parts of France. It is located in the north of the Paris Basin (see Map 9.1). The large farms in the south and east of the *departement* specialized in valuable crops such as sugar beet, wheat, rapeseed, etc. of the sort then being encouraged by French economic planning. Conversely, the small farms in the north-east of the *departement*, at the fringe of Lower-Normandy, focused on dairy.

The archive includes Guillemot's correspondence as Oise director extending over a decade, an outstanding source that sheds light on the day-to-day concerns of a DDSA in charge of the agricultural policy in a wealthy agricultural *departement*. The correspondence is unfortunately incomplete, consisting only of the DDSA's outgoing letters but, in spite of the absence of incoming replies, it does reveal the reasons for his correspondence. Unlike the practice in scientific correspondence, the DDSA exchanged letters with all sorts of people: with the Ministry of Agriculture, the INRA and foreign scientists, but also with cooperatives, farmers' unions (*syndicats agricoles*), firms, and very often with farmers. As we shall see, analysing this correspondence helps to understand the farmers' concerns and to identify the important actors in the network with whom they were directly or indirectly connected. The correspondence reveals that farmers were confronted with more than one sort of knowledge and expertise: they had to deal with a mass of information. It shows how acquiring knowledge was not a single or one-way process, but rather it was embedded in a complex and multidirectional network.[11]

The first section of this chapter describes, very briefly, the history of the Departmental Services for Agriculture and the post-war role of the DDSA in the Oise *departement*. The second analyses the correspondence of the director over a two-month period, from 10 May to 7 July 1950, which represents a total of 428 letters.[12] This section will demonstrate that the network of the DDSA was quite far-flung, and that the DDSA maintained a very active correspondence with farmers in his *département*.[13] In the third part, I will detail the various means the DDSA used to improve agricultural practices, including networking. The following section examines in more detail his correspondence with farmers, especially regarding the

---

11 Since the incoming letters are missing, it remains unclear whether the whole correspondence has been preserved. However, Guillemot seems to have been diligent in replying to his many letters.

12 As this figure proves, the DDSA answered several letters a day. Some outgoing letters are missing because they were classified separately in thematic files. It is impossible to determine the exact number of contacts or letters: the same letter could have been sent to several contacts and the number of contacts remains sometimes unclear. All identifiable contacts have been cited here.

13 AD60, 515W/10671. All the letters mentioned in this chapter belong to the same file. This chapter analyses a total of 428 letters, reports and administrative documents sent out by the DDSA between 10 May and 6 July 1950.

question of pesticides.[14] The final part goes deeper into the structure of the DDSA's network. This analysis allows us to distinguish two levels of knowledge, intended for two different types of farmers. In line with the introduction of this book, it also allows us to delineate more than one knowledge (sub-)network and determine the place of the director and the farmers within them.

The Departmental Services for Agriculture

Between the last quarter of the nineteenth century and the Second World War, the French Ministry of Agriculture created a number of institutions for developing agriculture. French historians have focused on the most important and famous of them: the IRA, renamed the INRA after the Second World War. They have paid much less attention to another institution devoted to agricultural improvement: the Departmental Agricultural Services. These decentralized institutions were created by the law of 16 June 1879, which appointed *professeurs départementaux d'agriculture* to each *departement*.[15] Their original purpose was to educate future school teachers in teacher-training colleges and, if necessary, to provide lectures for the instruction of farmers and schoolmasters (art. 6). A new law, of 21 August 1912, profoundly transformed the role of the institution. Its first article stated:

> There shall be established in every Department, a Service for Agriculture, to replace the Departmental Chair for Agriculture as established by the law of 16 June 1879 [... its responsibility] shall include: the diffusion of agricultural knowledge; agricultural teaching in the schools listed in ministerial decrees; the promotion of the economic and social cause of agriculture, of mutual insurances in agriculture[16] and of rural hygiene;

---

14   Rachel Carson's book, *Silent Spring*, published in 1962, marked the beginning of concerns about the massive use of organic pesticides. Environmental historians and historians of science have studied the effects of these new types of pesticide. Recent research allows their impact to be placed in perspective and emphasises that Carson's book conceals the unequal effects, both socially and racially, of the use of pesticides in the United States. See C. Montrie, *The Myth of Silent Spring. Rethinking the Origins of American Environmentalism* (Berkeley, CA, 2018). For France: N. Jas, 'Public Health and Pesticide Regulation in France after *Silent Spring*', *History and Technology* 23 (2007), pp. 369–88; N. Jas, 'Pesticides et santé des travailleurs agricoles en France. Questions anciennes et nouveaux enjeux', *Courrier de l'environnement de L'INRA* 59 (October 2010), pp. 47–59 (https://hal.archives-ouvertes.fr/hal-01196933/file/C59Jas.pdf); J.-N. Jouzel, *Pesticides. Comment ignorer ce que l'on sait* (Paris, 2019).
15   France had 87 *départements* in 1879.
16   This refers to various forms of insurance, such as fire and hail insurance, accident insurance for rural workers and old age pensions. See C. Gide, *Les Associations Coopératives Agricoles. Cours sur la Coopération au Collège de France.*

agricultural information, statistics and food supply; supervision of experimental fields; research and technical projects, and in general every service pertaining to agriculture.

At first glance, it may appear that the DDSA was given a universal responsibility, but the last paragraph of the same article added that 'The Veterinary and Forestry services and the agronomical stations are not included in the remits [of the DDSA]'.[17] Even after the enactment of the law, other institutions continued to spread agricultural knowledge within the French *departements*, but the Services départementaux de l'agriculture, directed as they were by agricultural engineers, became central to the knowledge and extension system for several reasons.

Firstly, the chief engineer worked directly under the Ministry of Agriculture's authority (art. 9 of the 1912 law). Second, he was charged with promoting accident insurances and old age pensions for farm workers, and by doing so he was in regular contact with the farming elite. Third, he was responsible for collecting statistics, and was thus well informed about the state of agriculture in his district. He also had to carry out economic surveys, in which a requirement was to take note of the profitability of crops, cattle breeding etc. Finally, through their teaching function, his services reached a great number of farmers. For all these reasons he was – unlike the central administration – to some degree in a position to organize and implement, at the departmental level, the agricultural policy of the French state.

From the end of the Second World War onwards, the DDSA became a key actor in the 'modernization' of French agriculture.[18] The authorities aimed, while continuing to feed the French population, to modernize French agriculture by reorienting it towards export crops such as wheat, sugar beet, barley and the like, to increase the domestic production of otherwise imported crops, such as rapeseed or maize, and, finally, to improve the quality of milk. However, at the same time it was necessary to maintain the equilibrium within French rural society. From these points of view, the *departement* of Oise was especially important. It was one of the biggest producers of sugar beet and wheat, and the western part of the *departement* provided milk for Paris. It was, moreover, one of the most advanced and mechanized agricultural areas of France, where

---

Décembre 1924–Mars 1925 (Paris, 1925). For accident insurance from the late nineteenth century onwards: Cl.-E. Michard, 'Les accidents, fléaux méconnus en agriculture. De la solidarité facultative à la solidarité obligatoire: pour une histoire sociale du monde agricole', *Ruralia* 14 (2004), http://journals. openedition.org/ruralia/966.

17 *Bulletin des lois de la République française* (1912), pp. 2455–6.

18 P. Muller, *Le technocrate*. For this modernization process and the role of advisers, Brunier, *Conseillers et conseillères*.

the adoption of the tractor had gone furthest, though change had come at a social cost. In the Oise, the number of farms shrank from 22,600 in 1929 to 8,700 in 1955 (−62 per cent); for the whole of France, the figures were 3,966,430 in 1929, and 2,267,701 in 1955 (−43 per cent). In the Oise, more than in any other *departement*, small farms disappeared rapidly between these two dates.

Nevertheless, even in *departement* as advanced as the Oise, French planners made use of a range of modernization strategies. One of the most important, and least costly[19], was the diffusion of knowledge. When Guillemot, sent the Ministry of Agriculture a plan to popularize the cultivation of the potato, he pointed out that there were two levels of knowledge:

The Oise is a Department dominated by high yields and advanced agriculture, where farmers are up to date with technical improvements and innovations in the various sectors of agricultural production. Accordingly, they always attend technical demonstrations, so long as they provide updates of scientific research rather than mere popularization. In fact, as far as popularization is concerned, the farming elite sets an example for others, and the work of popularization should concentrate on lectures and visits to farms that can be used as models.[20]

Thus, the efforts to spread knowledge should, firstly, give the more dynamic French farmers access to scientific knowledge to improve their profitability and, second, they should popularize that knowledge to help the bulk of farmers adapt to the new agricultural pattern and adopt best practices. This means that the Departmental Services simultaneously had to activate their scientific network and to advertise good farming practices. It is clear that these efforts could only succeed if the services, and especially their directors, had a very good knowledge of all agricultural issues within their *departement*, and could mobilize their expert network to give shape to their actions.[21]

---

[19] With the exception of the establishment of the INRA, French planners were reluctant to invest much in the modernization of agriculture. A large part of the agricultural budget served for the stabilization of prices: A. Chatriot, *La politique du blé. Crises et regulation d'un marché dans la France de l'entre-deux-guerres* (Paris, 2016); A. Chatriot, F. Conord and E. Lynch (eds), *Orienter et réguler les marchés agricoles: entre pilotage national et politique agricole commune. Des années 1960 au début des années 1980* (Paris, 2018).

[20] AD60, 515W/10671; DDSA to the Ministry, reply to a circular concerning the 'Programme d'action 'Pommes de terre', Campagne 1950/51.

[21] In December 1950, the services in Oise employed four engineers, two technicians, three teachers, and five administrative workers. AD60, 515W/10657.

The correspondence of the DDSA, from May to July 1950

While analysing the DDSA's correspondence, we can follow the efforts he took in reaching his goals, as well as identifying the networks he mobilized for this purpose. Firstly, we will address the connections of the DDSA with farmers, similar services in other *departements*, other services of the state, cooperatives, syndicates, etc., for the whole of France. Map 9.1 reveals the destinations of the letters and reports (428 documents in total) sent by the DDSA between 10 May and 7 July 1950, by *departement*. I have chosen this period for two reasons. Firstly, in 1950, the years of harsh post-war rationing had come to an end; the correspondence of 1950 thus allows us to examine the efforts of the administration in the early stages of the developing agricultural revolution. Secondly, springtime was a very busy season for farmers, during which they experimented with new material, specifically new pesticides, with or without the help of scientists, as we will see.

Attention needs to be drawn to three points. For obvious administrative reasons, the *departement* of the Oise was the main destination of the letters and documents (242). The DDSA, playing the key role here, was obliged to exchange letters with all the services of the French state

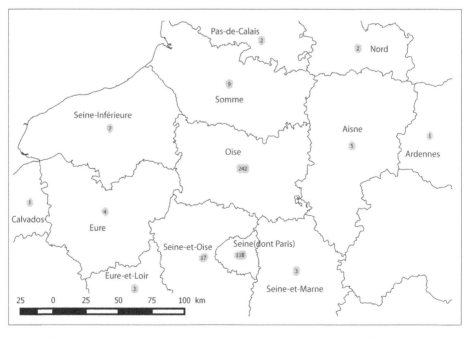

MAP 9.1 Letters and reports sent by the DDSA, number per *departement*.

in the *departement*. The second most important destination was Paris, and more particularly the Ministry of Agriculture and those experts who were able to give advice (118). The third most important destination was the *departement* of Seine-et-Oise (17) where the INRA and the École nationale d'Agriculture of Grignon, for the education of agricultural engineers, were located (near Versailles).

The DDSA of Oise of course also corresponded with DDSAs in geographically neighbouring and agriculturally similar *departements*: the Somme, Aisne, Seine-et-Oise (the present-day *departements* of Val-d'Oise, Yvelines and Essonne), Seine-et-Marne, Eure and Seine-Inférieure (now Seine-Maritime), and with more distant *departements* with a comparable agriculture.

Moreover, the DDSA was in contact with foreign countries. One letter was addressed to a Belgian farmer, and several letters were sent to the Netherlands. One of these is very interesting: it was a request to the 'Commission Gouvernementale pour l'Établissement de la liste des variétés de plantes de grande culture', at Wageningen University, asking for a list of the varieties of plants for field crops (potatoes, flax, peas, and so forth).[22]

If we analyse the DDSA's correspondence within the *departement* of the Oise, we can identify the location of the farmers with whom he was in touch (see Map 9.2). This correspondence covers nearly the whole *departement*, but the south-east (Valois et Multien) and south-west (Vexin Français), where few farmers lived, were over-represented. Conversely, the DDSA had fewer contacts in the north-west of his *departement*, a milk-producing area with more than a thousand dairy farmers and cattle-breeders.[23]

The District Services for Agriculture were supposed to have a thorough knowledge of the farming practices and highly diverse produce of their *departement*. The *Rapport sur la mise en œuvre du plan Monnet dans l'Oise*, written at the beginning of 1951, in which the DDSA discusses the

---

22 AD60, 515W/10671, 7 June 1950. 'Would you be so kind as to send me the pamphlets that you have published in French with descriptive lists of varieties of plants for field crops (potatoes, flax, peas, etc.). Thank you in advance for any documentation you can send me. If there are costs involved in sending them, would you be so kind as to inform me and indicate how I can settle them?'. The letter shows how impressed the French authorities were by the performance of Dutch agriculture and how they valued the expertise of Wageningen.

23 In Valois, Multien and Vexin, and to a lesser extend in Soissonnais – all areas devoted to wheat, barley and sugar beet cultivation – a few dozen farmers controlled the major part of the land. In the Valois, farms of over 100 ha covered 80 per cent of the arable land, whereas in the Pays de Bray where dairy and cattle breeding dominated, farms of over 100 ha represented less than 10 per cent of the agricultural surface.

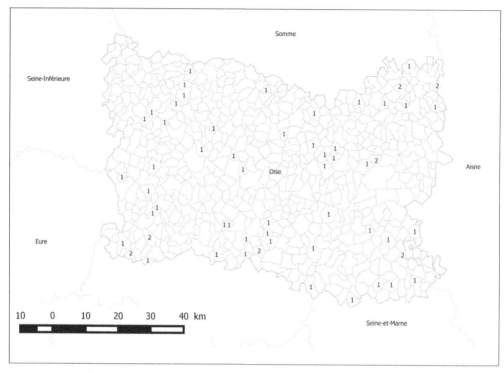

MAP 9.2 Correspondence with farmers located in the *departement* of the Oise.

agriculture of the *departement* and its various specializations in considerable detail, shows that he and his staff knew their territory.[24] The analysis of the correspondence over a two-month period allows us to come to the conclusion that the DDSA did indeed act as a disseminator of knowledge and influenced farming practices. The range of his contacts enables us to identify the links in the network in which he played an influential role. Moreover, his correspondence uncovers the extent of the body of specialized knowledge with which farmers were confronted with and how they reacted to it.

Dissemination of knowledge and networking

The Direction des services agricoles used various channels to promote the best varieties of wheat and other staples: experimental fields, articles in the press and leaflets, lectures (sometimes with films), visits to factories, cooperatives and experimental fields, radio talks, and meetings.

24 AD60, 515W/10719.

These different means to spread knowledge in order to change and improve farming practices were used both separately and in combination. The first role of the DDSA was to coordinate the extension effort. From this point of view, he was not really a free agent: often, he had to conform to the ministry's instructions and his freedom of action was very circumscribed. For example, on 20 June 1950, the DDSA sent, as requested, a report to the ministry about the propagation of fruit farming in which he explained in great detail the provisional programme. The instructions of the ministry reveal the degree to which the service was steered by the central administration.

This is to remind you that you must send me:

1. the attached Appendix with an indication of the sums requested

2. a short note listing proposed actions, indicating precisely whether you can carry out studies on yields and cost prices, and for which species

3. copies of leaflets published in the last three years

4. your suggestions for research to be undertaken by the INRA

A copy of your reply should be sent to M. Lenfant, Director of the National Horticultural School at Versailles, who is in charge of the extension programme for fruit farming.[25]

At the end of each year, the DDSAs were obliged to report what had been undertaken in their *departement* to improve farming practices for the whole range of crops. For example, on the 17 January 1953, the DDSA from Oise informed the ministry of his efforts to popularize the cultivation of barley and winter barley.[26] His list of activities for 1952 mentioned seven demonstration fields (one for manuring, six for varieties); 20 (or 25) collective visits for a total of 500 participants; 120 conferences for 2,400 participants; four articles in the press, 2,000 (or 3,000) leaflets, posters, brochures, etc. distributed on the use of manure and 50 on cultivation.[27] For animal production, the DDSA organized contests, in cooperation with the unions of livestock farmers, and distributed prizes for the best farm animal or stock-breeder.

---

25 AD60, 515W/10719, 5 June 1950. After collecting all the replies, the ministry sent out a circular on 27 July 1950, to inform all French DDSAs about the 'Allocation of funds: fruit, publicity: 1950–1951 campaign'.

26 I used the report for 1952 (AD60, 515W/10719) because the one for 1950 could not be located. There is a separate report for every single type of crop and for cattle breeding.

27 The document is a draft and not always very clear. Some of the listed activities gathered a large number of people. For the same year, the DDSA claimed that 600 people attended three demonstrations of potato harvesting; see AD60, 515W/10719.

The second role of the DDSA was to mobilize large numbers of stake-holders and integrate them into a network of informed and committed individuals, who would be able to influence the agricultural practices in their surroundings. For example, the DDSA planned an impressive 'Wheat Day' at Compiègne in the south-east of the *departement*, for the weekend of 8–9 July 1950. Sadly, the event was cancelled at the last minute after a storm destroyed part of the crop during the night of 4–5 July.

Nevertheless, the DDSA had worked very hard for two months to organize the event, in accordance with the goals of the French Economic Plan.[28] He called first and foremost for help from the unions and other professional organizations. On 5 May he wrote to other DDSAs of north-eastern France announcing that the Wheat Day was co-organized by 'the Director of Agricultural Services of the Oise, the General Association of Wheat Producers, the Federated Cooperatives and the Grain Merchants Associations'. Moreover, he had organized a number of farmers to set up demonstration fields. The second part of the Wheat Day would become an excursion to these experimental fields, where he hoped to welcome many interested people. To guarantee the security of all the participants, he asked the police to close off the roads in the south of the *departement*.[29]

That the DDSA aimed at furthering the networking between various stakeholders can be seen in his efforts to reach a varied public. In addition to the farmers and their professional organizations, he also invited to the Wheat Day the INRA and other scientific institutions, the DDSAs of the other French *departements*, as well as companies supplying farmers with fertilizers, machinery etc. Moreover, he organized thought-provoking lectures by experts in order to present the most advanced knowledge regarding numerous topics, such as seed selection.

In a letter of 20 May 1950, for instance, the DDSA invited Pierre Jonard from the INRA to present a new kind of wheat seed, called *Étoile de Choisy*, which was to become very popular among French farmers up to the 1960s.[30] His lecture was one in a series of three, each one taking from 20 to 30 minutes, and with an expert in a particular field, with firstly 'M. Romans who will speak about genetics and plant improvements', secondly 'M. Blondeau or Gilles Leclercq about methods of cultivation, sowing dates, quantity of seed, sowing depth, spring labour', and lastly

---

28 One of the most important aims of the French Plan after the Second World War was to turn the country into a major exporter of wheat, barley, etc.: see above.

29 He sent four letters to the *commissaires de police* (chiefs of police) of Beauvais, Compiègne, Senlis and Clermont. It is noteworthy to underline that this field day was planned in the big farming area of Valois, Multien, Vexin and a part of Beauvaisis.

30 Jonard was research director at the INRA. He published numerous works on wheat varieties during this period.

Jonard himself: 'The third lecture is yours; it can be, as it was in Lille, on crop varieties but also including the conference theme of baking quality'.[31]

This letter touches upon another important aspect of the network put together by the DDSA: the visibility of the enterprises that provided seeds, fertilizers and other inputs to the farmers. Manufacturers do not often appear directly in the correspondence, but they were a part of the knowledge network because their products were at stake in the experiments and demonstrations of the INRA and other institutions, and in the fieldwork of farmers. It is obvious that these enterprises sought an entry into and profit from the network as a powerful means to exhibit and sell their products. Several letters of the DDSA, sent to different firms, give an insight into the relationship between these commercial suppliers and the public service for agriculture. Three may serve as an example: they demonstrate that the contact between the enterprises and the DDSA had first and foremost to do with the plan to modernize the French economy, but also with the diffusion of knowledge.

In the first letter, addressed to a Mr Blondeau, the DDSA wrote:

> to thank you for your leaflet on different varieties of grasses and leguminous fodder plants that may be used together to create temporary or permanent meadows. This information will be very useful as at the moment there is not much documentation on this subject.[32]

In another letter, sent to Shell Française on 3 July, the DDSA thanked Mr Maisonneuve, a director of the company, for sending posters that could be useful to teachers in winter schools, and at the Centre d'apprentissage de motoculture (training centre for mechanical farming) at Rouvroy-lès-Merles. The DDSA also asked Maisonneuve to send films regarding mechanization, as farming in the *departement* of the Oise was strongly mechanized.[33] The third letter was addressed to the General Inspector of

---

31 On *Etoile de Choisy*, the role of Blondeau in seed selection, and the bread-making quality of wheat, see B. Belderok, H. Mesdag and D. A. Donner, *Bread-Making Quality of Wheat: A Century of Breeding in Europe* (Dordrecht, 2000). About the importance of seed selection after 1945, see C. Bonneuil and F. Hochereau, 'Gouverner le procès génétique. Biopolitique et métrologie de la construction d'un standard variétal dans la France agricole d'après-guerre', *Annales. Histoire, Sciences Sociales* 63 (2008), pp. 1303–40; C. Bonneuil and F. Thomas, *Gènes, pouvoirs et profits. Recherches publiques et régimes de production des savoirs de Mendel aux OGM* (Lausanne, 2009).

32 This letter was sent on 23 May 1950. The DDSA, who had met Blondeau some days before, invited him to give a lecture on Wheat Day.

33 For obvious reasons Shell was very active in promoting mechanization in French agriculture. Another example of this interest surfaced in a very different context (that of the small farmers of the mountain region of the Alps): see Brunier, *Conseillers et conseillères*, p. 107. Oil companies were not only interested in the use of farming machines, but they also manufactured

Agriculture to inform him that one of the agricultural engineers of the departmental services had been invited to visit Potasse d'Alsace, a large company producing potassium fertilizers.

Correspondence with farmers

When analysing the DDSA's correspondence with farmers, we have to take into account all the factors mentioned up until now: the French government's agricultural policy, the role of the DDSA, the various other actors in the network with their divergent levels of knowledge, and the varied channels of communication used by the DDSA.

A large part of the correspondence of the DDSA concerned districts with large farms, especially around Chaumont, Senlis, Betz and Saint-Just-en-Chaussée. In fact, it was easier for the DDSA to keep in touch with the farmers there because they were not very numerous. We cannot guarantee that the DDSA was acquainted with every single farm in that area, but it is obvious that he knew some farmers very well, especially those engaged in unions and cooperatives.

The content of the letters varies. The DDSA wrote to some farmers because they headed a union or a cooperative and/or because they gave an entry into a network of people sharing certain knowledge. For example, he sent several letters to P. Dumont, one of the co-organizers of the Wheat Day. In a second letter, after having received details from the Ministry of Agriculture, the DDSA answered Dumont's request for information about the cost of shipping '*gadoue*' (urban manure). In a third letter, the DDSA asked him to come to a meeting on the next harvest as Dumont headed a cooperative.[34]

But the DDSA did not direct his letters only to unions and cooperatives. As he had the authority of a public servant, and because he was familiar with official paperwork, farmers could ask him to help with financial or administrative matters. For example, the DDSA advised a woman that she could receive a grant of 10,000 francs in order to send her son to the Agricultural School of Neubourg (located in the nearby *departement* of Eure)[35], where the young man could take a course on

---

nitrogen fertilizers and pesticides. See P. H. Spitz, *Petrochemicals: The Rise of an Industry* (New York, 1988). For France there was an agreement between Texaco and Kulhmann to produce nitrogen fertilizers : see P. Martin, 'Mutation dans l'industrie des engrais azotés de synthèse et transfert de technologie américaine dans les années 1950: le cas du procédé Texaco aux Etablissements Kuhlmann de Paimboeuf', in T. Preveraud (ed.), *Circulations savantes entre l'Europe et le monde (XVIIe–XXe siècle)* (Rennes, 2017), pp. 121–41.

34 Letters dated 5, 6 and 23 June 1950.
35 During this period of two months, the DDSA sent only one letter to the agricultural school of Neubourg, but this demand for funding prompted

motorized farming.[36] This kind of correspondence is important from two points of view. First, it allows us to assess the influence of the DDSA: he had the authority to bestow benefits to farmers with good practices, or on those who, in his assessment, deserved some support. Secondly, it gives some insight into the priorities of French agricultural policy: mechanization was considered as crucial to the modernization of farming but was hampered by the lack of skilled machine operators.[37]

Three letters were addressed to the agricultural winter school, four to the agricultural home economics school for women and the agricultural school of Rennes. Two other letters related to the opening of a new agricultural school by a priest who asked for funding. These letters were of an administrative nature, rather than dealing with the teaching programmes or the number of students. Nevertheless, a letter to the ministry gave some details about the programme and the funding of the winter school. It is worth noting that school years in France ended in June and restarted in October (November for the winter school). It is likely that the exchange of letters with the DDSA regarding teaching and other school matters might have been more frequent in the autumn than in the chosen period for this analysis.

During the spring, the most interesting letters were those in which the DDSA answered questions from farmers about particular agricultural matters, and especially pesticides.[38] Sometimes his replies were elaborate and his advice very precise. On other occasions he lacked the answers. In such cases, he consulted other members of his network to gather information that allowed him to give a proper reply to the question posed. His correspondence reveals which issues troubled the farmers and help us to understand how the knowledge network operated.

Questions about pesticides were prominent in the DDSA's correspondence. The 'pesticide issue' appeared to be critical during the spring because farmers used these chemicals on their young crops during that season. Many submitted questions to the DDSA before, during and after spreading the pesticides. The DDSA answered, for instance, with a long letter to 'Fernand Lecointe, municipal delegate of Novillers-les-Caillioux (Oise)' in which he explained the best way to eradicate weeds such as charlock and thistles (*sanve* and *chardon*) in a field of oats in which alfalfa had also been sown.[39] He began his response with a general warning that shows that farmers did not necessarily understand the effect of the

---

three more letters: two letters to the mother of the candidate and one to the president of a cooperative.

36 Letters dated 26 May and 1 June 1950.
37 See Herment, 'Tractorization'.
38 He also gave information or advice regarding electric fences, donkeys, manure production, silage from fodder crops, and the like.
39 Letter, 31 May 1950.

weed-killers. 'I must inform you that hormones based on 2.4 D acid, such as Weedone, Herbasol, etc. [...] produce harmful reactions in oats and their use is officially prohibited'. Then, he continued to recommend some specific products:

> Specialized products such as Agroxone and Deshermone, which you will find at your supplier or cooperative, are better. However, in my opinion, the best are the *colorants nitrés* which give excellent results. I would advise you to use herbicides such as Herbogyl-Siox or Supersinox.[40]

Sometimes the DDSA asked for external advice from the INRA or other colleagues before answering. On 22 June he wrote to several farmers collectively ('Monsieur Laroche à Liancour-Saint-Pierre, MM. Pétillon à Enecourt-le-Sac, M. Gillouard à Monjavoult') to inform them that, according to Trouvelot and Régnier of the INRA, the parasite that attacked the colza fields seemed to be the 'cécidomyie des crucifères (contarinis)'.[41] He went on to tell them that nobody knew how to kill this little fly, and in the end he recommended a better crop rotation. It is noteworthy that his advice was often very precise. But, as the effects of pesticides were not entirely known, he remained sometimes very vague, as in this case. In fact, both the DDSA and the farmers were confronted with a body of knowledge that was difficult to master.

An exchange of letters with a beekeeper is symptomatic of this unease with the available information. Charles Bergeron, who lived in Senlis, had lost his bees after the spreading of a pesticide on a nearby rapeseed field. He sent a letter to the DDSA on 3 May. On 19 May, the DDSA replied that the pesticide could not have been the cause as it had been spread before the flowering of the rapeseed. However, the DDSA did not deny that pesticides were dangerous, and he explained:

---

[40] The advice was sometimes very precise. In a letter to Mr Chaussebourg, not a farmer but an engineer of the state Roadbuilding Service, he gave the following instructions on killing the 'sésie du peuplier' (the hornet moth, which attacked poplar trees): 'Moreover, the larva can be destroyed by pushing the insecticide into the holes from which the sawdust escapes, in matchstick form, sold as 'Fuscello Antitario' and manufactured by the Saffra company, Via Moscova 18, Milan, Post Box 1245' (letter, 5 July 1950).

[41] 'No practical way to fight it. It seems that nicotine treatments will ensure protection for the coming generations but dusting is difficult with colza. Also, humidity favours the growth of this insect. The only practical solution is to have a greater rotation of crucifers'. Regnier, the director of the zoological station at Rouen, played an important role in this network. He too gave advice about the hornet moth. The network was quite efficient, as shown by the date of the letter sent to Régnier (30 June) and that of the answer to Chaussebourg (5 July). (Underlining as in the original text.)

according to my information from the mayor of Montlognon, I can tell you that the treatment took place on 3 May 1950, that the population was warned by the ringing of bells and the farmers were individually warned to take all necessary precautions.

It would therefore appear that the poison you noticed in your hives did not come from the treatments carried out in Montlognon, so you should ascertain whether farmers in other municipalities were spraying in the week of April 17 to 22.

I must tell you that it will be difficult to establish this, given the delay in informing the farmers of your problem. However, I remain at your disposal if you are able to obtain additional information.

Finally, on 22 May, the beekeeper addressed a letter to the DDSA to tell that he had sent his bees to the apicultural research centre at Bures-sur-Yvette.[42] In his reply, the DDSA recommended Bergeron come to an agreement with a farmer located in Baron, another village close to Montlognon, who was suspected to have caused the loss of the hive.

Other letters demonstrated that the effects of a new range of products – DDT, hormones, and the like – required a learning process. A farmer had some trouble with a firm that distributed a pesticide that destroyed flax.[43] In yet another letter, the DDSA gave the following recommendation to Mr Haupin on using hormones to destroy thistles:

1) treat the cereal between tillering (*tallage*) and joint stage (*montaison*)

2) follow the dosage prescribed by the manufacturer

3) carry out the treatment on a sunny, windless day ....

And, as a final precaution, clean all equipment very carefully after use so as not to harm other crops.[44]

Among the letters related to the use of new products, three are very interesting. A Mr Brunier of Noyon enquired about the effects of a product called Atol.[45] On 12 May 1950 the DDSA circulated a letter among his colleagues in the *departements* of Seine-Inférieure and Meuse asking if they had encountered it.[46] On 19 May, after having received replies from

---

42   These last details come from the letter sent by the DDSA to Bergeron, 30 May 1950. For the history of the station of Bures-sur-Yvette, see J. Louveaux, *Chronique historique de la Zoologie agricole Française. Les abeilles et l'apiculture* (Versailles, 1996). For recent research on the effect of pesticides on apiculture in France, see L. Humbert, 'Résister à la "modernisation agricole", les apiculteurs-trices dans la lutte contre les insecticides de synthèse (1945–1965)' (mémoire de master EHESS, 2018).

43   Letter to M. Cotte, farmer at Hétomesnil. 27 June 1950.

44   Letter, 31 May 1950.

45   Letter, 19 May 1950.

46   Letter, 12 May 1950.

them saying that they had no knowledge of it, he wrote to his colleague in Seine-et-Marne asking whether he knew of it.[47]

Three points emerge from this exchange. Firstly, the manufacturer was eager to sell his product. Secondly, the services of the ministry and the DDSA were uncertain about its effects. Thirdly, the farmers were very receptive to the suggestion of using the new product. The DDSA made this last point very clear: in a letter of 12 May he wrote

> [A]ccording to my information, some farmers in your Department have already used this product, particularly around Jumièges. Would you be so kind as to tell me if you know about these trials and, if so, what you think of the results?.

Similarly, in his letter of 19 May, the DDSA wrote to his colleague of Seine-et-Marne: 'According to my information, some farmers in your department appear to have used this product already'.[48]

Levels of knowledge and networks

So, as the analysis of these two months of correspondence of the DDSA of Oise proves, French farmers in the early 1950s had access to an extensive network of expert knowledge. But as we have seen, this correspondence was first and foremost directed towards the wealthiest farmers. This necessitates a brief assessment of the other forms of dissemination that the DDSA used in areas where small farmers were numerous. For them, different methods were needed to spread knowledge, such as leaflets, contests and lectures. The content of a leaflet for distribution among farmers in dairying districts demonstrates that the information addressed to them was general advice for practical use:

> It is easy to keep a pasture in good condition and even improve it if the following principles are observed:
> 1. Keep the meadows well aerated. Just as barley must be harrowed, so pasture must be 'regenerated'.
> 2. Groom the grass regularly by scything the weeds and spreading the animal droppings.
> 3. Give back to the soil, in the form of fertilizer, what the consumption

---

[47] Letter, 19 May 1950.
[48] It is possible that the eagerness of farmers to use the product was a consequence of the sales talk of salesmen to convince them. But, taking into account the wide variety of dangerous pesticides the farmers used and the large geographical diffusion of the product as mentioned by the DDSA, it seems unlikely that this was the sole explanation.

of the grass has removed. A field is correctly maintained when it receives every year:

– 500 to 800 kilos of slag, using phosphate slag at least one out of every two years

– 60 to 100 kilos of ammonium nitrate, spread six weeks before the animals are put out to grass

– if you have acid meadows, add in ten tonnes of marl every ten years.

4. Use up your grass while it is young (about 10 centimetres high). This is when it is richest and least liable to be spoiled.

5. Ensile the fodder left in spring and use it up so as to economise on oilcake.

After having outlined these basic principles, the DDSA, on first sight paradoxically so, wrote: 'These few rules are well known to all livestock farmers. When applied to pasture that has never received fertilizer, they will increase the milk production considerably'.[49]

The content of this leaflet illustrates the difference between the two levels of knowledge identified above. What we observe here is an effort to turn scientific knowledge into vernacular know-how. In the French dairy sector, one of the best strategies to improve current practices was to deprecate old habits. Sylvain Brunier has explained how, during the post-war period, traditional practices were systematically labelled as primitive, and the new practices as advanced.[50] The DDSA seemed to use the same double language when he warned at the beginning of the leaflet: 'At the moment when your cows are eating grass at no apparent cost, you have to remember that pastures, like arable fields, can become impoverished'.[51]

Finally, and in line with the introduction by Leen Van Molle and Yves Segers, I can point to three types or models of knowledge networks that can be identified in the analysis of the correspondence of the Oise DDSA. In the first, the DDSA played the role of a 'cultural amphibian', bridging the gap between science and farmers. The model is reflected in the strategy of popularizing knowledge about fertilizers in the dairy and cattle breeding area. But popularization is not enough to clarify the complexity of the knowledge transfers during the post-war green

---

49 AD 60, 515W/10719: Leaflet sent to farmers in 1953 (dated Beauvais 22 June 1953). The Direction des Services Agricoles used the backs of unneeded leaflets for drafts. It has not been possible to locate a file containing all the leaflets sent out by the DDSA.

50 Brunier, *Conseillers et conseillères agricoles*, pp. 148–50.

51 On occasion, even with the elite farmers, the DDSA used very simple terms. For example, when organizing a meeting to combat the white worm of the sugar beet, he simply referred to the pest as the *ver blanc*.

FIGURE 9.1 The DDSA as the star in the network (model 2).

revolution, especially with regard to the arable farming area with large farms cultivating wheat, rapeseed, potato, sugar beet and the like.

The second puts the DDSA of Oise, Mr Guillemot, at the centre of a large network. Mr Guillemot is the star of this network (Figure 9.1). He has numerous connections with a wide range of stakeholders: firms, public services (including the DDSAs of nearby *départements*, the INRA and other scientific institutions), farmers' unions and cooperatives, and, finally, farmers. In this model, the farmers appear rather as peripheral elements. They are connected to the DDSA, but the model does not reflect the variety and the complexity of the links between the various actors of the network. Moreover, the juxtaposition of the groups of actors and the rather peripheral location of the farmers are unsatisfactory.

With all the information available in the correspondence of the DDSA, it is possible to delineate a third model (Figure 9.2). Indeed, the various stakeholders, far from being isolated, were interconnected. This last model comes close to the concept of 'entangled knowledge', as explained by Van Molle and Yves Segers in the introduction to this book. It situates the farmers at the crossroads, as the central intersection of a complex and interconnected body of expertise in which the DDSA did not take the central position. We can illustrate this by pointing in the first place at the Wheat Day: the correspondence concerning that day proves

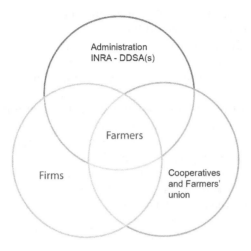

FIGURE 9.2 Interconnected model (model 3).

that cooperatives, scientific institutions, supplying enterprises and their products all played a key role in the network that aimed at implementing new varieties of seeds and improving the baking quality of wheat (*qualité boulangère du blé*). Indeed, the DDSA depended on a wide range of actors and products to participate in the event, in order to promote the best varieties. The 'pesticide issue' offers a second illustration: the producing companies displayed an aggressive commercial behaviour, but farmers for their part acted in some cases, at least partially, autonomously. Some farmers appealed to the DDSA and scientific institutions for advice or experiments with new products. Some had a direct link with suppliers, or indirect ties with suppliers via their cooperatives.

Conclusion

The analysis of the correspondence of the DDSA in the *departement* of the Oise for the two months from early May to early July 1950 reveals that the promoters of the new French agricultural policy after the Second World War had at least two forms of agriculture in mind, requiring two levels of knowledge to meet their goals.

The first type of farmer operated in the Paris Basin and raised cereals, sugar beet, rapeseed and similar crops on a large scale. The second type ran one of the innumerable mixed farms, or, as in the Oise, one of the many small and medium-sized farms producing milk and breeding livestock. For the former, the DSA could mobilize a vast network of producers and disseminators of scientific knowledge; for the latter he had to mobilize the rhetoric of change and the powers of persuasion to convince farmers to abandon old habits.

This first conclusion leads to a second one: the DDSAs were unable to promote the best practices all over their *departement*. Some were perhaps able to become acquainted with the big farmers in their area because there were so few, as was the case in the Oise *departement*. But the DDSA of the Oise could not deal personally with the multitude of small and medium-sized farmers. To attain his goal, he had to involve the farmers' unions and cooperatives, and consequently to promote these organizations. Because, accordingly, he oriented his networking to the needs of the farmers' unions and cooperatives, he paradoxically grew more and more estranged from the mass of small farmers. After all, as the sources demonstrate, the role of the DDSA was not that important in the 1950s, whereas cooperatives, unions and supplying companies became more and more central to the diffusion of knowledge, the adoption of innovations and the progress of agriculture.

Moreover, the analysis clarifies the role of the farmers in the process that in its entirety is labelled as an agricultural revolution. The numerous letters related to questions about pesticides, as described here, are symptomatic of the weak influence of the DDSA, of the eagerness of farmers to adopt these new products, and of the agency of commercial companies.

In the case of fertilizers and mechanization, the transmission of knowledge was to a large extent taken over by the unions and cooperatives. The issue of pesticides, however, was one of the last fields in which the DDSA's scientific and potentially very high level of expertise could be of use. But even in that field, he found himself competing with other stakeholders, especially the private enterprises. It is striking that it was not the DDSA, but the farmers who were at the centre of the knowledge network. Or, to be more precise, they were surrounded by a multifaceted body of expertise. And what is even more striking, perhaps, is that they could experiment with new pesticides without control. The authorities were not able to master the use of pesticides, even if they did promote them. As I have mentioned, the DDSA had to urge many farmers to comply with the instructions for the use of new products provided by firms and cooperatives. In some cases, he was unable to provide accurate information, and in one case he did not have the slightest idea about a particular pesticide used by farmers. Contrary to what happened with seeds, as Christophe Bonneuil has demonstrated[52], the state services seemed, at least in part, to be overwhelmed by the aggressive and tempting commercial strategy of chemical firms and the eagerness of farmers to use their products.

---

[52] Likewise, the organization of the Wheat Day by the DDSA, with the help of the INRA and cooperatives, illustrates how seed improvements were triggered by the state.

10

Technical Change and Knowledge Networks in England, 1945–1980s

Paul Brassley

An atomistic industry – one, such as agriculture, comprised of many small firms – has knowledge acquisition and transfer problems not found in more concentrated industries that are made up of a small number of larger firms. Large firms can afford specialized research and development departments; equally, whereas they can profit from introducing technical changes before their competitors, they stand to lose if their competitors find output-increasing technologies first. Neither of these considerations applies in more competitive markets. Few farmers operated on a large enough scale to carry out their own research, and virtually no farmers controlled such a large part of the market that their production decisions had any impact on market prices. Thus, the research had to be done outside the farm, and farmers had every incentive to adopt output-increasing innovations, so a network of some shape or form was needed to connect the research organizations and commercial firms that were developing the new techniques, machines, pesticides, seeds, etc. with the farmers and farm workers who would finally use them.

This chapter ignores the original production of scientific and technical knowledge, but concentrates on the way in which that knowledge, once produced and accepted as useful, was transferred to those who used it in practice.[1] It is important to remember, however, that agricultural research in the UK expanded between the 1940s and 1980s, in terms of the money spent on it, the scientists engaged in it, and the results it produced.[2]

---

[1] Both of these topics are discussed at greater length in chapters 2 and 3 of P. Brassley, D. Harvey, M. Lobley and M. Winter, *The Real Agricultural Revolution: the Transformation of English Farming, 1939–1985* (Woodbridge, 2021).

[2] G. W. Cooke, *Agricultural Research 1931–1981* (London, 1981); C. J. Doyle and M.

There was much discussion on what its function should be: whether to discover fundamental scientific principles or to produce rapid answers to current farming problems. This question was extensively discussed in a series of advisory councils (the Agricultural Improvement Council, the Agricultural Advisory Council, and finally the Advisory Council for Agriculture and Horticulture) which brought together prominent farmers and agricultural scientists between 1941 and 1979. The details of their deliberations are not discussed in this chapter, but the results are discussed further in the conclusions of this chapter. However, the chapter's main purpose is to identify the components of the agricultural knowledge network, to trace their development over time, and to show how the network was used.

The following account is based upon three types of source: the contemporary literature and official reports; the archives of the Ministry of Agriculture now in the National Archives at Kew; and interviews with farmers. Details of the first two of these are given in the footnotes, but it is convenient to provide more details of the interviews at this point. The farmers interviewed were identified from the surviving records of the Farm Management Survey held at the Centre for Rural Policy Research in the University of Exeter. The survey began in the late 1930s and carries on to the present day (now as the Farm Business Survey). The surviving fieldbooks for the period 1938–1985 contain details of the accounts of several hundred farms, in some cases for periods of 20 years or more. These were analysed between 2009 and 2012, and at the same time 29 farmers whose farms had been part of the survey were located and interviewed. Part of the interview was concerned with the farmer's training and acquisition of information, and it is this material that is used in this chapter. Those interviewed are identified by their code numbers in the survey, e.g. 'farmer 209' or 'farmer 3/1'. Transcripts of these interviews are currently held at the Centre for Rural Policy Research and will in time be transferred to Exeter University Library.[3]

Using this combination of sources enables us to examine the knowledge network from multiple perspectives. The chapter therefore traces the history of agricultural education, advisory services, and media in this period, before examining the experiences of individual farmers in the network and concluding with some general reflections.

S. Ridout, 'The Impact of Scientific Research on UK Agricultural Productivity', *Research Policy* 14 (1985), pp. 109–16; K. Blaxter and N. Robertson, *From Dearth to Plenty: the Modern Revolution in Food Production* (Cambridge, 1995).

[3] They are also available in the UK Data Archive at http//doi.org/10.5255/UKDA-SN-851111, 'Processes of technical change in British agriculture: innovation in the farming of south-west England, 1935–1985'.

Transmitting knowledge: the formal networks

Agricultural education

Most farmers acquired new technical information from a combination of education, extension workers, representatives of commercial firms, media sources and discussions with fellow farmers. For many farmers, education was probably the least significant of these, partly because relatively few farmers had much full-time agricultural education, and partly as a result of the time lag between their education and the point at which they took control of the management of their farms. The history of agricultural education reveals only small numbers of students in universities, national colleges and local agricultural training establishments in the early 1950s. Moreover, many of these students found work in the ancillary industries rather than on farms. The total number of agriculture, forestry and veterinary students in the UK increased from about 3,000 in the mid-1950s to just over 5,000 in the mid-1980s, but for an industry with over 200,000 farmers and twice that number of employed workers for much of this period, the numbers in formal training remained small.[4]

Although this low level of formal education may have attracted criticism in official reports, it was not generally perceived as a problem within farming itself, where attitudes to education exhibited a wide range of variation, as interviews with farmers reveal.[5] There was a long tradition of farmers learning from their fathers (as the majority of farmers were men), and many young people entering agriculture felt similar to farmer 209: 'I wanted to leave school and get to work on the farm, despite my parents' suggestion that I went to Seale-Hayne [a national agricultural college in Devon]'. There is interview data about the agricultural education of 25 farmers and, of these, 14 had no full-time agricultural education at all. Farmer 162 went to a local training institute for a fortnight's course while he was still at school, but he had no desire to go there for a course of any longer duration:

> I was never interested. I learned most from father, I suppose I must have admired what he did, and I wanted to be like him, so to be home here was the natural thing to do.

---

4   P. Brassley, 'Agricultural Education, Training and Advice in the UK, 1850–2000', in N. Vivier (ed.), *The State and Rural Societies: Policy and Education in Europe, 1700–2000* (Turnhout, 2008), p. 268.

5   The official reports were Lord Luxmoore (chair), *Report of the Committee on Post-War Agricultural Education in England and Wales* (Cmd.6433, 1943); Earl De La Warr (chair), *Report of the Committee on Further Education for Agriculture provided by Local Education Authorities* (Cmnd.614, 1958); C. I. C. Bosanquet (chair), *The Demand for Agricultural Graduates: report of an interdepartmental committee* (Cmnd.2419, 1964).

And neither had his father been to college. Farmer 101, however, provided an interesting insight into this:

> I learned a lot at home from father, about what he did, and when I went to college [he went to Seale-Hayne College] I learned *why* he did it. And when you learn why you did it, you learn to think about whether it can be done any other way to achieve results.

Farmer 466, who had a B.Sc. in agriculture from Cambridge University and an M.A. from Reading University, made the same point: 'it's an attitude of mind. What the university education does is to introduce you to the upcoming technologies but also give you the ability to deal with them'. Farmer 7/8, whose father had been at Seale-Hayne in the 1930s, and had done a cheesemaking course at the Somerset county farm institute at Cannington, himself went to Kingston Maurward, the Dorset county farm institute, but felt that 'if you were a farmer's son you knew a lot of it before you went down there', although he also 'learned about the feeding of cows, how much cake they really wanted, and fertilizer use, and that sort of thing. It was useful'. Farmer 3/1 was more decided in his conclusions. Asked if his OND (Ordinary National Diploma) course at Seale-Hayne in the early 1970s had taught him anything he replied:

> Certainly in that era agricultural colleges were regarded as a finishing school by most farmers [...]. In terms of what I brought back to my own dairy farm, I would have to say probably 'No'. It was just too general. Ideally, I would have been sent abroad [...]. I would personally send my son off to a big farm in New Zealand for two or three years

although he did admit that his industrial placement year on a big dairy farm in Dorset 'showed me how *not* to farm'.

Advisory services

Beyond formal education there was a wide variety of sources of information and training in the four decades after the war. Of these the most important, especially in the 1950s and 1960s, was the National Agricultural Advisory Service, more commonly known in the agricultural industry by its initials, NAAS. Before the war, agricultural advice was a county council responsibility, but the 1943 Luxmoore Report argued that the system had been inadequate, largely because it was underfunded, and proposed the creation of a national service.[6] The proposal was accepted, and the NAAS was created in 1946 with the aim of increasing

---

6   Luxmoore, *Post-War Agricultural Education*; C. J. Holmes, 'Science and the Farmer: the Development of the Agricultural Advisory Service in England and Wales, 1900–1939', *Agricultural History Rev.* 36 (1988), pp. 77–86.

the efficiency of the agricultural industry. It remained in existence during the 20 post-war years when agricultural output increased most rapidly. In 1971 the NAAS was brought together with the Agricultural Land Service, the Land Drainage Department and the ministry's Veterinary Service, to form the Agricultural Development and Advisory Service (ADAS), but its services remained essentially free to farmers until about the mid-1980s, after which it was gradually commercialized and its operations run down.[7] By 1950 NAAS was employing about 1,500 people, a number that remained roughly constant over the next 20 years. Some of these were specialists in a range of disciplines from animal husbandry to entomology and plant pathology, but the core of the service was the 460 or so district advisory officers. These were the general practitioners and the people that farmers contacted first. For farmer 3/1 in Dorset they were

> our biggest single contributor to farm information, they were the first port of call for new technical information, and within ADAS it was the District Adviser. We only rarely went beyond him to the specialist advisers, we used the District Adviser as a general practitioner, and they helped the industry a lot.

Similarly, farmer 2/21 was

> quite an avid supporter of NAAS, I had good friends who were in it [...] and I always valued their advice, which was free at the point of need, like the Health Service.

The annual reports of the county agricultural officers provide a useful survey of the activities of NAAS, and later ADAS, at a local level. Throughout the 1950s, 1960s and 1970s the basis of their work remained the individual advisory visits to farms, but in addition individual officers or county teams carried out their own research work – those in Devon worked, for example, on the use of wheat reed for thatching and control of the weed fat hen (*Chenopodium album*) in the kale crop in 1962–1963 – held advisory meetings, attended conferences and shows, cooperated with local authorities, bankers, and accountants, wrote articles for the press and appeared on radio and television programmes. They also played a major part in organizing emergency fodder supplies by airlift and road to over 300 farms during the blizzards in the cold winter of 1962–1963.[8] In his report for 1952–1953 the county officer for Devon emphasized the success of the informal discussion meetings that had been held in small village halls for an audience of 30–40 people, which 'have brought in

7   S. Foreman, *Loaves and Fishes: An Illustrated History of the Ministry of Agriculture, Fisheries and Food, 1889–1989* (London, 1989), pp. 117.
8   The National Archives (hereafter TNA), MAF 114/747, Devon County Advisory Officer's Annual Work Report, 1963.

many farmers who would not go to the local market town, and would not rise to ask questions at a formal meeting'.[9] This question of the success with which advisory services were connecting with farmers remained central to the concerns of both county and national advisory officers. The county reports always quantified the number of advisory visits, and a national report on the first eight years of the service's operation included a statistical survey of the activities of NAAS officers for the year 1953–1954, which included 375,223 advisory visits, equating to an average of roughly one per farmer per year in England and Wales. Of course, some farmers were visited much more often and others not at all. A six-month national study in the spring and summer of 1967 demonstrated that advisers had visited 25 per cent of 50–150-acre farms, but over 40 per cent of farms bigger than 500 acres. In Cambridgeshire, between 1954 and 1961, advisers had visited nearly half of all holdings of less than 50 acres, two-thirds of 10–150-acre holdings, and four-fifths of all holdings larger than 150 acres.[10]

NAAS officers were also responsible for running the 12 experimental husbandry farms (EHFs) located in various parts of England and Wales. These conducted developmental, as opposed to fundamental, research.[11] While some farmers ignored their work, others were enthusiastic. Farmer 570 in North Devon learned a lot about silage making from visits to Liscombe, the nearby EHF:

> Everybody got into the idea by going to Liscombe. They were doing research, but it was such down to earth research. You could look at the bullocks, and those that had been fed silage, and those that had been fed silage and meal, and then they always had a few outside, and you could see the difference between them, and you learned how to do it, and which improved grasses to put in.

The national advisory services were not the only sources of advice available to farmers. There were in addition several semi-public organizations concerned with the production and marketing of particular commodities. The Milk Marketing Board, for example, ran a low-cost production (LCP) service from 1962, which involved monthly visits by consulting officers to participating farms, of which there were 3,700 by 1973. It also had a scheme for an annual test of milking machines, to

9   TNA, MAF 114/241, Report of the Devon County Agricultural Officer on Advisory Work Apr. 1952-Mar. 1953.
10 N. F. McCann, *The Story of the National Agricultural Advisory Service: A Mainspring of Agricultural Revival, 1946–1971* (Ely, 1989), p. 73; see also R. J. Dancey, 'The Evolution of Agricultural Extension in England and Wales', *J. Agricultural Economics* 44 (1993), pp. 375–93.
11 J. A. Macmillan, 'Experimental Husbandry Farms: Review of Progress', *Agriculture* 59 (1953), pp. 459–62.

which a further 7,500 producers subscribed.[12] Other organizations, such as the British Sugar Corporation, the Home Grown Cereals Authority (HGCA) and the Meat and Livestock Commission (MLC) also provided technical information, although it was not the purpose for which they were specifically established. The MLC was established in 1967 and employed fieldsmen to visit farms and give advice, and also to run courses on specific topics, such as the on-farm artificial insemination of pigs.[13] The National Institute of Agricultural Botany (NIAB) was established in 1919 to provide advice on varieties of all farm crops, for which it carried out trials all over the country, issuing recommended lists of varieties for each crop with details of yield variations, disease resistance, suitability for different soils, and so on.[14] Any farmer could join NIAB and so receive these lists, as farmer 2/7 in Dorset did: 'I used to look forward every January to the NIAB leaflets coming out to see what was recommended for the spring planting'. In the Blackmore Vale dairy district of Dorset, however, farmer 3/1 felt that recommended lists were of more use to cereal farmers than grassland specialists, and instead

you'd ask the seeds rep – often the cake rep [the sales representative of an agricultural merchant], from the same firm – and he'd say 'I'll send you some bags of No. 4'.

On the other hand, many farmers regularly attended visits to grass and cereal demonstration plots arranged by NIAB. John Jemmet, the NIAB Senior Regional Trials Officer in the south-west of England, remembered arranging visits to trial sites and their enthusiastic reception by 'a pretty good cross section of farmers'. He also made the point that NIAB demonstrations served to pass information in the opposite direction, from those who used new varieties to the plant breeders.[15]

In 1966 the government established the Agricultural Training Board (ATB), one of a number of industrial training boards to provide training beyond that provided by the agricultural education system and the commodity organizations. What they provided was essentially in-service training for farmers and their workers. As farmer 3/1 recalled of the ATB:

I went on some courses, foot trimming, for example, and they were good, they were held on farms, very specific, so you went to look at

---

[12] S. Baker, *Milk to Market: Forty Years of Milk Marketing* (London, 1973), pp. 230–3.

[13] P. Wormell, *Anatomy of Agriculture: A Study of Britain's Greatest Industry* (London, 1978), p. 505; P. Brassley, 'Cutting Across Nature? The History of Artificial Insemination in Pigs in the UK', *Stud. History and Philosophy of Biological and Biomedical Sciences* 38 (2007), pp. 442–61.

[14] N. T. Gill and K. C. Vear, *Agricultural Botany* (London, 1958), pp. 78–9.

[15] The late John Jemmett, personal communication with the author, 29 June 2012.

one , how to stop dermatitis or whatever, and they would be a one-day course, fitted in between milkings.

Young Farmers' Clubs were another source of training used by many, although they were not specifically established for that purpose. Beginning in 1921, the movement reached a peak of 1,500 clubs and over 70,000 members in 1955.[16] Interestingly, although several interviewed farmers mention hearing speakers on technical matters at local branch meetings of the National Farmers' Union (NFU), these usually came after the formal business of the branch meeting was over. The NFU was never formally a partner or a participant in the technical knowledge network, but saw its role as a political one, representing farmers to government.

In addition to these official or semi-official organizations there were also commercial firms that farmers looked to for advice along with their products. One agricultural journalist estimated that in the 'heady days' of the 1960s and 1970s there were 'at least 50,000 people' calling on farmers, advising them, and arranging technical events for them.[17] Another estimate at the end of this period suggested that some 40,000 public sector employees worked in education and the civil service in areas related to agriculture, and they had their counterparts in the commercial firms too, so the numbers involved were of the same order of magnitude.[18] Farmer 2/7 in Dorset remembered having 'a chap called Doug Matthews, he used to sell Boots products, Isocornox etc, and we used to rely on his advice, he was the technical rep', and then in the 1980s 'we went on to the independent adviser [...] you would pay him about £3 an acre and he would do this farm and several others in the locality'. Farmers had often dealt with the same firm for years and trusted their judgement. As farmer 787 said, 'If you're interested in something you find out anyway, I ask people, I wanted some machinery for the corn, and I went and talked to a dealer'. Similarly, farmer 3/1 remembered: 'Everybody had a firm they dealt with. We had one at Bruton called Sheldon Jones, they were a compounder, but they expanded into dairy seeds. It was all very friendly'. Farmer 109's memories supported this:

> We didn't avoid reps, we still know some. There were a lot of reps about in those days, but we always had the same one, from Wyatt and Bruce [...] And there was Tuckers, we dealt with Tuckers as well, Mr Johnson, for seeds and feeds, and fertilizers.

16 Wormell, *Anatomy of Agriculture*, p. 460.
17 D. Montague, *Farming, Food and Politics: the Merchant's Tale* (Dublin, 2000), p. 111.
18 G. M. Craig, J. L. Jollans and A. Korbey (eds), *The Case for Agriculture: An Independent Assessment* (Reading, 1986), pp. 94–9.

Fertilizer producers such as Fisons and ICI, and feed firms such as BOCM, might charter trains to take 3,000 farmers at a time to demonstration farms or factories. Most farmers bought their feeds, seeds and fertilizers from agricultural merchants rather than directly from the producers, but many of the bigger producers nevertheless employed their own teams of technical representatives who would visit farms to advise on the use of increasingly technically complex products. These men (and they were then, in contrast to later, almost all men) not only knew about their own products but would also have called on numerous other farms in the district, so they often had a well-informed picture of technical changes beyond their own immediate commercial interests. Talking over such things was a way to capture a potential customer's interest, and many of these representatives were trusted by farmers and seen as a free and reliable source of technical information. British Oil and Cake Mills (BOCM), one of the larger feed manufacturers, was one of those that did not sell direct to farmers, but nevertheless there are 83 people in a photograph of its technical sales team taken in the 1960s. Firms such as ICI and Fisons were one of the bigger recruiters of agricultural students from universities and colleges during this period. At its peak, ICI had 5,000 people in its fertilizer operation.[19]

Agricultural media

Another, more traditional, source of information for farmers was the agricultural show. There was an enormous variety of these, from the local show to the county or regional shows such as the Royal Cornwall, the Devon, the Bath and West, the Great Yorkshire etc., and the national show, the Royal, which moved around the country until 1963 when it held its first show at its permanent showground at Stoneleigh in Warwickshire. Although in their nineteenth-century origins most or all of these had as their objective the promotion of technical change – 'improvement' in the language of the time – by the mid-twentieth century it was clear that the more local shows were essentially social events, where rural people met their friends and engaged in friendly competition showing all kinds of products from breeding animals to jam. The big regional and national shows were different. For traditional livestock breeders wishing to sell their animals at high prices, a presence and a good performance at such shows was essential, and for machinery manufacturers, seed firms, fertilizer and pesticide companies they represented an opportunity to present their latest products to farmers who operated on a big enough scale to be able to take one or more days away from the farm and travel some distance. Banks and advisory services also had a permanent

[19] Montague, *Farming, Food and Politics*, pp. 110–11, 260–1.

presence at such shows. Attendance at the Royal Show rose steadily to the mid-1970s, when there were around 200,000 visitors and exhibitors each year, and these numbers were maintained or even exceeded until the mid-1980s. While a proportion of those attending the Royal may have had little or no connection with agriculture and simply sought a day's entertainment, visitor surveys found that 36 per cent of all male visitors in 1975, and 43 per cent in 1983, were farmers, farm managers or farm workers. Sixty per cent of the male visitors in 1972 were, in some way, connected with agriculture, and in that year over 26,000 farmers and farm managers visited the show. Since they farmed a total of 11 million acres, which represented 423 acres each, it is clear that, as suggested above, they tended to be drawn from the ranks of those farming on a larger than average scale. And this minority of the farming population were there to do business: a 1986 survey found that two-thirds of the farmers, managers and workers attending the show within seven months made a purchase related to what they had seen.[20]

Agricultural shows, with the exception of the Smithfield livestock show and other local Christmas fatstock shows in December, were held in the summer months, but throughout the year the print and broadcast media aimed their output at farmers. As with the shows, agricultural journals aimed at farmers had existed from the eighteenth century. The market leaders in the 1950s and 1960s were *Farmer and Stockbreeder*, which had first been published in 1889, and *Farmer's Weekly*, which began in 1934. The former was effectively taken over by the NFU in 1971 and became *British Farmer and Stockbreeder* before closing in 1984, leaving the latter as the principal weekly farming publication, although by no means the only one.[21] There was also *Farmers Guardian*, published in the north of England, and a range of specialist magazines, such as *Dairy Farmer* and *Pig Farmer*. The Ministry of Agriculture had its own journal, *Agriculture*, published monthly (originally as *The Journal of the Board of Agriculture*) since 1894, until it was closed in 1972. It was probably read more by advisers and academics than by farmers in general, as was the *NAAS Quarterly Review*, published from 1948.[22] It was claimed in 1978 that there were 126 farming magazines or other publications in existence, and in addition the serious national newspapers and some of the regional newspapers such as the *Western Morning News* all had full-time agricultural correspondents. At that time *Farmer's Weekly* had a circulation of 130,000, and the combined circulations of the *Farmers Guardian* and the specialist publications such as *Dairy Farmer*, *Power Farming*, *Arable Farmer*, *Big Farm Weekly* and *Big*

---

20 N. Goddard, *Harvests of Change: The Royal Agricultural Society of England, 1838–1988* (London, 1988), pp. 264–7.
21 http://www.reading.ac.uk/merl/collections/merl-collections.aspx.
22 Foreman, *Loaves and Fishes*, pp. 90–2.

Farm Management amounted to as many again.[23] Even taking account of the fact that some farmers would read several of these publications each week, it would have been unusual, given these numbers, for a farmer *not* to have been exposed to some source of printed farming news each week. Certainly most of the farmers interviewed mentioned reading, often citing the *Farmers Weekly*, as a major source of information. As farmer 2/7 said, 'The *Farmers Weekly* has been my compulsion every Saturday morning for 50 years'.

Commercial publishers also found it worthwhile to produce books on farming technique, many of which sold well beyond the student market. *Farming for Profits*, the first edition of which was published in paperback by Penguin, was written by Dr Keith Dexter and Derek (later Sir Derek) Barber, both of whom worked for NAAS at the time. It sold 25,000 copies between 1961 and 1963.[24] In 1955 the Ministry of Agriculture published *The Farm as a Business*, giving advice on 'the principles underlying farm business analysis and planning', and from 1963 this was converted into eight booklets in an *Aids to Management* series, comprised of a general introduction to management and individual booklets on beef, sheep, pigs, poultry, labour and machinery, arable crops, and dairying, each available at 2s 6d (which was roughly the cost of a Penguin paperback in 1963).[25] Standard textbooks must have sold well too, for there were four new editions of Fream's *Elements of Agriculture* between 1948 and 1983, and four of Watson and More's *Agriculture* between 1945 and 1962.[26] As far as the press and the publishers were concerned, agriculture was clearly a market worth catering for.

Radio farming programmes began before the Second World War and continued during the war. A radio soap opera, *The Archers*, designed to provide a combination of instruction, information and entertainment, became a fixture on BBC radio from 1951.[27] By 1958 BBC radio was broadcasting a market report for farmers in the early morning. In July 1962 the early morning market report was incorporated into a 10-minute *Farm Bulletin* of news items broadcast from 6.40 a.m. each weekday. By 1965 the programme had become *Farming Today*, broadcast from Monday to Saturday between 6.35 and 6.50 a.m., still with market prices at the beginning, and continuing to attract favourable comments from the

---

23 Wormell, *Anatomy of Agriculture*, pp. 541–50.
24 K. Dexter and D. Barber, *Farming for Profits* (London, 1967).
25 Ministry of Agriculture, Fisheries and Food, *Aids to Management: Dairying* (London, 1967), pp. iv, 1.
26 C. Spedding (ed.), *Fream's Agriculture* (16th edn, London, 1983); J. A. S. Watson and J. A. More, *Agriculture: The Science and Practice of Farming* (11th edn, Edinburgh, 1962).
27 S. Laing, 'Images of the Rural in Popular Culture', in B. Short (ed.), *The English Rural Community: Image and Analysis* (Cambridge, 1992), pp. 133–51.

Ministry of Agriculture.[28] There was also a weekly radio programme, *Farm Fare*, which soon changed its title to *On Your Farm*, and was broadcast on Wednesday lunchtimes, but later became a regular fixture on early Saturday mornings until the twenty-first century.

BBC Television farming programmes began on 3 October 1957. The programme was simply called *Farming* and usually consisted of three items, linked by a chairman, who was always a farmer with the kind of large farming business that (according to one of them) allowed him to be absent from the farm for up to 50 days each year.[29] By the autumn of 1960 it had settled into a Sunday lunchtime slot and had evolved into using much more film and outside broadcast material. Independent (commercial) television began in 1955 but did not initially cover the whole country. In the west of England, the regional company Westward Television began broadcasting in 1961 and immediately introduced a half hour *Farming News*. Like the BBC farming programmes, it was aimed at an agricultural audience with little attempt to relate to the wider population. Unlike the BBC, it included advertising, a significant amount of which was for products targeted at the agricultural audience, especially livestock health products.[30] Initially a relatively low proportion of farmers listened or watched. In 1961 the BBC commissioned an audience research report on farming programmes, based on a sample of nearly 3,000 farmers selected at random from NFU and Scottish NFU members. It revealed that only about a third of farmers were regular listeners (i.e. at least three or four times a week) to the early morning radio farming programme and concluded that about a quarter of farmers saw the BBC television farming programme regularly. The audience for the ITV farming programmes was even smaller.[31] This relatively small audience reach was probably affected by the restricted availability of mains electricity supplies on farms at that time. When a public supply of electricity became available, a television was often one of the first things to be purchased.[32]

These early programmes had a largely technical focus, one reason for which was almost certainly the composition of the committees advising the programme makers, which were dominated by producers. Both the BBC and ITV had advisory committees overseeing their

28 TNA, MAF 197/44, Minutes of the BBC Central Agricultural Advisory Committee, 21 Jan. 1965.
29 J. Cherrington, *On the Smell of an Oily Rag* (London, 1979), p. 145.
30 Jennie Constable, South West Film and Television Archive, Plymouth, personal communications with the author, Feb. and Mar. 2013.
31 TNA, MAF 197/40, BBC Audience Research Report, 1961.
32 P. Brassley, 'Electrifying Farms in England', in P. Brassley, J. Burchardt and K. Sayer (eds), *Transforming the Countryside: the Electrification of Rural Britain* (London, 2017), pp. 105–7.

agricultural output. Most of those on the BBC's committee were farmers or landowners, but in 1958 there were also two civil servants from the Ministry of Agriculture, a publisher and the Professor of Agriculture at Leeds University. The committee was chaired in 1958 by Clyde Higgs, a prominent farmer who had also been involved in making radio programmes, and in 1965 by Tristram Beresford, a farmer and agricultural journalist.[33] The chair of the Agricultural Advisory Board for Westward TV from the 1960s until the end of its franchise in 1981 was R. G. Pomeroy, a north Devon farmer and a member of the Milk Marketing Board. There were also three farmers, one from each of the counties of Devon, Cornwall and Dorset, representatives of the Ministry of Agriculture and the NFU, an independent agricultural adviser, and the Director of the Agricultural Economics Unit at Exeter University.[34] The impact of these advisory committees on the decisions of programme makers deserves further investigation.

Knowledge and its reception: the evidence from interviews with farmers

If, as the above discussion suggests, the supply of information and training available to farmers increased dramatically in the 40 post-war years, what happened to the demand for it? To judge from the uptake of agricultural education, it was not always enormous, but the extent to which commercial firms were prepared to keep technical representatives ('reps') in the field in the 1960s and 1970s suggests that they were providing something that many farmers valued. The problem is that the relationship between farmers and technical training and information is not easy to measure because much of it is an informal process, and what evidence there is tends to be anecdotal. The evidence from the sample of farmers interviewed in the south-west is that, as in many other aspects of farming, there were considerable differences from one farmer to another. As with their experiences of education, what worked for one farmer might be anathema to another.

Few farmers among those interviewed used no sources of advice or information whatsoever, and it is perhaps significant that those nearest to being complete non-users were no longer farming when they were interviewed. Farmer 692 belonged to a Young Farmers' Club, where he learned to shear sheep, but apart from that he

> didn't have much to do with ADAS or demonstration farms [...] didn't often read *Farmers Weekly* [...] I used to watch the farming

33 TNA, MAF 197/40, BBC Audience Research Report, 1961; MAF 197/44, Minutes of the BBC Central Agricultural Advisory Committee, 21 Jan. 1965.
34 Constable, pers. comms.

programme on TV but I didn't get a lot of information from it [...] you gradually learn from each other.

Farmer 162, who had a 132-acre livestock farm on the edge of Exmoor, used to read the literature sent to him by the advisory services and the ministry but he 'never asked for any help', and although he was a keen member of the Young Farmers', it was 'more a social thing' than a source of information or training. On the other hand, he was always heavily involved in a sheep breeding society, and farming newspapers and magazines were 'very important when I was leaving school, I used to read everything that was going'. His father used to listen to the early morning radio programme for the fatstock prices, and both his father and mother followed *The Archers*, but more for the story than for any technical information. The 'best guide of the lot', he felt, was the Exeter University Farm Management Survey (FMS) report, because it 'showed you where you were earning a pound'. Farmer 826 also felt that he received useful advice from the FMS Investigation Officer, Estelle Burnside, who visited him regularly, and farmer 782 found that the FMS figures were 'very useful, they influenced my decisions to a certain extent'. Farmer 209 found that 'sometimes it wasn't good reading, because you weren't doing as well as you thought you were, but it told you what to stop doing'.

Farmer 162 also emphasized the importance of the informal knowledge network:

> Generally speaking, the farmers round here got together and talked among themselves, what their plans were, and one of them would say that he'd tried something, and the others would look over the hedge. [*Interviewer: were they formal meetings?*] No, if they met on the road, or rent day, or harvest festival.

Farmer 243, with a small dairy farm in East Devon, made the same point:

> I got my information by asking people who I thought knew something about it, neighbours and so on [...]. I very rarely went to demonstrations. You used to pick up hints from the Young Farmers' Club, talking to people you met there. And for machinery we had Medland Sanders and Twose who had a base at Plymtree, and several of their workmen used to live round here, and you'd say 'Bob, come and have a look at this', and they'd say 'You want this' or something, and they'd make it up for you. So it was an informal way of doing things.

As farmer 782 said, 'You pick up things talking to other farmers, chatting at market for example'. Farmer 2/7, who had a 680-acre farm in Dorset, emphasized the importance of 'meeting the other members of the family socially, who are all farming, that gave me a lot of my information', rather than any published sources:

You learned by a process of osmosis, I suppose, when you were chatting to farmers, you learn on the shooting field, you say 'That's a good crop there, or what have you done about so and so, how did you plant that, why are you growing that?' You don't know you are learning or taking it in.

A. G. Street made similar points about learning and sources of information when discussing the years before the First World War.[35] As farmer 535 put it:

from journals, and Young Farmers' Club, and NFU, you get lectures, and you meet people – you are living in a sea of information and you pick out what you want […] and I would talk with my cousin, and my wife's brother – it was a network.

However, without further investigation of the way in which agricultural research workers communicated with farmers, advisers, and those in the ancillary industries, it is difficult to know how much this network influenced research priorities and activities.

At the opposite extreme from those farmers who emphasized the informal knowledge networks were those who seemed to use all possible sources of information and training. Farmer 209, who began with a 34-acre rented farm in Cornwall in the 1940s and by 2012 was farming over 700 acres, was never a full-time agricultural student, although he did day release classes, and read farming textbooks. He went to NFU meetings with his father, which often ended with a technical talk in those days, read farming periodicals, watched farming television programmes and used

quite a bit of ADAS advice back then, either at a meeting or somebody coming here. It was free then, it would be from the District adviser, Truro office. Back in the '50s and '60s there were many more reps coming round to farms, feeding you information.

Farmer 466 had a very different educational background, with degrees in agriculture and agricultural economics, but he and his father also used a wide range of information sources. In addition to the normal farming periodicals he read NIAB leaflets, used ADAS and MLC demonstration farms, went on study tours to the Netherlands and Israel, and emphasized the importance of technical reps.

They ran things like grassland clubs, and we all trotted off to [meetings of] the grassland society, and it was very effective technical extension work, […] very practical extension work at no cost to the farmer except his time.

---

35   A. G. Street, *Farmer's Glory* (London, 1959), pp. 40, 81–2.

Conclusions

This chapter has sought to identify the various components of the agricultural knowledge network that existed in the UK between 1945 and the mid-1980s, the period in which national agricultural policy, despite increasing surpluses in European agriculture, was unequivocally in favour of output expansion. It has also attempted to explore the ways in which farmers used the network to acquire information and expertise.

The chapter began by demonstrating how the expenditure and effort devoted to agricultural science and technical development increased markedly in the 40 years after the end of the Second World War. However, governments, scientists, advisers, firms in the agricultural supply industry and farmers did not always have the same objectives and priorities. Writing at the end of this period, the Economic Development Committee for Agriculture, part of the government's National Economic Development Office, found that the value of research 'was too often judged on the publication of research papers with lack of regard for the practical value of the end product'. This was not surprising, for the committee also argued that 'In public sector research, the motivation of staff is often directed towards an improvement in general scientific understanding rather than to dealing with the specific identified needs of users'.[36]

Perhaps because of this difference in priorities, scientists did not always communicate well with farmers. The report contained several case studies on the adoption of specific technical changes, that

> showed the continuing difficulty of presenting research findings to the industry in a meaningful way. They are often presented as scientific papers, written in the language of the researcher, and do not indicate how the research might be applied in farming systems.[37]

This is reminiscent of Jonathan Harwood's identification of the 'tension between the worlds of scholarship and practical agriculture', which, he argues, leads to a process of 'academic drift' in which scientists ostensibly serving an economic community seek professional status by increasingly taking their research questions from the basic sciences.[38] As far as the knowledge network is concerned, what matters here is not so much the priorities of the scientists *per se* but the language or, as others

---

[36] Agriculture EDC [Economic Development Committee], *The Adoption of Technology in Agriculture: Opportunities for Improvement* (London, 1985), pp. 31, 14.

[37] *Ibid.*, 18.

[38] J. Harwood, *Technology's Dilemma: Agricultural Colleges between Science and Practice in Germany, 1860–1934* (Oxford, 2005), pp. 19, 31.

might put it, the different discourses used by different groups.[39] Scientists communicated with each other in a technical language using scientific periodicals and academic conferences that were not read or attended, or perhaps even understood, by farmers. Although from time to time they might write articles in the farming press, in general it was more likely that farmers would hear about new technologies through intermediaries in the knowledge network in the form of advisers, journalists, technical representatives or even other farmers.[40] These intermediaries might be seen as 'cultural amphibians', capable of relating to both elitist/scientific and popular cultures.[41] An alternative term is 'translators', defined as those who

> pass information between worlds by selecting information from one world [agricultural science] which is relevant to another [practical agriculture] and present it in a format that the second world will understand.[42]

In addition to transmitting information about science and technology from the laboratory and research station to the farm, one of the functions of these translators or cultural amphibia – advisers, journalists, technical representatives – was to inform scientists and technologists about reactions to their efforts and the requirements of farmers. Much of the evidence upon which this chapter is based comes from interviews with farmers, whereas many fewer interviews with researchers and advisers exist. And to analyse them fully might require another chapter of similar length to this one. However, this chapter should have made it clear that both formal and informal pathways of information exchange existed to transfer thoughts and information from farmers to scientists, just as they did to pass knowledge in the opposite direction. In the author's experience of working in an agriculture faculty for 30 years, agricultural scientists were usually well aware of farmers' ideas and viewpoints. They read the same trade press publications, they encountered farmers at all sorts of meetings, and those working in the universities regularly took students on farm walks to commercial farms. These sources of information were one of the factors influencing their decisions about the research that they would carry out.

---

39   See Brassley, 'Cutting across Nature?'.

40   For an example of a research scientist writing for the farming press, see C. Polge, 'AI may soon help you to breed better pigs', *Pig Farming* (Nov. 1954), p. 27.

41   The term 'cultural amphibians' is taken from M. Macdonald, 'The Secularization of Suicide in England', *Past and Present* 111 (1986), pp. 50–100.

42   J. Marie, 'For Science, Love, and Money: the Social Worlds of Poultry and Rabbit Breeding in Britain, 1900–1940', *Social Studies of Science* 36 (2008), pp. 919–36.

Another way of looking at these relationships between those who initially produced new technologies and those who eventually used them is in terms of formal and informal linkages. This chapter has been structured to follow the formal linkages: scientists produced new knowledge, which was then transferred via education, extension, and the print and broadcast media, each of which might be seen as a formal, and in some cases sequential, link with the farming community. For example, Blaxter and his colleagues in the 1960s developed a new system of livestock rationing, the metabolizable energy system, to replace the starch equivalent system that had been in use since the beginning of the century.[43] Those in formal agricultural education at the time learned to use the new method, and it was discussed in the latest textbooks.[44] Then, as some of them took up their positions in the extension services or as technical representatives or farming journalists, they began to explain to farmers how to use it. This was how a new technique was spread through formal linkages. But, as the remarks of farmers recounted earlier show, there were many ways of learning about new technologies that ignored these formal sequential pathways but instead relied upon chance meetings, informal conversations, and snippets of information acquired from a range of sources, which eventually meant that a farmer was in a position to make a judgement on whether a specific new technology was worth adopting – or not.

The role of this complex and multi-layered knowledge network is thus revealed as crucial to the transmission of new technologies. It was unlikely that any one pathway would work for all technical changes and all farmers. As we have seen, the level of formal education in the agricultural industry was generally low, with some significant exceptions, and in any case, farmers were unlikely to be taking significant management decisions about their farms so soon after their formal education had been completed. Farmers with different levels of education, experience and expertise responded to different stimuli, so there is a distinct impression (albeit difficult to prove statistically) that small farmers with little training were more likely to consult or take notice of those with lower levels of technical training such as neighbours, salesmen and popular farming journals, whereas those with higher levels of education farming on a larger scale were more likely to use more professional advisers, specialist publications, conferences and peer group meetings.

The important feature of the years from the mid-1940s to the mid-1980s was that for much of the time government was prepared to fund large numbers of people to operate in the various pathways of this knowledge network, while at the same time commercial firms also found it profitable

---

43 Blaxter and Robertson, *From Dearth to Plenty*, pp. 231–2.
44 P. McDonald, R. A. Edwards and J. F. D. Greenhalgh, *Animal Nutrition* (Edinburgh, 1966).

to do so, so most of the requirements of most of the farmers were met by one organization or another. The ways in which farmers learned about new crop varieties, or new animal husbandry techniques, were different from those in which they acquired familiarity with machinery. The complexity and variability of the knowledge network over time, type of farmer, and system of farming therefore makes any generalization difficult and open to question. But if that makes us realize the dangers of assuming that a knowledge transmission policy that worked in one set of circumstances will be effective in another, it might be no bad thing.

11

Communicating an Innovation: Building Dutch Progeny Testing Stations for Pigs

Steven van der Laan

In 1926, as one of a succession of protectionist measures, England prohibited the import of all fresh meat from continental Europe.[1] This was a serious blow to Dutch pig farmers, who had sold over 36 tons of fresh pork to the English in 1925, more than half of the total export of pork.[2] Processed meat such as bacon was left out of the import restrictions. As a result, Dutch pig farmers were more or less forced to breed pigs that yielded good quality bacon, instead of the fresh meat pigs that had been bred up to then. Yet by switching to the export of bacon, the Dutch had to compete with Danish pig farmers who controlled the London bacon market. To meet this competition, Dutch pig farmers built progeny testing stations in which the offspring of breeding sows were fattened in a controlled environment. The results of these testing stations were used to determine the breeding value of the individual sows.

Many, very different groups of people were involved in the process leading up to the progeny testing stations, including pig breeders, scientists, livestock consultants, journalists and veterinarians. This chapter will consider the exchange of information between these groups and will show how an innovation like progeny testing stations can be explained as a result of a broad change in breeding practices, rather than as the outcome of a straightforward, top-down implementation of (scientific) knowledge.

---

[1] Anon., 'Onze vleeshandel op Engeland', *De Veldbode* 1226 (3 July 1926); Anon., '80ste Nederlandsche landhuishoudkundig congres', *De Veldbode* 1337 (8 September 1928).

[2] *Verslagen en medeedelingen van de Directie van den landbouw, Verslag over den Landbouw in Nederland over 1925* 2 ('s-Gravenhage, 1926), p. 91; J. Bieleman, *Boeren in Nederland. Geschiedenis van de landbouw 1500–2000* (Amsterdam, 2008), p. 416.

In recent years, there has been a growing number of publications dealing with similar issues in the history of twentieth-century breeding. In this literature, the influence of Mendelian genetics on breeding practices is often the subject of investigation. It has become clear by now that the influence of Mendelian theory on early twentieth-century developments within breeding was small. The laws of inheritance were not easily applicable to characteristics such as milk yield, egg production and meat growth.[3] Still, in the Netherlands, Mendel's theory was well understood at the time among pig breeders and, as shall be shown, they did not hesitate in applying this knowledge in their daily practice. However, this was done not to 'rationalize' pig breeding in the way geneticists and some livestock consultants had in mind, but rather to understand and gain control over very specific qualitative characteristics such as skin colour. At the same time, they were well aware that although progeny testing was rational from a Mendelian perspective, the theory itself had very little to add to the discussions leading up to the implementation of progeny testing stations.

The goal of this chapter is to explain the establishment of progeny testing stations in the Netherlands. This will be done by showing how the rationalization of pig farming in general, and the implementation of progeny testing in particular, can be understood as a diffuse process of knowledge exchange between different groups of people, spanning over a period of several decades. It is argued that the formation of this knowledge network and the exchange of knowledge played an important role in the acceptance of this innovation as a rational development.

The road to progeny testing stations

The Dutch selection of breeding pigs was based on external examination and data provided by the herd books. Although herd books for pigs had only existed since the early twentieth century, the general idea behind them was much older. A pig's ancestry was deemed very important: if a pig was a descendant of a prize-winning boar, it was expected to have inherited at least some of the qualities of its father. The idea behind an external examination is that external characteristics are indicative of

---

3   Examples include: Chr. Bonneuil, 'Mendelism, Plant Breeding and Experimental Cultures: Agriculture and the Development of Genetics in France', *Journal of the History of Biology* 39 (2006), pp. 281–308; Th. Wieland, 'Scientific Theory and Agricultural Practice: Plant Breeding in Germany from the Late 19th to the Early 20th Century', *Journal of the History of Biology* 39 (2006), pp. 309–343; B. Theunissen, 'Breeding for Nobility or for Production? Cultures of Dairy Cattle Breeding in the Netherlands, 1945–1995', *Isis* 103, 2 (2012), pp. 278–309; K. Cooke, 'From Science to Practice or Practice to Science? Chickens and Eggs in Raymond Pearl's Agricultural Breeding Research, 1907–1916', *Isis* 88, 1 (1997), pp. 62–86.

high-quality meat, resistance to diseases, efficient food conversion and fertile sows.[4] Making the connection between the exterior of a pig and these qualities was the result of years of experience in pig breeding. With this experience, the breeder acquired the so-called breeders' eye, which allowed him to see instantly if a certain pig should or should not be used for breeding.

Although the establishment of herd books for pigs was part of a wider development around the turn of the century (the first cattle herd book was established in 1874 and sheep followed in 1907), it appears that pig breeders had specific reasons for establishing herd books. These were an attempt to gain control over the many mixed breeds in the Netherlands, which were the result of so-called wild crossing that had been practised on a large scale by Dutch breeders in the nineteenth century.[5] Many publications at the end of the nineteenth and beginning of the twentieth century pointed out that Dutch pigs were a mishmash of all kinds of breeds, which made a successful breeding programme virtually impossible.[6] Herd books were thus set up to create some order among this chaos.

The herd books operated on a provincial level, and it was soon decided that there was a need to quantify the breeders' eye as the entry requirements for pigs had to be the same for the whole province. The first attempt at the quantification of an external appraisal consisted of short descriptions of the characteristics of the major breeds: the ears of the Yorkshire breed for instance had to be 'erect', while the Improved German Landrace had to have 'floppy ears'.[7] The herd books of both the Gelderland and Overijssel provinces developed a next step in this quantification of breeds by means of an elaborate grading system. In this system, herd book officials awarded points for a number of external characteristics and, at the end, if the total number of points was above a certain pre-determined level, the pig was allowed to be entered into the herd book. The grading system was greeted with much enthusiasm, mostly because it was thought that this would enable a more objective way of grading pigs. For one, the system allowed for comparing the grading of a single pig by different officials, which made it less dependent on 'personal preferences'.[8] In 1923, the Centraal Bureau Varkensfokkerij (the CBV, a national

4   C. Grasseni, 'Designer Cows: the Practice of Cattle Breeding Between Skill and Standardisation', *Society and Animals* 13 (2005), p. 37.

5   H. Kroon, *Maatregelen ter bevordering der varkensfokkerij in Denemarken*, 1902, Nationaal Archief: 2.11.05–22.

6   A. ter Haar, *De Veldbode* no. 225 (27 April 1907); H. Kroon, *De tegenwoordige richtingen in de fokkerij der landbouw-huisdieren in Nederland* (Maastricht, 1913), p. 172.

7   J. Timmermans, 1913, as quoted by A. Paridaans, *75 jaar varkensfokkerij in stamboekverband. Invloed van de stamboekorganisatie op de kwaliteitsverbetering van het varken in (zuid) Nederland* (S.l., 1987), pp. 21–2.

8   E. Dommerhold, *Het uitwendige voorkomen van het varken*, Goedkoope

cooperative of all provincial herd books) standardized the grading system and imposed it on all Dutch herd books, meaning that every pig in the Netherlands was graded by the same criteria.

The selection of breeding pigs in Denmark was not only based on external qualities and ancestry, but also on *production* and *progeny*. Pig breeders who wanted to have a sow graded on its progeny had to sell four of the sow's piglets, preferably two boars and two sows, to a progeny testing station. These four piglets were fattened during a period of weeks in a highly controlled environment and weighed on a regular basis. At the end, the four now fully-grown pigs were slaughtered by butchers who wrote a report on the quality of the pork. This report, together with the results of the fattening period, were made public and gave an indication of the breeding quality of the sow.

Selection based on progeny meant that pigs were tested on their ability to pass on desired qualities such as external characteristics, fast growth and meat quality. In principle, this was not a novel procedure. It was, for example, one of the most important tools of the famous eighteenth-century breeder Robert Bakewell.[9] However, progeny testing is a tedious way of selection compared to pedigree evaluation. In pedigree evaluation, one can immediately judge the parents of a certain animal, whereas in progeny testing the animal first has to be mated and deliver offspring, which then have to be raised before anything can be assessed about both their quality and the breeding value of the parent. During the nineteenth century, the general method used in livestock breeding was based on genealogy and external characteristics, rather than progeny testing.[10] In the early years of the twentieth century, Dutch breeders occasionally referred to the 'breeding value' of pigs, which implied that a pig was able to transfer its characteristics to its offspring.[11] Although breeding value was part of the craftsmanship of breeding and was undoubtedly used by good breeders for selecting the best breeding material, it was not formalized by the herd books or breeding societies. Agricultural journalist E. van Muylwijk thus typified the determination of breeding value as 'unofficially looking around [...] at the neighbours, in the country, at the market, etc.'[12]

In 1923, the CBV attempted to make progeny testing an official

---

geïllustreerde Land- en Tuinbouwbibliotheek van 'De Veldbode', no. 110 (1921) 10.

9   R. Wood and V. Orel, *Genetic Prehistory in Selective Breeding: A Prelude to Mendel* (Oxford, 2001), p. 82.

10 M. Derry, *Masterminding Nature: Approaches to Artificial Selection in Livestock Breeding, 1750–2010* (Toronto, 2015).

11 A. van Leeuwen, 'Fokmethoden', *De Veldbode* 486 (27 April 1912). State agricultural teacher (*Rijkslandbouwleraar*) of Noord-Holland to Inspector of Agriculture, 19 March 1915, Nationaal Archief: 2.11.05–134.

12 E. van Muylwijk, 'De moderne erfelijkheidsleer en de practische fokkerij', *De*

requirement. This was largely motivated by the need to grant extraordi-
narily good pigs a predicate with which they could be distinguished from
the average breeding pigs in the herd books. An experiment was set up
in which the progeny of three boars, who were thought to be excellent
breeding material, was examined. Two of the three boars were deemed
to have 'exercised a resounding influence in favour of breeding.'[13] It took
some years to develop a workable list of criteria and in 1930 the CBV
began issuing the 'preferential' (*preferent*) predicate. From the herd books,
a couple of excellent boars (i.e. boars with high grades for their external
characteristics) were chosen, after which a representative of the CBV and
of the herd book inspected a minimum number of 12 of their offspring.
If the offspring was deemed to be good enough, the boar was declared
to be preferential. The predicate thus was awarded solely on the basis of
external qualities.

Around the time the CBV awarded its first predicates, it became clear
that much more was needed to improve the reputation and the quality
of Dutch bacon on the English market. To breed bacon pigs of the
same quality as Danish pigs, two options were proposed: either Danish
pigs were to be imported and used for breeding in the Netherlands, or
the Danish system of breeding was to be implemented to change the
Dutch pig breed to a more bacon-type pig. Both options were chosen by
different people and institutions. This chapter however will focus on the
implementation of progeny testing stations.

Prior to the implementation of these stations, Henri Leignes Bakhoven,
livestock consultant of Friesland, and Wieger de Jong, livestock consultant
of Gelderland and director of the CBV, undertook a study trip to Denmark
during which they inspected the workings of a testing station. Before the
report containing the results of this trip was published, Leignes Bakhoven
had already convinced the Friesian Society of Agriculture to build a
progeny testing station, and most of the other Dutch provinces followed
suit within the next year.[14] The procedure of fattening, slaughtering and
appraising in the Dutch testing stations was identical to the way it was
done in Denmark, and the development was lauded as 'a turning point'
in the breeding of pigs.[15]

Veldbode 1346 (10 November 1928). Dutch: '*onofficieel, rondkijken [...] bij de buren in 't land, op de markten, enz.*'.

[13] Minutes meeting CBV, 17 December 1926, Archive Veeteeltmuseum Beers: k13, 20A box 342.

[14] Friesche Maatschappij van Landbouw to Minister of the Interior, 1929. Tresoar: 2.1.2.14.3.2–719.

[15] Minutes meeting CBV, 18 Dec. 1931, Archive Veeteeltmuseum Beers: k13, 20A box 342. Dutch: '*Aan een keerpunt in de fokkerij zijn gekomen, nu ook de dieren naar productiegegevens worden onderzocht*'.

The livestock consultants

The implementation of progeny testing stations in the Netherlands appears to have happened quite smoothly. This innovation, like most other developments within pig breeding, was mainly led by livestock consultants. They had been appointed for the first time in 1909 by the government to 'provide council, hold lectures, arrange courses, to visit livestock inspections and breeding exhibitions and to promote the founding and organization of societies', in order to improve the breeding of livestock in the Netherlands.[16] Candidates for the position of livestock consultant were mostly agricultural teachers and, with few exceptions, graduates from the Wageningen agricultural college. This college had been reformed several times since the beginning of the twentieth century to give students a more scientifically adequate education in agricultural science. As of 1904, for example, students had to attend elementary courses in physics, chemistry and mathematics in the first part of the curriculum.[17] Later in their studies they could regularly be found in the laboratory, experimenting with plant hybridization. Generally speaking, they were considered part of a 'scientific institution'.[18] Livestock consultants were thus made familiar with developments in science and with a scientific way of thinking and working.

How did these consultants come to believe that progeny testing stations would improve the position of the Dutch bacon industry on the London market to the extent that it legitimized the large investments involved? An obvious factor is the success of the approach to pig selection in Denmark. This certainly provided the consultants with a convincing argument, but also because Denmark had always figured as a role model for Dutch pig breeders.[19] In the report of their study-trip, Leignes Bakhoven and De Jong listed ten recommendations from their research in Denmark. Their third recommendation explained the benefits of the Danish selection procedure: 'The [...] selection [of pigs in the Netherlands] should not only be based on external characteristics, but also on weight gain, amount of fodder needed and quality as a bacon-pig.'[20]

---

16   R. Strikwerda, 'Veeteeltconsulenten: tachtig jaar in touw', *Veeteelt: magazine van het Koninklijk Nederlands Rundvee Syndicaat NRS* 25 (2008) 32. Dutch: '*Door het geven van raad, het houden van voordrachten, het geven van cursussen, het bezoeken van keuringen en fokveetentoonstellingen en het bevorderen van het verenigingsleven*'.

17   J. van der Haar, *De geschiedenis van de Landbouwuniversiteit Wageningen*, Deel 1 (Wageningen, 1993), p. 121.

18   *Ibid.*, 124.

19   See for instance: *Rapport omtrent de vraag: is het mogelijk en gewenscht om met de varkensfokkerij den weg op te gaan dien men in Denemarken gevolgt heeft?* (1904); Nationaal Archief: 2.11.05–22.

20   H.L. Bakhoven and W. de Jong, *De varkensfokkerij en -mesterij in Denemarken*

Moreover, Leignes Bakhoven and De Jong put much emphasis in their report on the selection of pork quality. This 'interior appraisal' could only be executed after slaughtering, meaning that the pig in question could no longer be used for breeding.

It was 'breeding based on production', as Leignes Bakhoven and De Jong characterized the Danish method of selection, that explained the success of the Danish progeny testing stations, and thus they recommended it as a 'rational' addition to the methods of the herd books.[21] Determining the breeding value of a pig on the basis of its production, defined above as weight gain, amount of fodder needed and quality of pork and internal appraisal, instead of on its external characteristics, was conceived as the major innovation in pig breeding brought about by the progeny testing stations.[22]

Geneticists and useful knowledge

Although the initiative to establish progeny testing stations was largely taken by the livestock consultants, they were certainly not the only ones discussing new breeding methods. The rediscovery of Mendel's law around the turn of the century initially led early geneticists to promise a never-never land to breeders of livestock.[23] Dutch geneticists most notably propagated progeny testing, which they thought to be a more rational way of selecting than on the basis of ancestry.[24] Until about 1920, these scientists quintessentially approached practising breeders in this manner: what breeders had achieved so far was admirable, but their practice, or 'the art of breeding', was ridden with prejudices and misunderstandings.[25] It was up to the geneticist to raise breeding to a higher level by removing these prejudices and explaining the misunderstandings with their theoretical knowledge. This is how, in 1912, the previously mentioned geneticist Arend Hagedoorn addressed breeders

---

('s-Gravenhage, 1929), p. 23; Nationaal Archief: 2.11.05 134. Dutch: *'Geschieden op overeenkomstige wijze als dit in Denemarken geschiedt met behulp van proefmes- terijen'*, *'De [...] selectie [van varkens in Nederland] moet niet alleen plaats hebben naar exterieur, maar ook naar gewichtsvermeerdering, voederverbruik en kwaliteit als baconvarken'*.

21 *Ibid.*, 13. Dutch: *'Teelt naar prestatie [...] rationele'*.

22 Other sources draw the same conclusion, see: R. Anema, 'Selectiemesterijen en hun beteekenis voor de varkensfokkerij', *De Veldbode* 1427 (21 June 1930); C. Van Vloten, 'Welk varkensras is het beste?', *De Veldbode* 1435 (2 August 1930); A. van Leeuwen, 'Van 'de Woestenij' tot 'de Kamp' te Heelsum', *De Veldbode* 1415 (15 March 1930).

23 Cooke, 'From Science to Practice or Practice to Science?', p. 81.

24 Theunissen, 'Breeding Without Mendelism', p. 663.

25 B. Theunissen, *De Koe. Het verhaal van het Nederlandse melkvee 1900–2000* (Amsterdam, 2010), p. 17.

in the introduction to his book *Judicious Cultivation and Breeding*: 'I (i.e., science) will tell you how you should acquire these [desired] qualities and how you should maintain them in your animals.'[26]

From 1915 onwards, the application of genetics as a practice was the self-appointed task of the newly established Society for the Improvement of Scientific Cultivation.[27] From the inaugural lecture held by geneticist Marius Sirks, it became clear that the society held similar views on the possibility of improving practice through science. Sirks acknowledged that breeders had achieved a lot on the basis of their practical experience, but at a certain point they had inevitably got stuck. It was at this point that the society came to the rescue 'by making information obtained from pure science suitable for use in practice.'[28]

This goal, the application of genetics in breeding, however, turned out to be difficult to realize. The realization that Mendelian laws were difficult, if not impossible, to translate into practical guidelines for obtaining desired characteristics of breeding animals arose shortly after the formation of the society. Prior to this, it was already clear that many practical obstacles had to be faced if livestock was to be bred on a Mendelian basis. Especially in the case of cattle, horses and sheep, the small number of offspring was a problem, since this made it difficult to draw significant conclusions about the breeding value of these animals. With about 10 piglets per litter, this was not so much of a problem for pigs, yet they were large animals that were costly to keep, which hindered an easy experimental setup. Most experiments concerning Mendelian inheritance were performed on plants, mice, rabbits and chickens, but geneticists knew that the results from these experiments could not readily be translated to larger animals.[29] To set up experiments that would allow geneticists to draw solid conclusions about the inheritance of characteristics of larger livestock would require a 'very extensive institute', according to veterinarian Hendrik Kroon, 'that would cost millions and millions'.[30] Setting up an institute of such proportions was not possible at the time, which precluded the initiation of breeding programmes by scientists.

From the early twenties onwards, a change in attitude of scientists can be discerned in the literature. Whereas people like Hagedoorn first tried

---

[26] A. Hagedoorn, *Oordeelkundige zaadteelt en fokkerij* (Middelharnis, 1912), preface. Dutch: '*Ik (wetenschap) zal U vertellen hoe ge aan die [gewenste] eigenschappen moet komen en hoe ge die in Uw dieren moet vast houden*'.

[27] Dutch: *Vereeniging tot Bevordering van Wetenschappelijke Teelt*.

[28] M. Sirks, *Vereeniging tot Bevordering van Wetenschappelijke Teelt - Voordrachten, gehouden in de oprichtingsmeeting te Utrecht, op 7 Mei 1915*, 3. Dutch: '*Door de zuivere wetenschap verkregen gegevens voor de praktijk geschikt te maken*'.

[29] H. Kroon, *De Beteekenis der Genetische Eigenschapsanalyse voor de Teelt der Huisdieren* (S.l., 1922), p. 13.

[30] *Ibid.*, Dutch: '[...] *een zeer omvangrijk instituut [...] dat miljoenen en miljoenen zou kosten*'.

to intervene in the practices of breeders on the basis of their theoretical knowledge of inheritance, later on these men started to think more like the breeders themselves, fully acknowledging that their theories of inheritance did not have the power to transform the practice of livestock breeding. Hagedoon is again the most apt example. Many other sources from around 1920 also affirm that Mendelian theory had contributed little to the breeding of livestock.[31] The main achievement of geneticists, it was noted, was to provide a rational analysis of existing breeding methods.[32] Therefore, geneticists at the time could hardly do more than play an advisory role, and hope their advice was taken to heart when breeders made their decisions: 'A rather substantial understanding of the methods used in practice is needed', Hagedoorn stipulated in the agricultural magazine *De Veldbode*, 'in order to provide practitioners with advice on their work, without proposing impossible solutions.'[33]

Besides giving advice, holding lectures and publishing books and periodicals, experiments were also commissioned by the Society for the Improvement of Scientific Cultivation. For pigs, a relatively large experiment was set up in 1917, concerning the inheritance of skin colour. The experiment looked into whether it was possible for domesticated pigs to inherit the striped colour of wild boars, and if the alleged immunity of the wild boar to the much-feared spot disease (*vlekziekte*) could then also be transferred to domesticated pigs.[34] If the latter had been possible, it would without doubt have been a major development in breeding. Yet in the report on the experiment that was sent to the Minister of Agriculture in 1921, this particular goal was no longer mentioned. The report emphasized that the research on the inheritance of colour could 'lead to the development of important combinations', for which the society made a request for additional funds. However, an investigation into the inheritance of characteristics, thought to be useful for breeders and which included 'constitution, -wide and slender animals, animals with floppy

---

[31] E. Dommerhold, 'Practische toepassingen der erfelijkheidsleer in de veeteelt', *De Veldbode* 1432 (12 July 1930); A. van Leeuwen, 'Practische toepassingen der erfelijkheidsleer in de veeteelt [response to the article of Dommerhold]', *De Veldbode* 1434 (26 July 1930); J. Reimers, *Die Bedeutung des Mendelismus für die landwirtschaftliche Tierzucht* ('s-Gravenhage, 1916), p. 3; E. Muilwijk 'De moderne erfelijkheidsleer en de practische fokkerij, *De Veldbode* 1346 (10 November 1928).

[32] Theunissen, 'Breeding Without Mendelism', p. 660.

[33] A. Hagedoorn, 'De toepassing van wetenschap, in het bijzonder van erfelijkheidwetenschap', *De Veldbode* no. 1301 (24 December 1927). *De Veldbode* was one of the most widely read Dutch national agricultural magazines in the first 30 years of the twentieth century and featured articles from most authorities in the world of farming.

[34] A report on this experiment can be found in a brochure of the Dutch Genetical Society: R. Houwink, *Proeftuin te Meppel* (Assen, 1920).

ears, with hanging tails and curly tails [...] are not to be considered by the society, but rather by professional breeders', the report concludes.[35]

It thus appears that the ambitions of the society to further the practice of pig breeding with this experiment were rather low on the agenda. The inheritance of economically important characteristics, such as the constitution of pigs, were left to be investigated by the breeders themselves, while scientists working for the society focused on genetically more manageable issues, such as skin colour. The goals of the experiment as formulated in the 1921 report, though, did have an accidental connection to an issue that was topical among pig breeders. This was the so-called 'spot question' *(vlekjeskwestie)*. It pertained to the pig breeds in the Netherlands that were supposed to be of a white colour, but which occasionally produced offspring that had black spots of hair on their skin. Breeders interpreted these spots as an indication of impurity within the breed.[36] Pigs with spots were thus scrupulously avoided by most of the breeders and a number of herd books had, as an entry requirement, the condition that a pig had to be spotless.[37] It appears, however, that there never was a connection between the society's experiment and the spot question, especially as geneticists were of the opinion that breeders should not base their breeding on exterior characteristics such as skin colour.[38] Whether the experiment was set up to make theories of inheritance applicable for practical breeding is thus to be doubted. Instead, it appears that the society considered it as an experiment of which the outcomes mostly benefitted the field of genetics itself.

The pig breeders

The actions and thoughts of the scientists and livestock consultants are relatively well documented. They published books, spoke their mind at meetings of which minutes were made, and wrote papers and article for magazines. For breeders there is significantly less material available, as they did not usually write for a wider audience.

Fortunately, there was a handful of breeders who, from time to time, did explain their view on pig breeding in various magazines. Also, from

35 Rapport *Vereeniging tot bevordering van wetenschappelijke teelt,* send to the Minister of Agriculture, Industry and Trade, 15 April 1921; Nationaal archief: 2.11.05–134. Dutch: '[...] het ontstaan van nieuwe belangrijke combinaties [kon] leiden. [...] lichaamsbouw, -breede en smalle dieren, dieren met hangooren en staande oren, met hangende staarten en krulstaarten [...] ligt niet op den weg onzer vereeniging, doch op dien der praktische fokkerij'.

36 The spot question was purely an aesthetic feature, unlike the above-mentioned spot disease.

37 Verslag over Het Boekjaar 1931 van 'Het Limburgsch Varkensstamboek', p. 7, Archive Veeteeltmuseum Beers: k13, 29g, box 385.

38 Reimers, *Die Bedeutung des Mendelismus,* p. 35.

1918 onwards, veterinarian and editor of *De Veldbode*, Aryen van Leeuwen, regularly visited pig breeders to report on their way of working. It should be mentioned that the breeders who were visited by Van Leeuwen were in many cases the same breeders who voiced their opinions in writing. It was these very breeders, however, for which the progeny testing stations were built. These 'progressive' breeders, who made serious efforts to rationalize and improve their breeding methods and who led the way in many innovative breeding techniques, determined in many aspects the Dutch pig breeds. Less progressive breeders and pig multipliers preferred to have their sows coupled with the best breeding boars available, so their herds were also influenced considerably by the breeding animals of the group considered as the top pig-breeders.

While these top-breeders were all well-informed about their business and not afraid of introducing novelties, they could still differ in their opinions about a variety of aspects of pig farming. Firstly, different breeders could breed for different purposes. Whereas some of them already bred for bacon pigs in 1920, others focused on the production of fresh meat. Also, the application of technical innovations could be a basis for vehement discussion among breeders. There were, for example, breeders who opposed the mechanization of the feeding of pigs; they felt this would impede the indispensable contact farmers had with their pigs.[39] Conversely, some breeders led the way in these developments and sent in self-designed feeding systems for evaluation to *De Veldbode*.[40] What all top-breeders had in common, however, was their organized way of working. With no counterexample to be found, they were members of a herd book, whose records they used in order to keep track of the many different bloodlines in their area. For some, the information stored in the records was insufficient, so they kept their own record in which they entered every pig that went in or out of their herd, supplemented by precise information about important production numbers.[41]

Also, selection on the production figures of progeny, which was to be done in progeny testing stations, was already applied by several pig breeders. An example of this is pig breeder C.R. van Vloten of Heelsum (Gelderland). In an article in a 1926 issue of *De Veldbode* he gave his opinion on breeding exhibitions, wondering whether it was 'practically and scientifically impossible' to 'focus more on progeny' instead of on

[39] A. van Leeuwen, 'Automatische voederbakken voor varkens', *De Veldbode* 1097 (12 January 1924).

[40] C. van Vloten, 'Automatische varkensvoederbakken', *De Veldbode* 1108 (29 March 1924).

[41] A. van Leeuwen, 'De beste varkensfokstallen van Nederland. Het fokstation voor het VDL op de boerderij Twickel te Delden', *De Veldbode* 1184 (5 September 1925).

the selection of exterior characteristics, as was customary in these exhibitions.[42] In his article, he asked Hagedoorn to respond, to which the reply came that he agreed that exhibitions of livestock breeding in general were far too focused on exterior appraisal. Hagedoorn had observed that prize-winning pigs were too fat to be used for breeding, though these were problems that anyone with experience in breeding would notice and which, according to Hagedoorn, did not take a geneticist to solve,. He thus concluded that breeding exhibitions fell short of improving livestock breeding, though he did not venture to put forth an alternative.[43]

With their feeding experiments, mechanization, progeny testing and ideas on pig breeding in general, breeders like Van Vloten thus appeared to have been at the forefront of the modernization of pig farming. Additionally, from various discussions in magazines, it appears that such breeders were well aware of Mendel's theory and its usefulness. An example of such a discussion, appearing in 1926 in *De Veldbode*, concerned the heritability of black hair on white pigs. As mentioned, breeders conceived skin spots to be an indication of impurity. The discussion was instigated by the boar keeping association Vooruitgang, which had bought a breeding boar from another association that turned out to have spotted offspring. This was quite a setback for Vooruitgang, as the boar had already been coupled with all 50 sows owned by its members, the result of which would be about 500 piglets that no one would want to use for breeding.[44] The discussion was about whether the association from which the boar had been bought could be held accountable for selling an impure boar, and whether the impurity of the boar could indisputably be deduced from the characteristics of the piglets, or whether it was actually the Vooruitgang sows which were impure. The first series of letters from the two associations was accompanied by comments from veterinarian Van Leeuwen who tried to clarify matters with pre-Mendelian notions of breeding such as 'blood' and 'pedigree'. Vooruitgang responded to this with an evaluation of the case from a Mendelian perspective, which clearly demonstrated the knowledgeability of the association in this matter. Van Leeuwen objected to this evaluation that 'the Mendelian rules are not hard and fast rules, from which one would never ever be allowed to diverge'.[45]

42 C. van Vloten, 'Large Black en V.D.L.', *De Veldbode* 1236 (11 September 1926). Dutch: '[…] *praktisch en wetenschappelijk onmogelijk* […] *meer op afstammelingen te letten.'*

43 A. Hagendoorn, 'Over tentoonstellingen en onze fokkerij!', *De Veldbode* 1240 (9 Oktober 1926).

44 A. van Leeuwen, 'Een interessante erfelijkheids- en rechtskwestie', *De Veldbode* 1230 (31 July 1926).

45 A. van Leeuwen, 'Een interessante erfelijkheids- en rechtskwestie', *De Veldbode* 1236 (11 September 1926). Dutch: '[…]*de Mendelsche regels nog geen weten van Meden en Perzen zijn, waarvan nooit en te nimmer zou mogen worden afgeweken'.*

This led Engelbert Dommerhold, livestock consultant of Overijssel, to join the discussion. He was of the opinion that it had been 'confounded' by 'layman and semi-experts'. Dommerhold's contribution, however, will not have helped to clarify the discussion. To illustrate his point that a spotted skin was not linked to an animal's performance, he mentioned three famous black-and-white piebald breeding bulls that had produced red-and-white pied offspring several times. From his statement, it seems that Dommerhold supported the geneticists' point of view: exterior characteristics such as skin spots were not useful for selection; instead, breeders had to select their stock on the basis of the production of its offspring. Yet, in his conclusion, Dommerhold propagated the breeding of 'pure herdbook piglets', especially because they cost only little more than the '[spotted] ordinary pigs'.[46] Pig breeder H.W. Schilt of Groenekan (Utrecht) disagreed, fuelling the discussion by stating that all herd books had registered many pigs that may well deliver spotted offspring. It had already come up in the discussion that spots were a recessive trait to the dominant white colour of pigs. From an external appraisal of a white pig it could therefore not be determined whether it was a homozygote or heterozygote white. Only extensive progeny testing would allow breeders the right to say something about the probability of a pig being a pure homozygote, but even then there was always the chance that it carried the gene for black hair. Schilt therefore made it clear that he could not care less if his pigs gave spotted offspring, even proclaiming that one of his own herd book sows was indeed spotted.[47]

Yet Schilt's attitude to spots appears to have been the exception, also among the progressive breeders. The Zuid-Hollands herd book, in which Schilt had entered his alleged spotted sow, sent in a disconcerted response in which they wanted to make it absolutely clear that the spots on Schilt's pigs were due to a pigmentation, and that pigs with actual dark hairs were without exception excluded from breeding in Zuid-Holland.[48] It is thus certainly not the case that pig breeders only focused on production numbers of pigs. A pig of the Great Yorkshire breed, which figured in the discussion, was supposedly spotlessly white, according to the breed description. In the history of cattle breeding, in which the question of spots also features, this has been linked to the branding of a breed as

---

[46] E. Dommerhold, 'Veel geschreeuw, weinig wol', *De Veldbode* 1237 (18 September 1926). Dutch: '*Vertroebeld [...] leeken en halve kenners*', '*zuivere stamboekbiggen [...] (bonte) gebruiksvarkens*'.

[47] H. Schilt, 'Een interessante erfelijkheids- en rechtskwestie', *De Veldbode*1240 (9 October 1926).

[48] H. Roest, 'Een interessante erfelijkheidskwestie', *De Veldbode* 1234 (30 October 1926).

pure, and thus of a guaranteed quality.[49] Pig breeders also wanted to be able to advertise their pigs as purebred, and the absence of spots would avoid any doubt over this purity, even though there was no direct relationship with production qualities. The whiteness of the Yorkshire was thus a marketing requirement.

The breeders obviously understood the Mendelian inheritance of skin colour. Only a limited number of genes determined the colour of their pigs, and the effects could be expressed in a few rules of thumb: the white colour of the Yorkshire was dominant over the black of the Berkshire breed, while the black of Sussex pigs was dominant over the white of the Landrace.[50] The breeders also clearly understood that they had nothing to gain from Mendel's theory when it came to improving the production qualities of their pigs. Production characteristics such as meat growth, resistance to illness, and fertility are not only dependent on a greater number of genes, they are also crucially influenced by the food pigs are fed and the environment they live in. Therefore, geneticists were not able to formulate rules which could then be laid down as guidelines for breeders to follow. The heritability of production characteristics could only be empirically determined by means of controlled progeny investigations, as was done at the progeny testing stations. Around the time that the first testing stations were built, virtually everyone in the world of pig breeding made this distinction: in the articles, books and minutes discussing progeny testing stations, Mendelian theory was never used as an argument. In contrast there was a widespread understanding of the use of Mendelian theories in relation to the colour of pigs. Genetics was thus only considered useful in the context of the management of a breed as a distinct brand. Economically important production characteristics on the other hand were not dealt with on the basis of a specific scientific theory, but rather by what was conceived as a scientific way of working: the quantitative testing of these characteristics in a controlled environment.

The foundation of progeny testing stations and the way they operated corresponded to the organized way of breeding as it had developed in the first 30 years after 1900. Like many breeders, these testing stations operated with a carefully put together pig diet and elaborate tables that monitored the day-to-day growth of piglets in detail. Through this organized way of working, both breeders and the testing stations attempted to gain control over the genetically elusive production figures of pigs. The development of a 'rational' way of breeding was the major

---

[49] Theunissen, 'Theory and practice of dairy cattle breeding', p. 656.
[50] E. Dommerhold, 'Veel geschreeuw, weinig wol', *De Veldbode* 1237 (18 September 1926).

innovation in pig breeding in the early twentieth century, and progeny testing stations were a tangible result.

Conclusion and discussion

The establishment of progeny testing stations in Dutch pig breeding at the end of the 1920s is a clear indication of a growing need for control among Dutch pig breeders: good breeding practices required a rational, controlled way of working. This development was a reaction to the haphazard crossing of pigs in the nineteenth century. The introduction of herd books was meant to stabilize the breeds of pigs and to create a uniform basis from which their improvement could begin. As their holdings grew larger, pig farmers began to look for various ways of enhancing the productivity of their animals. Improving the diet of pigs through experiments with pig fodder was a first and relatively easy approach, as compared to attempting to control the genetically elusive individual characteristics such as growth, fertility, and resistance to illness. Progeny testing stations were a next step in introducing rational ways of working.

The establishment of progeny testing stations was not simply the result of a top-down application of (scientific) knowledge and methods. Information transfer from the scientists to livestock consultants to pig breeders was undoubtedly involved. Livestock consultants had enjoyed scientific training, and at least some of them had heard the early calls of Hagedoorn and his colleagues for the implementation of genetic thinking and progeny testing. In their turn, livestock consultants informed pig breeders about Mendelism and the benefits of progeny testing stations.[51] Yet this is only part of the story. The testing stations were only one element in a prolonged debate that also addressed traditional breeding methods, which were anything but replaced by the newer methods and which continued to be seen as indispensable by all parties involved. What is more, Mendelian theory was not pivotal in the acceptance of progeny testing, which did not depend on any specific insights into heredity.

This conclusion fits into the framework drawn by recent studies of innovations in rural settings. Notions such as 'multi-dimensional processes',[52] 'cultures of breeding',[53] 'perspectives of social groups',[54] or

---

51 R. Anema 'Selectiemesterijen en hun beteekenis voor de varkensfokkerij', *De Veldbode* 1427 (17 June 1930).

52 P. Brassley, 'Cutting across nature? The history of artificial insemination in pigs in the United Kingdom', *Studies in History and Philosophy of Biological and Biomedical Sciences* 38 (2007), p. 457.

53 Theunissen, 'Breeding for nobility or for production?', p. 309.

54 Bonneuil, 'Mendelism, Plant Breeding and Experimental Cultures', p. 284

simply 'different levels'[55] are indicative of a similar perspective that is taken in all these studies, in which innovation is not a linear top-down process, but rather the result of multifarious interactions and discussions between the parties involved. It is impossible, for instance, to pinpoint the position of the different groups in the debate – scientists, consultants and farmers – solely on the basis of their background. Firstly, individuals within the three groups might entertain different ideas. Different breeders bred different pigs and had divergent opinions on what constituted good breeding and feeding, some being more progressive, others more traditional. Some breeders were happy to employ Mendelian insights if it suited their purposes. Even while they agreed with the scientists that the banning of spotted pigs lacked any rational scientific basis, it was nevertheless their economic rationality that induced them to do so, simply for the marketability of their own breeding stock. The Mendelian rules helped them to accomplish this. Similarly, scientists and livestock consultants had different ideas about possible improvements in pig breeding. Veterinarian Van Leeuwen for instance insisted on the usefulness of non-Mendelian notions such as bloodlines and ancestry. The sometimes heated debates at the CBV also provide examples of this divergence of opinion.

Secondly, many of the actors involved adopted new views or changed their opinion over the years: pig breeders began to look for a more quantitative way of selecting their pigs. Hagedoorn and some of his colleagues realized that Mendelian theory could not be turned into a breeding programme, that they had to be involved in the world of practical breeding if they wished to be of assistance, and livestock consultants struggled with the relationship between external appraisal and selection on production characteristics.

Progeny testing turned out to be a method by which opinions ultimately converged towards a consensus, as all parties saw it as a rational way to improve productivity. While it dated from long before Mendel's work and thus in no way depended on it, for Hagedoorn the method was rational in the scientific sense because Mendelian theory was fully consistent with it and explained its effectiveness. For breeders, its rationality found its basis in its practical efficacy, as demonstrated by the Danish example, which had clearly shown its capacity to help increasing productivity. What had been lacking so far was the means to put the principle to work in a practical context, and it was here that the consultants stepped in by stimulating the development of progeny testing stations, which made its effective implementation feasible for the first time. Progeny testing stations were an innovation in which convictions about scientific and practical rationality came together, the

---

55 Wieland, 'Scientific Theory and Agricultural Practice', p. 337.

former supplying a theoretical explanation and justification, on which the latter, however, did not depend on for its effectiveness. The debates surrounding the establishment of progeny testing stations thus testify to the diffuse nature of the circulation of knowledge and practices. By following key-players in the debate, we have seen how practical concepts were transformed (progeny testing), new concepts were put into use (Mendelism), and older ones were partially retained rather than replaced (exterior evaluation). The end result was a new, controlled way of working that was deemed rational by all those involved.

INDEX

Printed and bound by CPI Group (UK) Ltd, Croydon, CR0 4YY

24/04/2025

14661368-0001